PRAISE FOR TERRY FOSTER AND *BREWING BARLEY WINES*

"Terry Foster's command of traditional English beer styles and how to brew them is unrivaled. Enjoy as he turns his expert eye on the malty complexity of barley wine, one of England's true classics."

—Brad Ring, publisher, *Brew Your Own Magazine*

"This book is a culmination of literally centuries of information that Terry has accrued over decades and decades of research. If you are a casual beer fan or are serious about the depth of information here, grab a copy and a glass of barley wine and sit back—this is a great read."

—Jeffrey Browning Sr., owner and head brewer,
Brewport, Bridgeport, Connecticut

"For decades Terry Foster has been sharing the fascinating history of British beer and brewing with readers through a meticulously researched, straightforward, and easily digestible style. His books are invaluable resources filled with brewing techniques and recipes that set brewers of every level up for success in mastering classic styles."

—Dawson Rapuzzi, editor, *Brew Your Own Magazine*

"I've known Terry for over twenty years and having access to a legend in the brewing industry is a very comforting feeling. It's intimidating to be around a master of your profession, but it is always a pleasure being with Terry. I love pouring Terry a beer we've made—often one where he's literally written a book about the style—and we're just two guys in a pub sharing a pint. As much as you think you know about a style of beer, you're going to learn some things with a Dr. Terry Foster book. Whenever Terry tried a beer I made and liked it—now that's a great feeling. In *Brewing Barley Wines*, he shares his truly next level knowledge about beer and its history."

—Rob Leonard, owner, New England Br~~~~ ~~.,
~t

Doctor Who? My draft line at Brewport Brewing Co., Bridgeport, CT.

BREWING BARLEY WINES

ORIGINS, HISTORY, AND MAKING THEM AT HOME TODAY

TERRY FOSTER

Skyhorse Publishing

Skyhorse Publishing books may be purchased in bulk at special discounts for sales promotion, corporate gifts, fund-raising, or educational purposes. Special editions can also be created to specifications. For details, contact the Special Sales Department, Skyhorse Publishing, 307 West 36th Street, 11th Floor, New York, NY 10018 or info@skyhorsepublishing.com.

Skyhorse® and Skyhorse Publishing® are registered trademarks of Skyhorse Publishing, Inc.®, a Delaware corporation.

Visit our website at www.skyhorsepublishing.com.

10 9 8 7 6 5 4 3 2 1

Library of Congress Cataloging-in-Publication Data is available on file.

Paperback ISBN: 978-1-5107-6693-8
Ebook ISBN: 978-1-5107-6694-5

Cover design: Brian Peterson
Cover photo: Getty Images

Printed in China

AS ALWAYS, MY THANKS GO TO MY WIFE FOR PUTTING UP WITH my obsession for brewing beer and brewing history. She encouraged me to go off and search brewing archives in London, Oxford, New Haven, and on the internet while she was left to her own devices. Neither did she complain about the time I spent brewing at home, at BRüRm@ BAR, and now at Brewport, nor at the time I spent writing about beer and brewing, as well as a little fiction. Thank you, Lois!

I must also thank Jeff Browning, the brewer at BAR and now brewer and part owner at Brewport. He has been a good friend for many years, and I am grateful for his insight into producing good beer and his willingness to adapt some of my experiments to a commercial scale, especially the old beers we have re-created. He says he has learned from me, but so have I from him—I think the score is tied and we are now into overtime.

CONTENTS

Introduction   *1*

Chapter 1: *Definitions and Examples of Barley Wine*   *3*

Chapter 2: *History of Barley Wine*   *29*

Chapter 3: *Barley Wine Ingredients*   *89*

Chapter 4: *Brewing Barley Wine*   *131*

Chapter 5: *Barley Wine Recipes*   *161*

Bibliography   *270*

A Selection of Other Sources Searched   *277*

BREWING BARLEY WINES

INTRODUCTION

I STARTED BREWING MY OWN BEER IN ENGLAND JUST AS THE craft of homebrewing was beginning to be revived there and developed sufficient knowledge to start my "career" as a beer writer. I then moved to the United States just as homebrewing was legalized here and became embroiled in the craft in the early stages of its development, both through writing and lecturing on various aspects of brewing. I wrote *Pale Ale*, the first book in the Brewers Association portfolio on Classic Beer Styles, which was responsible for me being told at a meeting of the New England Brewer's Association that I was the "father" of all the members present, a dubious accolade at best. In my "other profession" of technical service in the minerals processing field, I traveled to many of the world's countries and, of course, managed to drink a great many different beers in many different places. After I retired from that profession I took to commercial brewing with Jeff Browning, first at BRüRm@BAR in New Haven and then at Brewport in Bridgeport, where I now enjoy the title of Consultant Brewer. But my roots are in homebrewing, which I still practice, sometimes assiduously, although I still enjoy drinking the outputs of the many craft breweries which have established themselves in North America since I came here in 1978.

My writings on brewing have been centered on English ales, most notably on pale ales and IPAs, porters and stouts, with but little reference to barley wine. Yet it is a beer which I have often brewed over the years, and if you consider the variety of beer styles as a tree, barley wine represents the top branch of that tree. Yet commercial brewers offer it only occasionally, for it is truly a specialty beer with relatively low sales. Many home brewers do not tackle it because it is not an easy beer to make and it is expensive to do so. Beer drinkers, in general, cannot break the habit of drinking beer in quantities of a pint or half-liter and cannot accept the idea of a beer which is drunk only a few ounces at a time, and must be sipped and savored slowly. They say that a beer at up to 14% abv or even more is too strong, yet what wine drinker refuses a cabernet sauvignon at 14% abv?

Defining barley wine and brewing it are challenges and I hope I have answered the first in this book. I also hope I have helped home brewers to overcome the second and to turn out a beer of which they can be proud. I have tried to show the diversity and complexity of this great style and perhaps convince you and others that this is a beer that is truly worth brewing. If you have successfully brewed a good barley wine, you are as near as you will ever get to having completed your brewing education.

CHAPTER ONE

DEFINITIONS AND EXAMPLES OF BARLEY WINE

Boy: Would I were in an alehouse in London! I would give all my fame for a pot of ale and safety. (William Shakespeare, *Henry V*, act 3, scene 2)

I THOUGHT THAT THE DEFINITION WOULD BE THE EASY PART OF this book, but the more I considered it the less certain I became. For the style seems to have had something of a murky past, with modern definitions being somewhat arbitrary. We do know, of course, that it is originally an English style, but one which has been taken up in relatively recent times by American craft brewers. So, let's start by looking at how Americans look at barley wine, by considering the definitions given by the Brewers Association (BA).

This program gives us two versions of this beer: American-Style Barley Wine Ale and British-Style Barley Wine Ale. The essential difference between the two is that the American version (Surprise! Surprise!) is more highly hopped than the British version. Otherwise, original gravities (OG) and alcohol content are pretty much the same at 1.085–1.120 (20.4–28.0ºP), 8.5–12.2% abv. Further details are available on their website: www.brewersassociation.org/edu/brewers-association-beer-style-guidelines/. But do note that the hop rates given for the American version means that a double (or even triple) IPA would actually fit this category—more on that later.

But if it is an English style, what do the British authorities say? The revered Michael Jackson (*New World Guide to Beer*, 1988) gives no definitive statement on strength, but merely quotes several examples. He does, however, point out that there are both pale and dark examples of the style (the latter would not fit into the BA definition). Roger Protz, editor of CAMRA's *Good Beer Guide*, writing with Graham Wheeler in *Brew Your Own Real Ale at Home* (1993), is unusually terse on the style. He writes "Barley wine is a modern, euphemistic term for a very strong ale. . . . I suppose a barley wine should have an OG of at least 1090 (*sic*)."

The well-respected British beer historian and beer author Martyn Cornell has this to say:

> In the early twentieth century, ales of 1080 (*sic*) or greater became known generically as "barley wine," although this blanket characterization cut across a wide variety of beer styles. This means that today "barley wine" can have any of the very different characteristics of a sweet dark ale, a super-strong stout, a strong Burton or a strong bitter ale.

In order to try to clarify some of this confusion, let's look at some beers that would fit Cornell's loose definition:

Table 1 Barley Wines?

BEER	ref	OG	Plato
American Tonic Ale C 1896	WH	1.086	20.8
American Tonic Ale G 1896	WH	1.091	21.7
Queen's College Chancellor Ale 1937	HLH/TF	1.140	32.0
Coppinger Strong Ale 1810	TF	1.107	25.1
Coppinger Dorchester Ale 1815	TF	1.136	31.2
Amsinck No. 15 Dorset XXX Old Ale 1868	TF	1.085	20.4
Amsinck No. 6 London Ale 1868	TF	1.110	25.9
Olde English Ale 1901	WH	1.089	21.4

BEER	ref	OG	Plato
Somerset Ale 3-year-old 1882	WH	1.095	22.6
Worthington Burton Ale 1890	WH	1.103	24.2
American Ale 1887	WH	1.081	19.4
Brakspear 140/- 1810	DP	1.100	23.7
Flower's Brewery XXX March Beer 1872	DP	1.120	28.0
Old Burton Ale 1824	DP	1.134	30.9
October Pale Ale 1743	DP	1.110	25.9
Simpson's March Beer 1854	DP	1.100	23.7
Bass Strong Ale 1896	RP	1.102	24.0
Ballingall Old Barley Wine 1955	RP	1.075	18.1
Bass Prince's Ale 1934	RP	1.113	26.5
Bass No.1 Barley wine, Red Label 1965	RP	1.107	25.1
Bass Strong Ale 1896	RP	1.102	24.0
Bodger's barley wine, 1993	RP	1.080	19.3
Courage Russian Imperial Stout 1983	RP	1.109	25.7
Scotch Ale E 140/- 1837	WHR	1.127	29.4
Scotch Ale E 120/- 1837	WHR	1.127	29.4
Scotch Ale E 100/- 1837	WHR	1.106	25.0
Scotch Ale E 80/- 1837	WHR	1.090	21.6
Everard's Old Bill Barley Wine 1993	RP	1.070	17.0
Friary Audit Strong Ale 1951	RP	1.084	20.1
Godson Stock Ale 1983	RP	1.084	20.1
Edmonds Audit Ale 1955	RP	1.083	20.9
Hall & Woodhouse Stingo Barley Wine 1959	RP	1.077	18.6
Hammonds Stingo 1992	RP	1.110	25.9
Harvey Elizabethan Ale 1959	RP	1.085	20.4
McEwans Scotch Ale 1955	RP	1.088	21.0
McEwans Scotch Ale 1940	RP	1.080	19.2
McMullen Coronation Ale 1953	RP	1.089	21.2

Continued

BEER	ref	OG	Plato
Morgans Brewery Barley Wine 1953	RP	1.072	17.4
Reid KKK Ale 1839	RP	1.089	21.2
Reid SSS Exp Stout 1867	RP	1.094	22.3
Ridley Bishops Barley Wine 1983	RP	1.080	19.2
Scarborough & Whitby Barley Wine 1953	RP	1.064	15.7
Tamplin Cheer-i-o No.1 Barley Wine 1959	RP	1.063	15.4
Tennant Bros. Gold Label No.1 Barley Wine 1954	RP	1.102	24.1
Whitbread KKK 1891	RP	1.086	20.6
Whitbread Final Selection 1965	RP	1.079	19.0
Young & Co., Celebration Ale, 1955	RP	1.076	18.4
Truman S1 Barley Wine1931	RP	1.105	24.8
Truman XXXXK Ale 1832	RP	1.118	27.5
Barclay Perkins KKKK Strong Ale 1870	RP	1.106	25.0
Whitbread KXXXX Stock Ale 1837	RP	1.113	26.4
Thomas Hardy's Ale 2005	TF	1.125	29.0
J.W. Lees Harvest Ale 2010	TF	1.120	28.0
Fuller's Vintage Ale 2016	TF	1.090	21.6
Bluepoint Brewing Old Howling Bastard 2017	TF	1.107	25.1
Firefly Twinkler Barley Wine 2016	TF	1.091	21.7
Rogue XS Old Crustacean Barley Wine 2017	TF	1.106	25.0
Sierra Nevada Bigfoot® Barleywine-Style Ale 2017	TF	1.097	23.0
Anchor Old Foghorn® Ale 2001	BA	1.100	23.7

WH = Wahl-Henius
HLH = H. Lloyd Hind
BA = Beer Advocate
WHR = W. H. Roberts
TF = Author
RP = Ron Pattinson
DP = Durden Park

This list is not intended to be comprehensive; rather, I have put it together to illustrate some points about barley wine. You may have wondered why I did not include Samuel Adams's Utopias, which could be regarded as being the biggest barley wine of them all, coming in at around 25% abv (it varies somewhat from year to year). At this strength some might question whether it is really a beer at all, but my point in omitting it is that this kind of alcohol level can only be achieved by means of special techniques. Since I don't know these techniques in any detail I have taken an executive decision and concluded that brewing this beer is beyond the scope of this book. I have not included in the table any details of color, finishing gravity, or alcohol content; that was just because I did not want the table to be too complicated.

From the table, OG of these beers runs from 1.063 (15.4°P) to 1.134 (30.9°P). Yes, I know there is one at 1.136 (31.2°P), but that is an approximation which I calculated making an arbitrary assumption as to the brewhouse efficiency attained in its production. Of the eight beers with an OG below 1.080 (19.3°P), five were designated as barley wines by their respective brewers. That puts these below the lower BA limit and below Cornell's bottom limit, so can they really be called barley wines? That raises an important question, namely that if a brewer calls his output a tangerine isn't that what it is, even though style guidelines say it is an orange? After all, the BA designations are intended as competition requirements, and Cornell's merely reflects general custom. Of course, the real answer lies in the taste of these beers. If you were to drink one and found it thinner and less satisfying than barley wines produced at higher OG, then you would be justified in saying it was not a barley wine, wouldn't you? Besides, we do not normally judge a beer by looking at its brewing parameters, do we? No, we taste it and decide whether it is a "good beer," which is to say we decide whether we enjoy drinking it or not, and not whether it fits any relatively arbitrary description.

What I am saying is that all these definitions are nothing more than guidelines, and as brewers we should not follow them slavishly so long as we actually like the beer. However, I would, in fact, say that we should take 1.080 (19.3°P) as our target for the lower end of the starting gravity range. With that settled, what do we do about the top end? Well, the table shows only three beers above 1.120 (28.0°P), which is the top end given by the BA. No, because again that is for competitions, and there is no reason why you should not go higher if you wish. Except for the reason that it is very difficult to get much above this figure! I have brewed an all-grain version of the Queen's College Chancellor Ale, but it took a lot of time and hard work, and a procedure that few craft brewers would consider, on economic grounds alone. For the home brewer, there is an easier way and I shall detail this and my all-grain procedure in the brewing section.

The table includes one stout and several Scotch ales, just to demonstrate what kinds of beers *could* fall into this category. I think most people would say that an imperial stout is just that and cannot be called a barley wine, so let's dismiss that. But the Scotch ales present a different problem. The examples in the table mostly start at higher gravities than in the BA definitions for this style, and I would have no problem in calling them barley wines, with the caveat that they generally finish at a higher gravity than other beers in this category. That makes them taste sweeter, and I think that the real art of brewing barley wine is to minimize sweetness in the finished beer. Also, in Scotch ales hop levels are traditionally quite low, perhaps as little as 30–40 IBU, so that there is not much bitterness to offset the malty sweetness in this style. But if that kind of flavor is your bag, and you want to call it barley wine, I'm on your side. Also in the table is Truman's XXXXK Ale from 1832, which I note because it was called Mild Ale (even Imperial Mild Ale by Ron Pattinson). But the "K" in its designation signifies that it was a keeping beer, meant to be long matured before going to the customer. Which is odd, since in 1832 "Mild" meant that the beer was put on sale while still quite new, say not more than a month old after brewing. Ah, how brewers love to blur the lines with their labeling!

BARLEY WINES AND HOP BITTERNESS

That brings me onto the subject of hopping rates for barley wines. It's difficult to know what bitterness levels beers had in the eighteenth and nineteenth centuries. That's because brewers in those times had no knowledge of alpha acids, let alone means to measure them. And it is difficult to track back from what we know of the alpha acid content of modern hops because cultivation methods have improved since then and today's brewers have access to new hop varieties. So, first let's look at some modern barley wines.

Fuller's Vintage Ale at 8.5% abv has 40 IBU, according to Martyn Cornell (blog, *The mystery of the vanishing 2016 Vintage Ale*). Perhaps the most famous modern version of the style, Thomas Hardy's Ale is variously given as 12% abv, 50–70 IBU (R. Protz, *Beer Drinker's Almanac, 5th Edition, 1997*), 72 IBU (*BeerSmith Recipe Cloud*), and 43 IBU (*All About Beer, July 2004*). Do note that the last analysis was of the later version brewed by O'Hanlon's, and not the original version from

Thomas Hardy's Ale, a beer with romantic connections but a checkered history.

Eldridge Pope. On the other hand, Truman's S1 Barley Wine (1931) is quoted as having 137 IBU, at 9.7% abv (*Ron Pattinson, The Home Brewer's Guide to Vintage Beers, 2014)*; that is probably higher than can be obtained in practice, so must be a calculated number, not an analysis. Bass No.1, the first beer to be called barley wine, is given as 10+% abv and 60–70 IBU (*Fal Allen and Dick Cantwell, Barley Wine, Classic Beer Style series).*

In contrast, Rogue's XS Old Crustacean at 10.6% abv is given as 110 IBU by the brewer. Similarly, Smuttynose Barleywine Style Ale is at 65 IBU (though at 11.6% abv it is close in strength to the Rogue beer), whereas Otter Creek 20th Anniversary Ale at the slightly higher 12.0% abv has only 55 IBU. Sierra Nevada Bigfoot Barleywine-Style Ale at the lower level of 9.6% abv comes in at 90 IBU. But Avery Hog Heaven Imperial Red IPA (formerly called Barleywine-Style Ale) at 9.2% abv is quoted as having 104 IBU, compared to Free State Brewing's at 10.5% abv and 150 IBU (*America's Best & Top 10).* Again, the latter is presumably only a calculated figure. The case of Hog Heaven is revealing, since it was originally styled as a Barleywine-Style Ale as there was at the time no other suitable classification for it. Later, Avery (perhaps my favorite Colorado brewery) changed the name to Imperial Red IPA, seeing that designation as a better fit for this beer. All of which underlines my point about the difficulty of defining Barley Wine. I am tempted to argue that "Imperial" should not be coupled with "IPA," but that would be a digression. Lastly, a version of Ballantine Burton Ale brewed in 2015 contains 11.3% abv, at 75 IBU. You will see that a Burton ale is quoted in the table, and this is obviously a pale beer, and well-suited to the category.

BA guidelines state that for the American style of the beer bitterness should be in the range 60–100, while the British style range is much lower at 40–65 IBU. That may be true for modern versions of barley wine, but what about English beers brewed in older times? Dr. Keith Thomas has analyzed brewing records for 1903 from Hammond's Bradford Brewery, in Yorkshire, and suggests that Old Tom, XXXX was brewed at 7.5% abv and probably 72 IBU. But Hammond's XXXXX

Stingo was at the higher level of 9.5% abv and bitterness at maybe 119 IBU (Martyn Cornell, *Amber, Gold and Black*).

If we go farther back to a series of brewings performed in the 1860s in London *(George Amsinck, A Series of fifty Brewings in extenso, 1868)* we have quite detailed information on four barley wines. These range from 1.097 to 1.110 OG and from 8.1 to 9.3% abv. Amsinck does give the weight of hops added, but of course there are no figures on hop alpha acid, utilization, or IBU. We can assume that the hops contained 3% alpha acid, as suggested by Peter Darby *(personal communication)*. If we then further assume that utilization was only 15%, as might be expected with such high gravity beers, these four beers would calculate to 53, 60, 68 and 70 IBU. The last two would then be higher than the top limit of the BA range for British barley wines. In fact, alpha acid utilization might well have been higher than 15%, because Amsinck actually performed two boils. The first was of the higher gravity first wort and ran for two hours, and the second of the lower gravity second wort from the mash, re-using the hops from the first boil and lasting three hours. However, even the conservative 15% I have chosen does, I think, illustrate the point that British barley wines can have a higher level of bitterness than BA guidelines indicate.

Let's come back to a beer brewed in the twentieth century, namely Queen's College Chancellor Ale. This Oxford college first hired a brewer in 1341, the year it was founded, and brewing was carried out there using pretty much the same medieval methods up to 1937, when it ceased brewing. It was visited in 1927 by H. Lloyd Hind, a brewing scientist of some note who published details of the College's brewing procedure. Chancellor Ale was brewed at OG 1.135 (31.0ºP), 10.7% abv, and used 26 lb. hops to produce 2.5 barrels of finished beer. Again, we do not know the alpha acid content of the hops, but it is likely that this was higher than for those used by Amsinck some seventy years earlier. But if we use the conservative figures of 3% alpha acid and 15% utilization then calculation gives 130 IBU (*H. Lloyd Hind, Brewing Science and Practice, Vol.1, 1939; H. Lloyd Hind, "Brewing at Queen's College Oxford," The Brewer's Journal, 1927; T. Foster, Brewery History Journal No. 132*).

If I have gone on a bit about hop bitterness, it is simply that I am trying to demonstrate that this parameter does not really distinguish between so-called American and British barley wines. Sure, Many American craft-brewed versions are high in bitterness, but they are merely following long-standing traditions in British brewing. My good friend Jeff Browning, brewer at Brewport, a brewpub in Bridgeport, Connecticut, likes to say, "Brewing has been carried out for 10,000 years, so whatever you think of as 'new' has surely been thought of before." But there is a point about bitterness in barley wines that I should make, and that is that these beers tend toward sweetness, and a hefty level of hop bitterness helps to balance this and prevent the beer from being cloyingly sweet. So too does proper attenuation, but I'll get to that shortly. However, I must here mention Sierra Nevada Bigfoot, a beer often held to be iconic by American brewers and drinkers. The 2017 version, tasted in that year, I found to be intensely bitter, so much so, that even at 9.6% abv and 90 IBU it tasted thin and lacking in body. But it is a beer designed for long keeping and surely the bitterness will mellow out somewhat over time.

HOP AROMA AND FLAVOR

It is debatable as to whether these aspects of beer are desirable in barley wines. There are many components that go to make up the flavor and aroma of these beers, and ethanol itself is present in sufficient quantity to be noticeable on the palate. Then there will probably be some higher alcohols and esters which will give the beer something of a fruity character, and the residual sweetness which will add mouthfeel and "fullness" to it, as well as caramel, nutty flavors, and even some butterscotch notes from the dreaded diacetyl. So, hop aroma and flavor may well be hidden behind all these other attributes. If you take the attitude that this means that all you need to do is to follow the current approach to IPA brewing and throw in yet greater amounts of hops in the later stages of brewing and dry-hopping, I advise you not to do so. Because if you do, all you will have produced is a double or even "triple" IPA, rather than a barley wine!

However, that does not mean that you should not attempt to add some hop flavor and aroma to your barley wine. That is nothing new, for both the Amsinck brews and the chancellor ale were dry-hopped in the cask. But, bear in mind that these are attributes which diminish with age, and that these beers, especially the "big" ones starting at over 1.090 (26.1°P) and upward are meant to be keeping beers. Chancellor Ale was routinely kept a year before drinking, for example. And in Table 1 there are some beers, such as those of Whitbread and Truman, that have the letter K in their designation, which stands for "Keeping." Thomas Hardy's Ale specifically states on the bottle label that it will last for *at least* twenty-five years. Very big barley wines are often somewhat harsh and unbalanced when first brewed and need time to mellow out and come into balance. Some, indeed, will develop oxidized, sherry-like notes on long keeping, an often much-desired attribute. And "long" can mean years, by which time any hop flavor and aroma will have dissipated.

In short, if you want hop flavor and aroma in your barley wine, you are best to brew at the lower end of the range, say OG 1.080–1.085 (19.2–20.3°P), and keep your late hop additions fairly modest. You can use whatever hop you like, even strong flavored ones, like those of the "citrus" family, or be less daring and use more delicate hops, such as (perish the thought) the more traditional Goldings or Fuggles. Just remember barley wine should not just be all about the hops, but primarily it should be all about the flavors of malt, caramel, esters and so on.

ATTENUATION

Brewers most often talk of this aspect of beer, but they do not mean true attenuation. This requires measuring the gravity of the beer after distilling off ethanol and replacing it with an equal volume of water. That is because ethanol has a lower density than water so that the measured final gravity of the wort is higher than the true final gravity. Most of us find it much easier to use "apparent attenuation," which is simply the difference between the original and final gravities divided by the original gravity and expressed as a percentage, with the "gravities' expressed only as the figures after the decimal point. In other words, in the case of a beer with OG 1.130 (29°P), FG 1.028 (7.1°P) we would have:

$$\text{Apparent attenuation} = \{(130\text{-}28)/130)\} \times 100 =$$
$$(102/130) \times 100 = 78.5\%$$

This is a very important factor in brewing barley wines. Apparent attenuation is the figure that yeast suppliers provide, and what you want to look at when selecting a yeast. It takes a lot of effort and cost to make a big beer like this, so you surely do not want to be disappointed with the result. Getting this sort of attenuation with a high alcohol beer is not easy, because yeast is inhibited by the very alcohol it produces. You must choose a yeast that gives good attenuation, and above all ensure that you pitch with a sufficient number of yeast cells, something I shall deal with later.

But what level of apparent attenuation should you be looking for? Well, you want a level of attenuation where the inherent sweetness of a barley wine would not swamp all other flavors. Low levels of attenuation, that is, high finishing gravities, will result in a beer that may be one-dimensional. Residual sugars may also be a target for beer-spoilage organisms in a barley wine stored for long periods. So, in this case it would seem that there is a lot to be said in favor of the BA designation of a maximum finishing gravity of 1.028 (7.1°P).

But, in the example above that is quite a high level of attenuation which you may find difficult to achieve, and I would suggest that a more reasonable FG number would be 1.035 (8.8°P), 73% apparent attenuation with OG 1.130 (29°P). If the FG is much higher, then sweetness starts to take over the palate. For lower OG beers, 1.085 (20.3°P), say, then getting down to FG 1.028 (7.1°P), or even less is quite feasible, and low enough to keep the sweetness in check. There are ways to reach low finishing gravities other than using a single pitching of an ale yeast, such as adding a champagne yeast at the end of the main fermentation. I'll discuss that later. Just remember that checking the numbers on attenuation is a useful guide, but that is all it is. That does not mean you should not pay attention to trying to achieve good attenuation, but, as always, the real point is whether the finished beer tastes good, not whether it fits the numbers!

Very low finishing gravities, as quoted above, were much less common in the past. If we go back to 1868 and Amsinck's four beers he

Sam Adams Utopias, a huge beer, sherry-like in its alcohol content, and dressed in an appropriate but unusual bottle.

achieved 72% for one with OG 1.097 (23°P), 70% for a second at this same gravity, 67% from OG 1.100 (23.8°P), and 65% from OG 1.110 (25.9°P). Further, the chancellor ale brewing overseen by Lloyd Hind in 1927 achieved attenuation of only 61% from OG 1.135 (31°P). So clearly these earlier brewers produced beers that were much sweeter than is nowadays considered as ideal for barley wine. But, luckily for us we have access to a wide range of yeast strains and a good bit more knowledge as to how to make them attenuate a barley wine efficiently.

COLOR

BA guidelines previously gave a fairly narrow range of color for Barley wines: 11–18 SRM for the American version and the even narrower 14–18 SRM for the British style. In recent years, the BA guidelines have kept the American range at 11–18 SRM while expanding the British range significantly to 11–36. I found the narrower guidelines rather odd since British barley wines have had some notably dark versions, such as Bass No. 1 and Thomas Hardy's Ale. The Hammond's Old Tom from 1903, which I mentioned earlier, actually used a tiny amount of black malt for color, so the updated range better reflects the true variety of British examples, but most barley wines are brewed with only pale malt, perhaps with a small proportion of caramel malt in the grist. So-called pale barley wines tend to be copper in color, but others can be of a deep chestnut shade, right through to red-brown, such as Samuel Smith's Yorkshire Stingo. You can achieve darker colors, should you so wish, by incorporating specialty and high-roast malts, but I'll discuss that in the brewing section.

There is surprisingly little information to be found on barley wine color in terms of actual numbers, although Rogue's Old Crustacean checks in at 57 SRM. That may be because these are beers produced on special occasions and the production methods probably ensure color variation from brew to brew. That is because they often require a long boil, during which Maillard browning reactions and caramelization occur and are responsible for the color of the beer. Which means that barley wines at the stronger end of the spectrum and which require longer boiling will be deeper in color than their lower gravity counter-parts. But this does depend on the methodology of the brewing such as whether sugar or malt extract is used to achieve the final gravity—I'll discuss that further in the brewing section. In the meantime, I shall deliberately ignore numbers for the color and use only descriptors for this parameter.

DEFINITION

My final suggestions are given below, but I want you to understand that these are my numbers and mine alone and reflect my dislike of trying to pin down beer styles too precisely. I know I have written previously on putting numbers to beer styles in my books, but I have always regarded such attempts as mere guidelines—no one ever handed me stone tablets with specific instructions carved into them. But do remember that BA style guidelines are for competitions and you need to adhere to them if you enter competitions sponsored by BA. Alternatively, if you enter competitions sponsored by the Beer Judge Certification Program (BJCP), you will need to adhere to their guidelines for English Barley Wine and American Barleywine, which are similar, but not identical, to the BA definitions.

So, Barley wines should have OG 1.080–1140+ (20–32°P), FG 25–35 (6.1–8.8°P), abv 8.5–13.5% +, IBU 40–100, color copper to dark red-brown.

But, this says nothing about flavor, which is surely the most important attribute of beer. It is a topic I shy away from, for three reasons. First, because each person's palate is different from any other, flavor perception and description will also be different. Second, because beer flavor *is* a perception which can alter due to a wide variety of effects, even down to the time of day when the tasting takes place. Indeed, many professional brewers consider that 11 a.m. is the time when most person's palates are at their highest level of perception, and some schedule their quality control tasting at this time. Third, because the words used by many writers to describe the taste of a beer are often vague, fluffy, and meaningless; I have seen beers described as tasting of tobacco or of soap, as though these were actually positive flavors. I would throw away any beer I brewed that tasted of either of these two flavors! Attempts have been made to define beer flavors on a scientific basis, such as those by the American Society of Brewing Chemists (ASBC *Methods of Sensory Analysis*, Sensory Analysis-12), which gives definitions of words used to describe flavors and puts them together in the form of a "flavor wheel" showing the relationships between flavor descriptors.

Unfortunately, systems such as the flavor wheel are complicated and designed for use by well-trained tasters, and are not easily interpreted by lesser mortals, such as home brewers and drinkers. Also, there is another factor to consider and that is that there is a difference between carefully tasting a beer to decide what are its component flavors and just drinking a beer to enjoy it in a pub or at home. In the latter case, you are looking at the overall flavor of the beer, rather than trying to pick out specific flavors. In light of that, I shall try to define what I expect to find when I drink a barley wine, purely for pleasure. It should be rich and full in body, coating the mouth with a luscious sweetness, though it should not be so sweet as to be cloying; it should taste of caramel or perhaps toffee or raisins, and especially if matured for long periods have an oxidized, sherry-like flavor. It should certainly have some hop bitterness, the intensity of which will vary according to the brewer's own taste. The overall effect should be that it is too rich and full-flavored to be drunk quickly; it should demand to be sipped slowly and not be gulped down.

WHEAT WINE

This is a beer "invented" by American craft brewers and meets the brewing parameters for barley wines given above, and the BA and BJCP numbers pretty much coincide with those given for barley wines. However, wheat wines do differ in one very important aspect. This is that it is brewed with 50% or more of the grist being wheat malt, which often results in it being fruitier (containing more esters) in character than barley wines. The examples I have tasted tend to be somewhat thinner and less full-bodied than a similar beer made from all malt although only relatively so, for they are still big beers. They generally do not have the phenolic "clove" character typical of many German wheat beers and are usually (but not necessarily) low in bitterness much like the English barley wines as defined by the BA. Wheat wines also tend to form a bigger head when poured than do their barley malt relations, where head formation is not normally a characteristic, because of the effect of their high alcohol content. I do not think this really makes it fundamentally different from barley wine, and I look at it as just a subspecies of this style. I do, however, like the name very much since it accurately reflects the difference between this and "regular" barley wines. In this respect it avoids solecisms, such as the dreadfully oxymoronic "Dark IPA"! Having said all that, Wheat wines are not very common, and I have come across only a few, the first being at Church Brew Works (Pittsburgh, Pennsylvania), though that was some years ago and it is not on their current menu. The second, which I was able to purchase locally, is White Oak, from The Bruery (Placentia, California). This was a 50:50 blend of a barrel-aged wheat wine and an "Ale" and has now been retired. It may be that this style is simply not favored by Connecticut and other New England craft brewers, for Beer Advocate does list over two hundred examples brewed in North America.

OLD AND STOCK ALES

There is often confusion as to what these beers are and whether they fit into the barley wine classification. Old ale is generally thought of as being a strong ale, but not as strong as barley wine, and darker in color than the latter. Which is still a somewhat vague description, although it seems to be accepted by many home and craft brewers. BA guidelines suggest old ales can be up to 9.1% abv, which overlaps their barley wine definition. In addition, they have a Strong Ale category with OG ranging from the bottom of the old ale level to above the top of the barley wine range! No wonder there is confusion about these styles! And of course, old ale should be old by definition, and traditionally aging would have taken place in wooden casks. But that also applies

to barley wines. Today it is generally customary for old ales to be bottled or canned relatively soon after brewing, in which case they are not
really old at all! I am therefore reduced to giving you a vague description of this type of beer and say that it should have OG 1.060–1.080
(15.0–20.0°P), be low in bitterness (about 40 IBU maximum), dark in
color, and sweet in flavor at 1.015–1.025 (4–6°P).

Stock ale is another quite vague term; it is very similar to old ale
in strength and in the sense of being a long-stored beer. It tends to be
paler in color and to have a higher level of bitterness than the latter.
But its most significant character trait is that it should have those odd
flavors associated with the presence of *Brettanomyces* yeast strains. After
all, this yeast was first cultured from an English stock ale by N. H.
Claussen in 1903, which is why the name carries the prefix "Brettano."
If it is called "stock ale" by the brewer, comes in at 8.0% abv or more,
and does not have that "Brett" flavor, it is more properly called "Barley
Wine." *Brettanomyces*-produced flavors may also be present in old ales,
but at a low level, and they should certainly not be present in barley
wines. In case you are not aware, the flavors from *Brettanomyces* are
often described as being like "a sweaty horse blanket." I do not know
who first described it in this unfortunate way, but I do know that Brett
flavors are in no way appealing to me!

To expand on this last paragraph, consider three beers I have before
me. First is Triple Bag, described by the brewer (Long Trail Brewing,
Bridgewater, Vermont) as "a triple amber ale," weighing in at 11% abv
and 65 IBU. Second comes Old Stock Ale, from North Coast Brewing
Co. (Fort Bragg, California) at 11.8% abv. Third we have Curmudgeon from Founder's Brewing Co. (Grand Rapids, Michigan), described
as an old ale with 9.8% abv and 50 IBU. My opinion, which some
might find to be of debatable worth, is that all three are really barley
wines, and that is exactly how they drink. Calling them anything else
is mere semantics, although there is a long history of brewers using
beer style designations that are somewhat imaginative. Of course, the
various titles used in these three cases may have been applied by the
brewers because that is exactly what they intended to brew, and there
is an argument that they are entitled to use those descriptions. And

it may be that they preferred to avoid the clumsy phrasing of barley wine–style ale and use a simpler designation. I should note here that as far as I can discover the US Food and Drug Administration (FDA) and the Alcohol and Tobacco Tax and Trade Bureau (TTB) require the use of the full term barley wine–style ale; apparently, the term barley wine is considered misleading and thought to indicate that the labeled product is a wine (as in grape) rather than a beer.

FINAL COMMENTS AND EXAMPLES

There are, or in some cases have been, a lot of barley wines out there, for it seems that many craft breweries see it as a point of honor to produce their own version of this style. Indeed, Beer Advocate list just under 1,400 examples on their website, and it will not surprise you that I have not yet managed to taste them all. One that I shall especially look out for is Arquebus Barleywine Ale, from Will Meyers, brewer at Cambridge Brewing Co. (Massachusetts). The reason is that a base beer is brewed at 1.083 (20°P), honey is added, and when it has fermented down to 1.040 (10°P) white wine juice and a champagne yeast (see section on Ingredients) are added, and the beer finishes at around 13–14% abv (Will Meyers, "Barleywine Designed for the Occasion," *Craft Beer and Brewing*, Dec. 2017/Jan. 2018). This is a beer that truly bridges the gap between beer and wine!

Since, for various reasons, my traveling around the United States is restricted, rather than try to catch up with these beers on their home turf, I decided to catch up with those that are available on my home turf. I simply bought all the examples I could find at liquor stores within fifteen miles of my Connecticut home. I came up with some forty different beers which I considered could be classed under the barley wine category. Some of them will be discussed below, but my list included some seventeen US barley wines and nine different years of J. W. Lees Harvest Ale from Lancashire in England, some of the latter matured in a variety of oak barrels, such as calvados, scotch whisky, port, and sherry casks. Also along for the ride were a couple of English barley wines, Harvey's Elizabethan Ale and Meantime Barley Wine.

And of course a bottle of Thomas Hardy Ale from 1992, when it was still brewed by Eldridge Pope, the brewers who originated this beer but later renounced their traditions and gave up brewing altogether! In addition, there were two American wee heavys from Alesmith Brewing Co. (San Diego, California) and Wulver Wee Heavy, aged in bourbon barrels and brewed by Thirsty Dog Brewing Co. (Akron, Ohio), at an appropriate wee heavy level of bitterness, 22 IBU. I also have one Scotch Ale, the latter brewed by Berkshire Brewing Co., South Deerfield, Massachusetts, aged in a bourbon barrel and brewed in honor of Greg Noonan, founder of the Vermont Brewery and Pub and one of the pioneers of craft brewing in the United States. Most famously, I also found the 2017 version of that doyen of American barley wines, Bigfoot from Sierra Nevada (Chico, California), which I discussed earlier. There is also 20-TON ALE from Two Roads Brewing Co. (Stratford, Connecticut), produced right on my doorstep. It weighs in at 12% abv, but I have no other details, as the brewmaster, Phil Markowski, is notoriously tight-lipped about his recipes. It is, however, billed as an English-style barley wine ale, but "highly hopped." One other Connecticut barley wine I did not buy was brought to me by the brewer as it is only available from the brewery, Alvarium Brewing Co. in New Britain, Connecticut. It was brewed in 2018 as an English barley wine, with the addition of wildflower honey. It was aged in a mix of two- and ten-year old bourbon barrels and weighs in at 8.7% abv and 53 IBU. Some 576 22-oz. bottles were produced, and the bourbon flavor is somewhat forward now, but should mellow out nicely with time.

An interesting beer I have here is HELLDORADO 2017 from Firestone Walker Brewing Co. in Paso Robles, California. It is self-described as a "Blonde Barley Wine Ale" with OG 24.3°P (1.103), 24 IBU, 12.8% abv, 11 SRM ("Golden Blonde"), and aged in bourbon barrels. I do not see it as really blond, more of a red-gold in color, but that is subjective, of course. It has some hints of bourbon, though not overdone, and some sherry-like, nutty, fruity flavors. But the alcohol comes through very strongly as heat on the back of the palate, and to me it lacks some body for a beer brewed at this OG. That may be because the finishing gravity is listed as only 1.87°P (1.007), representing an apparent attenuation of no less than 93%, all achieved with "A British Ale Yeast." All very intriguing, especially as I always thought Paso Robles was a ballroom dance.

Bringing up the rear were two versions of Ola Dubh from Harviestoun in Scotland and a couple of versions of Fuller's Vintage Ale from London, England. These last three actually do not fit the alcohol range for my definition of barley wine, but I felt they were near enough and interesting enough to include them. Note that because of their limited availability this does not include those from brewpubs in Connecticut, such as Brewport in Bridgeport, where we currently have a second version of Cute Fat Kid on tap. BrüRm@BAR and Willimantic Brewing have also been known to offer a draft barley wine. One of the interesting things is that a number of the American-brewed beers came in 22-ounce bottles, a philosophy I do not understand. This is just too great a volume of a beer very high in alcohol for any one person to handle in an evening. And, given the cost of such beers it is a great waste if you open it and find you do not like it! I think the Brits got it right

A selection of US barley wines, not all of them named as such.

when they opted for the ⅓ pint "nip" bottle, just the right volume for a couple of wineglassfuls of the nectar they contain.

A curtain comes down for a moment, then is raised again to reveal some beers particularly worthy of discussion. To begin with, we have a beer I have only sampled at the brewery, namely Double IPA from Firefly Hollow Brewing Company in Bristol, Connecticut. It is an excellent beer, brimming with malt character as well as hop flavor, and the brewer, Dana Bourque, said to me that it was really a hoppy barley wine, a statement that backs up my argument that the dividing line between a very strong IPA and a barley wine is a very faint one and is really determined only by what the brewer decides to call it. And, of course, these days IPAs are in great demand in New England and elsewhere.

Next, I want to discuss a beer that is actually designated as a barley wine. This is Olde School from Dogfish Head Craft Brewery Inc. (Delaware) and I mention it here because it is rated at no less than 15% abv, an alcohol level that is difficult, if not impossible to achieve by "normal" barley wine brewing methods. Barley wines are mostly brewed from pale malt, sometimes with the addition of a proportion of specialty malts, or with some sugar. Olde School, however, claims to use dates and figs in its brewing, but I do not see that as disqualifying it from the barley wine category, rather I see it as another example of Dogfish Head's propensity for brewing innovations. For the record, it claims on the label that "This beer ages with the best of 'em," raising the topic of barley wine aging, which is something I shall deal with later.

Four other beers sit before me. None are labeled as barley wine, yet they could be so designated. I have already mentioned Otter Creek Twentieth Anniversary Ale, but what about Scotch on Scotch from Boulevard Brewing Co. (Missouri)? It claims to be an "Oak aged Imperial Scotch Ale," is 9.6% abv, and has 25 IBU. The low hop level does fit Scottish-style beers since these usually have a fairly low level of bittering, as historically, hops were not grown in Scotland and had to be imported from England, making them somewhat expensive for Scottish brewers. But "Imperial" Scotch Ale is surely unnecessarily misleading? When did Scotland ever have an Emperor?

Next, let's look at Burton Ale from P. Ballantine & Sons (Minnesota) This rare beer purports to be 11.3% abv and 75 IBU, so has a significant level of bitterness. It is said to be a reincarnation of a beer brewed by Ballantine in the 1930s which could be kept for up to twenty years and was mostly given away to a select few, rather than being sold on the open market. Michael Jackson suggests it was actually an IPA, but it is too high in alcohol for that, and it is too pale to be a true Burton ale, since these latter were much darker in color. So, it must be a barley wine, mustn't it?

The fourth beer I want to consider is The Maharajah from Avery Brewing Co. (Colorado). This weighs in at 10.0% abv, and although I do not have a number for IBU, it is a beer which uses several different hops, is dry-hopped, and has a big hop character when drunk; it is called an "Imperial IPA." For my money, it is a hoppy barley wine, and would be an exemplar for an American-Style Barley Wine Ale in the BA system (you already know my ideas on that!). And needless to say, I find the use of the term "imperial" loose, incorrect, and meaningless. And note that many so-called double IPAs would actually fit the barley wine category, too. But should highly hopped beers really be seen as barley wines? The latter, high in alcohol, are designed as keeping beers, whereas those high in hop character will lose that on long storage (over a year or more) and become something quite different. Maybe they should be drunk while fresh from the brewery and be called double or triple (not imperial!) IPAs, but that's an argument for another day!

I do not want to bore you by endless repetitions of this kind of statement, but, in case you think I have deserted my English roots in talking only about American beers, let's briefly consider some English ones. Some of the more famous ones are Thomas Hardy's Ale, Harvey's Elizabethan Ale, Fuller's Vintage Ale, and the series of Harvest Ales brewed over several years by J. W. Lees, some of which have been matured in casks which previously contained various spirits. You have probably noticed that they are all termed "Ale" plus some other descriptor; not one of them calls itself barley wine, although that is exactly what they are. There are other barley wines produced by small brewers in England, but the above-mentioned are probably the most well-known English barley wines. Barley wine is now a rare product in England because the tax system works against such strong beers, as I shall explain in the history section. In fact, the Elizabethan Ale from Harvey's at only 7.5% abv is a little too low for a barley wine; the reason for this is directly related to that tax system, which heavily penalizes beers at greater than 7.5% abv. Note, however, that Meantime Brewing is an exception to this rule with an 8.5% abv barley wine. However, although it still operates as a relatively small brewery Meantime can no longer be regarded as a craft brewer since it was bought out by SAB Miller in 2015.

My own approach, which is perhaps rather nit-picking, is that if we are going to use style designations they should be reasonably accurate, since they are an important guide for the drinker and for their expectation of what is inside the bottle. But, you argue, what about something like Long Trail's Triple Bag, which is not actually described by any traditional name and might even represent a completely new style? To which I would reply that thanks to the BA and BJCP, we already have more than enough so-called styles and do not need another. Indeed, an interesting thing came to light

Bass No. 1, the first named barley wine; the glass is authentic, but, unfortunately the beer in it is not!

while I was writing this. That is, the results of competition at the 2017 Great American Beer Festival came out, and barley wines won medals in four categories! Shipfaced, from Silver Harbor Brewing Co. (Saint Joseph, Michigan) won the Barley Wine-Style Ale category, while Barrel Aged Barleywine from Charleville Vineyard & Microbrewery (Sainte Genevieve, Missouri) came third in the Wood- and Barrel-Aged Strong Beer category behind the gold medal winner, Hurly Burly Port Barrel

Aged Barleywine. More mystifying, to me at least, was the fact that the winner of the Old Ale or Strong Ale category was 10&2 Barleywine from Fifty West Brewing Co. (Cincinnati, Ohio). Even more mystifying is that the winner in the Pumpkin/Squash Beer category was 5 Phantoms Pumpkin Spice Barleywine from Phillipsburg Brewing Co., Phillipsburg, Montana. I think these results nicely make my point, but I won't take this any further. Instead, let's have another beer and continue this contentious discussion later.

CHAPTER TWO

HISTORY OF BARLEY WINE

Iago: I learn'd it in England, where, indeed, they are most potent in potting: your Dane, your German, and your swag-bellied Hollander—Drink ho!—are nothing to your English.
(William Shakespeare, *Othello*, act 2, scene 3)

THE ABOVE QUOTATION MAY BE SOMEWHAT BIASED AS, OF course, Shakespeare was himself English. But, although other nations have brewed strong beers, the title "barley wine" first appeared on the label of a beer brewed in England in the late nineteenth century, and it is generally accepted that barley wine is indeed an English style in origin. But the term had seen some use even outside England long before that.

Xenophon of Athens, writing in the fourth century BCE, says that the Armenians, as well as a neighboring people called Urartians, had a drink called barley wine (*A History of Beer and Brewing*, I. Hornsey, 2003). Hornsey further suggests that, drawing from Polybius, who wrote some two hundred years after Xenophon, the Scythians (in essentially what is now Ukraine) made and drank a barley wine. An English writer, James Fletcher, in 1750 published a tendentious, scholarly work, *A Dissertation on Barley Wine*. Fletcher agrees that Xenophon used the term, but further asserts that Aristotle, who was contemporaneous with Xenophon, also used it. However, none of these writers, including Fletcher's more modern work, had anything to say about what "barley wine" may have been like or how it was brewed.

Therefore, my interpretation of what these writers meant by "barley wine" was simply that it was an alcoholic drink produced from barley which was analogous to wine produced from grapes.

A contemporary of Fletcher, George Watkins (*The Compleat English Brewer*, 1768) also mentions barley wine, but gives no definitions or recipes for it. Instead he refers to strong beer as being intended for keeping, ale a strong malt liquor not designed for keeping, and small beer "which can be kept a considerable time." The last phrase seems a little odd, but the recipe he gives suggests this latter beer would have been unlikely to be any stronger than perhaps, 4% abv.

A much later reference comes in about 1830 (W. Brande, *Town and Country Brewery Book*). Brande mentions barley wine twice, bracketing it with Dorchester ale in the second note, but giving no definition or recipe for either beer.

EARLY BEERS

But I am jumping ahead of things here, and we should go back a few centuries. It is generally held that it was common English practice to make two or more brews from one batch of malt. For not until the nineteenth century did English brewers adopt the sparging technique of mashing, then washing the extract out of the grain bed by trickling hot water over it (actually a Scottish invention). Instead, they would mash the grain with hot water, and after a rest they would collect all the wort from this mash, then mash again and collect that wort. They would often repeat this practice once or twice more. The worts could be boiled separately and joined together to make one beer, or the first wort would go to make a strong beer, the second wort to make a middling beer, and the third and fourth worts were often combined to make a small beer. And, obviously, the strong beer would be the forerunner of our barley wine, and, in fact, this technique of making several beers from one batch of malt is perhaps the most common approach to brewing barley wine today.

While it was common practice to use this multi-mash procedure, it was not always the case that it was arranged to make several different beers, for there are instances where the worts were combined to make just one beer. A common myth is that porter was "invented" in 1722 by multi-mashing and combining the worts from each mash into one, which was called "entire" and, later, porter. But in 1502, one Richard Arnold (*The Customs of London*) gave his recipe for brewing 60 barrels of "sengyll," or single beer from 10 quarters malt, 2 quarters wheat, and 2 quarters oats. Clearly, this was an "entire" procedure, over a century before porter came on the scene. Allowing for a fairly modest rate of extraction, this beer would have had an OG of perhaps 1.040–1.045 (10–11.2°P). It would not have been very bitter; assuming the hops were low in alpha acid, perhaps 3%, so the IBU for this beer would have been about 17.

Somewhat later on, William Harrison (*The Description of England*, 1587) gave an account of a brewing carried out by his wife. She produced 3 hogsheads of beer, apparently also a single beer, from 8 bushels malt, 0.5 bushels wheat, and 0.5 bushels oats. Using yields as in the previous paragraph, this beer appears to have been stronger, with an OG perhaps as high as 1.055 (13.6°P).

Making a calculation as above, this beer would have had 17–18 IBU, so also not very bitter.

By Harrison's time, the brewing of ale (that is, a malt-based liquor brewed without hops) was in decline. In fact, it would not be long before the designation "ale" disappeared almost entirely, then later came back into usage and was applied to hopped beers, especially those that were made from pale malts and excluded brown malt. But the battle between ale and beer was a long one, for ale (often flavored with various herbs) was England's original malt beverage. Hopped beer was an import from Europe and was originally brewed in Europe by "aliens," notably Dutchmen. Beer and hops began to be imported into England perhaps as far back as the thirteenth century but only slowly became popular, largely because of the preservative action of hops. This meant that beer would not deteriorate and become sour as quickly as ale might, but perhaps the biggest point in favor of beer was that from a given quantity of malt a greater volume of beer could be produced than was the case for ale. One historian (Judith M. Bennett, *Ale, Beer and Brewsters in England*, 1996) states that ale brewers generally drew about 7½ gallons of ale from 1 bushel of malt. That means that if we assume a modest yield from the malt, the OG of that ale could be as high as 1.120 (30°P), in the region designated for barley wine. Another writer (Reginald Scott, *A perfite platform of a hoppe garden*, 1576) confirms this, saying he would expect to get 8–9 gallons "of indifferent ale" from 1 bushel of malt, whereas he considers you could get as much as 18–20 gallons of very good beer from the same amount of malt. Making a calculation on the same basis as before, that 9 gallons of ale would have OG 1.103 (28 °P), still in the barley wine range, while the 20 gallons of beer would have come in at OG 1.046, about the level of many of today's standard beers. Note that the latter figure is comparable with those I suggested for the beers brewed by Arnold and Harrison. Be careful about these figures—they are based on assumptions as to what the yield of extract from the malt might be, a number we have no way of determining.

Another point to be borne in mind is that although the above figures suggest that ale of those days was very strong, that may well not have been the case. For we do not know what sort of attenuation brewers then achieved, attenuation referring to how much of the sugars in the wort were actually converted to alcohol. Even now, with our much better understanding of the behavior of yeasts and the handling of them, fermenting a wort with OG 1.120 (30°P) is quite a tricky procedure (see the section on barley wine ingredients). Given good attenuation, such as we can now achieve, wort at that gravity will yield around 10–11% abv. But it seems unlikely that sixteenth- and seventeenth-century brewers who had no knowledge of the true role of yeast in fermentation could ever have achieved anything like that level of attenuation. That would mean that those strong ales were not particularly potent and would have contained significant amounts of unfermented sugars, making them both very sweet and susceptible to infections by bacteria and wild yeasts.

Little else appears in the seventeenth century concerning barley wine. There was a publication which made three interesting points, however (James Lightbody, Philomath, *Every Man His Own Gauger*, 1695). The writer states that double ale or beer is made in the same way as single, but by using the first wort from a mash as the water to mash fresh malt but gives no other details of the procedure. His second point was that the capacities of casks were now fixed by law at 32 English gallons (about 38 US gallons) for a barrel of ale and 36 English gallons (43 US gallons) for a barrel of beer. His third point I'll mention later, but it is clear that a wort of very high OG could be obtained in this way, although it probably made for a very long brew day!

A book on brewing appeared in 1692 (W. Y. Worth, *Cerevisiarii Comes*) which is of little importance here as regards details of brewing. I mention it because it contains a short piece on bottling beer, a topic rarely mentioned elsewhere until much later. Worth recommends priming the bottles with sugar solution, adding a little alcoholic spirit, and even a "few Christals of Tartar"!

In 1691 there appeared a book by Thomas Tryon (*A New Art of Brewing Beer, Ale, and other sorts of Liquors*) which sheds some light on hopping levels. Beer meant to keep for six months should have 6–7 lb. hops per quarter of malt, while beer or ale meant for present drinking should use 2, 3, or 4 lb. hops per quarter of malt. Oddly, though, he does not recommend boiling the wort; instead he says that the hops should be added and the wort brought to near boiling, then cooled. That would mean that the beer would have little hop bitterness, but it might mean that it had quite a bit of hop character!

Almost at the end of the seventeenth century there was a proposal to Parliament (*An Essay upon Excising . . .*, Dec. 1699) which is apparently anonymous. It appears to be a diatribe against "big" brewers, accusing them of making excessive profits as compared to their lesser brethren, and recommends a tax increase for these "giants." It does however, mention "Stout and Double Beer, or Double Ale," without further explanation. ("Stout" in those days meant any especially strong beer, not the black beers with which we associate the name.) Later, the author states that from a quarter of malt the brewer can draw 2¾ barrels of ale and 4 barrels of strong beer. Using the same assumptions as above, that would indicate an OG of 1.075 (18.2°P) for the ale, and 1.050 (12.4°P) for the beer, neither of which would fit our barley wine category.

A year later, brewing instructions were received from Edward Whitaker (*Directions for Brewing Malt Liquors*, 1700). He quotes 6–7 bushels of malt to yield 1 hogshead of good strong beer and 1 hogshead of small beer. Another publication (*A Guide to Gentlemen and Farmers for Brewing the Finest Malt-Liquors*, by a Country Gentleman, 1703) appears to be almost a direct transcript from Whitaker, except that it recommends 11 bushels of malt for a hogshead of strong ale or beer. Whitaker said to use only wort from the first mash for strong ale, which would put it at an OG of ± 1.090 (21°P). Interestingly he differentiates between strong ale and March or October beer, by boiling the latter for 1½ hours and the strong for 1 hour. He also says that strong ale should use ½ lb. hops/hogshead, and 1 lb./hogshead for ordinary strong beer, but 2 lb. hops/hogshead for March or October beer. These are quite low hop rates, so presumably these beers were not very bitter. But the interesting thing is that although the ale is more lightly hopped than the beers, it *is* now hopped. A further point is that it is now beer, especially March or October versions, which is stronger than ale.

The next item of interest to us came about 1715 (the date is uncertain), possibly by Edward Ward and entitled *A Vade Mecum for Malt-Worms*. It is essentially a guide to pubs in London and lists the beers they serve. First, the Peacock on Whitecross Street is described as the "House of Humming Stingo." Stingo was (and is) a form of barley wine; two examples are listed in table 1 in chapter 1, and I shall return to it later. Second, a pub on Milk Street where "Large quantities of Burton Ale are swilled" is noted. Again, this is listed in the table, and is a form of barley wine we shall also come across later.

AUDIT ALES

So far, I have looked at ales and beers produced either commercially or for the brewer's domestic use. But there is another group of ales/beers we should consider, the so-called audit ales brewed at Oxford and Cambridge colleges. These were especially strong ales brewed once a year and drunk at the feasts held to celebrate the annual audit of the respective college's accounts. I should note that other organizations held audit feasts and had audit ales, such as abbeys and cathedrals, trade guilds, and so on, but most of these had died out by the sixteenth or seventeenth centuries. That was not the case with the Oxbridge colleges, where the custom continued into the twentieth century; by then few of the colleges still brewed themselves but had local commercial breweries produce a special brew for them (John A. R. Compton-Davey, "Audit Ale—A Short History," *Brewery History*, no. 128). We do not know when the custom of brewing a special audit ale arose, nor when these ales became hopped beers, but Queen's College, Cambridge, had such a beer in 1580.

Perhaps the most important example is that of Queen's College, Oxford, which had established a brewery as far back as 1340 and continued to brew there up until 1937. We do not know what the early beers were like, but we do have some quite specific details of what came to be known as chancellor ale. That is because H. Lloyd Hind, a brewing biochemist and respected brewing author, visited the brewery in 1927 and was taken through the process by the brewer as well as carrying out analyses of the beer (H. Lloyd Hind, "Brewing at Queen's College, Oxford," *Brewer's Journal*, Nov. 15, 1927; H. Lloyd Hind, *Brewing Science and Practice, Vol. 1*, 1938). There is also on article on reproducing this beer, using Lloyd Hind's information, which we shall get to later (T. Foster, "Queen's College Chancellor Ale," *Brewery History*, no. 132). This was probably not the original brewery, but was still at least four hundred years old, and the beer Lloyd Hind saw brewed was produced by techniques, methods, and brewing vessels little changed from that time.

This continuity, and the fact that the beer was brewed using only pale malt and Goldings hops, might be taken to indicate that chancellor ale itself had changed little for some hundreds of years, but that is probably a somewhat imaginative interpretation. I could argue that this statement is supported by the fact the attenuation of the 1927 chancellor ale was only 60% (as defined in chapter 1), much less than the 70–80% a modern brewer might look for. Yet, the real points I want to make here is Lloyd Hind found that this batch came in at 10.7% abv, which clearly means that chancellor ale was a barley wine, and it is likely that all of the other Oxbridge audit ales were also at 8% abv or above. Finally, chancellor ale was only drunk when a year old and only brewed once a year, in October. Alfred Barnard (*The Noted Breweries of Great Britain and Ireland*, 1889–1891) stated the casks were never tapped until the beer was two years old. He tasted the 1884 brew in 1890 and averred that it was so strong that "two wine-glasses would intoxicate a man." However, he says elsewhere that he was not fond of very strong beers, and in a report on one of his many brewery visits he claimed not to be a beer drinker!

OCTOBER AND MARCH ALES

Through the seventeenth and into the eighteenth century, brewing was still carried out on a small scale commercially but was widely practiced domestically. Gervase Markham (*The Husbandman's Jewel*, 1620) gives only one recipe for a brew, which yields 1 hogshead of "ale or beer" made from 1 quarter of malt and using only ½ lb. hops. That is on the face of it a huge amount of malt for such a volume of ale/beer, which would surely have resulted in a very high OG (but see discussion below). Markham also states that "the best time for brewing is March or October."

A century later there came another book not aimed at commercial brewers (A Country Gentleman, *A Guide to Gentlemen and Farmers for Brewing the Finest Malt Liquors,* 1724). The author states categorically that it was general practice to use the first wort alone to brew ale or strong beer. He says it is necessary to use 11 bushels (1.4 quarter) of malt to give a hogshead of beer or ale. Since he recommends use of only the first wort, these figures are less outlandish than those of Markham and might indicate these brews would have had OG of 1.080–1.090, thus fitting our barley wine numbers. He appears to differentiate between beer and ale by his suggested hop additions per hogshead of ½ lb. for strong ale, 1 lb. for ordinary strong ale (not intended for keeping), and 2 lb. for March or October beer.

At some stage in this period ale had changed as brewers recognized that adding some hops would help their brew to keep without souring. So even ale was now a hopped brew, although much less so than was beer (Martyn Cornell, "Contending Liquors," *Brewery History*, no. 144). James Lightbody (see above) stated earlier, in 1695, that for brews made from 1 quarter of malt, 3 lb. of hops were used for ale, while 6 lb. were required for beer. But the distinction between the two remained—Cornell estimated that in the early eighteenth century that ale brewers used only about a quarter of the amount of hops used in beer brewing. What had become a trend, especially in many of the great country houses, was the custom of brewing a "big" or special beer in March and October. These could be either pale or brown and were brewed for keeping, October being the best month of the two since the beer would ferment out during the cold months of the winter when there was less chance of infection (remember they had no refrigeration in those days!). Such beers would likely have been brewed with the wort taken from the first mash and would therefore have an OG fitting our barley wine designation. If they were taken from the worts collected from both first and second mashes, they would have been somewhat weaker and less likely to keep well. Indeed, one writer (William Ellis, *The London and Country Brewer*, 1736 edition) suggests that some brewers would keep the wort from a third mash and use it the next day in brewing a strong beer.

William Ellis published several editions of this book anonymously, but, for example, the 1737 edition included an advertisement for a book on agriculture under his own name. He also published a book under his own name, in which he admitted he was the author of *The London and Country Brewer* (William Ellis, *The Country Housewife's Family Companion*, 1750). Ellis's book has often been regarded as seminal to the history of brewing, especially as far as the origin of porter is concerned. I have cast doubts on his account of porter brewing (T. Foster, *Brewing Porters and Stouts*, 2014), but here we are concerned with his recipes for October and March beers.

In *The London and Country Brewer*, Ellis quotes 11 bushels (1.4 quarter) of malt and 3½ lb. hops to give 1 hogshead of October or March brown beer and 14 bushels of malt plus 6 lb. hops for 1 hogshead of October or March pale beer. In *The Country Housewife's Companion*, he states more baldly that for March or October beer you should use 10–16 bushels (1.25–2.0 quarters) of malt and 4–10 lb. hops for 1 hogshead of "good beer." He does not say whether he used only the first wort, or whether this was an "entire" brew and used all three mashes. That makes it difficult to work out what sort of OG he would have got for these beers. But a modern brewer might expect to brew a hogshead of beer with OG 1.120 (30°P) using about 200 lb. malt for an entire brew and up to 300 lb. or so if taking only the wort from the first mash. Ellis used 460 lb. malt for the brown beer and 588 lb. for the pale beer. This apparent discrepancy may simply be due to his malt quality and brewing methods being much more inefficient than those of today. Note that in calculating Ellis's weights I took the figure of 336 lb. to the quarter, which is now standard but may not have been the case in his time. However, it does mean that his beers were of the appropriate strengths (as defined only by OG) to fit the barley wine category. Assuming that the hops contained 3% alpha acid calculation indicates that the brown beer had around 50 IBU, and the pale about 80 IBU. So, the latter was quite well-hopped, but the former was only modestly so, and when you consider that the final gravity was likely quite high they would surely have tasted very sweet to the modern drinker.

Strong October beer appears again in two books by Hannah Glasse (*First Catch Your Hare*, 1747; *The Compleat Confectioner, 1762*). In a very brief section on brewing in the first book, she quotes the use of 5 quarters of malt for 3 hogsheads (1.7 Quarter/ hogshead) and 24 lb. hops, both figures being higher than those given by Ellis and suggesting that this beer had an even higher OG than Ellis's. In contrast, her ale was made with 1 quarter of malt and 5 lb. hops for a hogshead of ale, along with one hogshead of small beer. Still, the distinction between strong beer and ale is that the latter uses a much smaller proportion of hops. The second book is intriguing, for the section on brewing is separately titled "The New Art of Brewing and Improving Malt Liquors" and attributed to William Ellis, "Late of London, Brewer." Ellis proposes a method for brewing strong ale without boiling the wort, but later gives a recipe for ale or strong beer which does involve boiling and which he describes as being the "Best Method" for doing so. This uses 4.5 bushels (0.56 quarter) of malt to give 0.75 barrels of beer, and he says the malt may be brown, amber, or pale; he collects two worts, boils them separately with the same hops, then combines the two in the cooler. This is somewhat less malt than was described in *First Catch Your Hare* or in *The London and Country Brewer*. Even so, making the assumptions I used earlier, this might correspond to an OG of 1.150 (about 36°P), which would make for a very powerful beer if fully attenuated in fermentation,

In this section Ellis also refers to "Double Ale or Strong Beer, called Norfolk Nog." The latter is a name for a modern English barley wine, which I shall return to later. The details of the procedure are rather sketchy, even vague, but he does say that it is brewed from 5 bushels malt and 2 bushels wheat bran to give a yield of 1 hogshead. Using a calculation on the same basis as before suggests that this beer could have had an OG of 1.120. Ellis does not say how many times the malt was mashed, or whether the wort(s) were combined, but compared to the strong ale in the paragraph above, this surely does not warrant the name "Double Ale."

Ellis also describes a strong or double beer, brewed by an Innkeeper. Again, the details of the brew are somewhat vague (as might be expected from an oral account), but it seems that it was made by separate mashings of two batches of malt, each of 12 bushels (1.5 quarters). Further, wort from the third mash of the first batch was used as liquor for the second mash, a procedure well suited to barley wine brewing. The second mash was also mashed a second time but it is not clear how this second wort was used, for the yield was quoted as 2 hogsheads sixpenny beer, 1 hogshead groat ale, "with but little small beer." A groat was fourpence, so this beer was still relatively expensive, and presumably quite strong. It is not possible to estimate the strength of the sixpenny ale, but with that amount of malt it must surely have been brewed to an OG well above 1.100.

Another interesting brew quoted by Ellis was from a Mr. Weller, who in 1738 produced 9 hogsheads strong pale beer and 2 hogsheads small beer, of which Ellis said, "He had the thinnest, lightest and best pale ale in Kent." Apparently, Weller used a pale malt dried with Welch coal and coke, which is an early reference to the use of coke in malting, at a time when wood or straw was more commonly used to dry malt. Deciphering Ellis's account of Weller's brewing is difficult because it took place over three days and it is not clear whether the 9 hogsheads of pale and 2 of small beer represented the yield from one day, or from all three, although either way the pale ale would have been a very strong beer. In fact, the amount of water used in the mashing was not enough to yield 9 hogsheads from one day's brewing, so the yield must have been the total from all three days. Weller's procedure was to twice mash 30 bushels of malt, boil the first wort with 5 lb. hops, and boil the second separately on the same hops. He then made a third mash, with cold water, boiled the wort, and used it the next day for mashing a second batch of malt. But this time he used 27 bushels of malt, assuming that the wort from the third mash contained the extract from 3 bushels of malt. On what basis he made this assumption we do not know, as he had no real way of determining the strengths of any of his worts. Weller then repeated the procedure that day and the next and sold the beer for fourpence a quart (less than 1p. a pint in modern English coinage).

Weller's prices compared well with others at the time. An anonymous publication (*An Enquiry into the Prices of Wheat, Malt*, 1765) gave average prices in the period 1730–1760. Pale strong cost 1 shilling and 4 pence per gallon (fourpence a quart), while brown strong fetched 1 shilling per gallon (threepence a quart). In contrast, both brown and pale small beer came in at less than 1 penny a quart.

George Watkins, in his book *The Compleat English Brewer* (1768), mentioned the writings of "Ellis," a further clue to the identity of the author of *The London and Country Brewer*. Watkins's small beer, which I mentioned earlier, was likely to have had an original gravity (OG) around 1.040 (10°P), depending upon the quality of the malt and the brewer's efficiency. The recipe involved mashing the malt twice with hot water and combining the collected worts. This double-mash approach was also used for the Ale, but the proportions he quotes (1 quarter malt to give 1 hogshead, 54 barrels of ale) would have provided a very high OG, unless the malt was of very poor quality and/or his extraction efficiency was very low. His ale was brewed with 3 lb. hops per hogshead, only one-sixth of the amount he used for his strong beer. His recipe for strong beer used more malt (5 quarters malt to give 3 hogsheads of beer) and he did three mashes of 1 hogshead each. The worts were boiled separately, each with 6 lb. hops, but boiled for very short times, namely, 15, 25, and 25 minutes for first, second, and third worts respectively. Even with such short boil times and, therefore, little evaporation, the OG of the strong beer would have been very high—I can't give a number as there are even more assumptions involved in making such calculations with this beer. Of course, he had no knowledge of yields or mash temperatures—use of the hydrometer in brewing would come almost twenty years later, and he probably did not have a thermometer, since that had only been demonstrated by Michael Combrune as useful to the brewer a few years earlier.

OTHER EIGHTEENTH-CENTURY DEVELOPMENTS

The first big development occurred in the early part of the century with the invention of porter in London. Porter became extremely popular, and modern commercial brewing as we know it grew on the back of porter. Even by the middle of the eighteenth century, porter breweries were large concerns, producing up to 50,000 barrels of the beer. Obviously, this represented a major change in drinkers' tastes and a move away from the strong ales and beers which had formerly been so common. However, such a move may have been quite gradual, according to a manuscript by Michael Combrune (*An Historical Account of the English Brewery*, 1762). Combrune details production of beer by common brewers in the London area from 1689 to 1750, and these figures are added to by Pater Mathias (*The Brewing Industry in England 1700–1830*, 1959). Mathias's figures show that production of strong beer was always much greater than was the case for small beer. Roughly, strong beer production ran at 30–50% more than that of small beer, except for the years 1823–1830, when there was a significant decline in small beer production. These numbers do not change after about 1730, the period when porter was becoming popular, so there must have been a decline in the production of "traditional" strong beers, assuming that porter was counted as a strong beer itself. Unfortunately, neither writer makes a distinction between these two types of beer.

Combrune also lists production by private brewers in 1725. He does not define whether these numbers apply only to London or to a wider area, for the total for both strong and small beers is about 50% higher than that for the common brewers in London for that year. But for these brewers, the amount of strong beer brewed is almost 70% higher than for small beer, and, of course, at that time private brewers were unlikely to be producing porter. Combrune does not give the number of private brewers but does show that they produced no less than 3 million barrels!

Combrune was a Frenchman brewing in Hampstead (now part of London but then a separate village); he published two important books, one in 1758 (*An Essay on Brewing, with a View of Establishing the Principles of the Art*), and one in 1762 (*The Theory and Practice of Brewing*), the latter being an expansion on the former. These books were important, for it can be argued that the recommendations in them represented the first real step in brewing science, and this was the next great development of the eighteenth century. You see, prior to this time brewers had no measuring instruments of any kind, and all was done by sight and touch. For example, many authors have indicated that the temperature of the mash water before adding the malt was measured by adding boiling water to the mash tun. The brewer then waited until it had cooled enough for him to see his face reflected in the surface of the water before mashing in the malt. To today's brewers who carefully adjust the temperature of their mashes according to the type of beer they are brewing, this must seem very primitive, but there was no other choice in those days.

Combrune's great advance was to introduce the thermometer to brewers, as an instrument useful in the brewing process itself. Thermometers were well known by then and were nothing new to many brewers, who may well have used them for measuring things such as air temperatures but had not thought of them as a means to improve their brewing techniques. Through a series of sound scientific experiments, Combrune showed the value of the thermometer for determining mash temperatures. In particular, he came up with a series of suggested mash temperatures according to the dryness of the malt. He further carried out tests on the drying of malt and the color changes seen as the malt temperature increased. These showed that the malt went from white at the lowest temperature through yellow, amber, brown, blackish-brown, and finally to black at the highest temperature. Neither he nor anyone else at the time realized that this idea was to form the basis of our modern methods for producing roasted and colored malts.

In fact, Combrune's recommended mash temperatures seem to be rather low by today's standards, but he had sown the seeds which other brewers would nourish. Indeed, by this time many of the larger London brewers were competent skilled men and well capable of picking up on and developing Combrune's ideas. Indeed, a Kent brewer, James Best, purchased a thermometer from Combrune in 1763 for 1 pound 5 shillings (1 pound 25p in today's money, about $1.60 at the current exchange rate). Best apparently also corresponded with Combrune on porter brewing techniques and was clearly a man eager to improve his knowledge and his brewing skills (Peter Moynihan, *Kentish Brewers and the Brewers of Kent*, 2011). A much fuller account of Combrune's approach is given by James Sumner (*Brewing Science, Technology and Print, 1700–1800*, 2013).

But Combrune's ideas were not enough, for knowing the temperature of the mash did not allow the brewer to determine which temperature would give him the most efficient use of his malt. But steps were already being taken in this direction, for in 1760, W. Reddington (*A Practical Treatise on Brewing*) had experimented with a hydrometer but did not appear to have come up with a practical instrument. The hydrometer itself was not new as a scientific instrument, and indeed was already used by excise officers to determine the alcoholic strength of spirits. There had been several half-hearted attempts to apply it to analyzing beer. But the first successful attempt dated to 1965, when John Baverstock, son of a Hampshire brewer, began experimenting with a hydrometer at his brewery, despite his father's strictures against doing so. I have already written about this (T. Foster, *Brewing Porters and Stouts*, 2014, and a historical novel woven around these events, *The*

Hydrometer Code, 2010) so will not go too deeply into it here, but some account is necessary as it was a turning point in the science of brewing.

Baverstock developed a system for determining the specific gravity of beer and approached some of the big porter brewers in London, showing them his findings. One of the biggest, Samuel Whitbread, turned him away, but another, Henry Thrale, did show interest. It seems some experiments were conducted at Thrale's brewery, observed by the eminent lexicographer Dr. Samuel Johnson. Thrale was apparently impressed by the results, even presenting Baverstock with a silver hydrometer. But Baverstock made an elementary mistake by not publishing his results.

In 1784 John Richardson preempted him by publishing the results of his work (*Statical Estimates of the Materials for Brewing*). Baverstock did finally publish *Hydrometric Observations and Experiments in the Brewery* (1785), but it was too late, and it was Richardson's system that was adopted by British brewers, who kept on with it until well into the twentieth century, when specific gravity determination became the norm. Richardson's system was based on the excess weight of a barrel of wort (or beer) over the weight of a barrel of water and was expressed in units of pounds per barrel. It is, to me, a rather clumsy unit, but I suppose Richardson was better at marketing than was Baverstock!

The significant part about Richardson's publication was that it showed brewers both original gravity and final gravity of several samples of beer. His system allowed brewers not only to determine the strength of a beer, which in turn allowed them to determine the quality of the malt they were using, the efficiency of their mashing process, how well the beer had attenuated which was a measure not only of the efficiency of his fermentation but also a measure of alcohol content. Use of the hydrometer and thermometer together (specific gravities had to be measured at a given specific temperature) was to make the artisan brewer something of a scientist as well as allowing brewing scientists to unravel the mysteries of mashing and fermentation.

Of interest in the context of barley wine is that Richardson quoted eight examples of "Strong Ale." These are listed in Table 2; the black figures are those of Richardson, while those in red are my calculations from his numbers.

OG (lb.)	OG (SG)	FG (lb.)	FG (SG)	ΔG (lb.)	ΔSG (SG)	Attenuation (%)	Abv (%)
42	1.117	18.6	1.052	23.4	65	55.6	8.6
41.7	1.115	22.5	1.063	19.2	52	45.2	6.8
41.0	1.113	20.8	1.057	20.2	56	49.6	7.3
40.6	1.112	18.1	1.050	22.5	62	55.3	8.2
40.0	1.110	21.6	1.059	18.4	51	46.4	6.7
39.0	1.107	18.5	1.052	20.5	55	51.4	7.2
38.3	1.106	17.8	1.050	20.5	56	52.3	7.3
36.7	1.103	17.2	1.046	19.5	57	55.3	7.5
36.0	1.100	12.5	1.032	23.5	68	68.0	9.0

Table 2 Richardson Strong Ales

Note: (i) FG is finishing gravity—Richardson quotes it as "SG when clear."
(ii) "Δ" is the difference between OG and FG
(iii) Attenuation is (Δ/OG) x 100

These all fit into the barley wine category as far as OG is concerned. However, Richardson says nothing about hop rates. Only the last one fits our modern category in terms of attenuation. That range, as given in chapter 1, was 1.025–1.035 (6.1–8.8°P) and only the last sample at 1.032 (8.1°P) falls within that range. This isn't surprising, for it is difficult to get good attenuation when starting the fermentation at such a high gravity. It is possible, too, that whoever brewed these beers (Richardson says nothing of their source) might have mashed the malt at a high temperature. After all, the brewer(s) may not yet have got a good handle on mashing temperatures, and the wort(s) could have been rather high in unfermentable material. But it is much more likely that it was a problem of yeast handling, for at this time there was still little understanding of yeast and its requirements for producing good fermentations. It was not known and would not be known until the middle of the nineteenth century that yeast was actually a fungus, a living organism; there was still a school of thought that fermentation was merely a simple chemical reaction. One point in particular is the role of oxygen at the start of fermentation. We now know that yeast needs oxygen in the early stages of growth, before going into the anaerobic, alcohol-producing stage. Most modern brewers now oxygenate the wort as it goes to the fermenter and would consider it absolutely essential to do so with high-gravity worts such as these, because if there is not an ample supply of active yeast at the start it would quickly be killed off at high alcohol levels, since the very alcohol yeast produces is in fact poisonous to the organism.

Of course, not every eighteenth-century brewer took up the use of the thermometer and hydrometer right away. Benjamin Martin was an instrument maker who had tried to use the hydrometer in brewing and from whom both Baverstock and Richardson had bought their instruments. Martin commented that the thermometer was in use at a number of breweries as early as 1766 (*A Description of the Nature, Construction and Use of the Torricellian, or Simple Barometer*); however, there is no evidence to support this claim, and it was probably just a sales pitch. But William Ploughman (*Oeconomy in Brewing, Concise Instructions for Brewing in Private Families, 1797*) stated baldly that the thermometer was too expensive to be used in brewing by private families. A treatise before that in 1793 (*The Theory and Practice of Malting and Brewing, by A Practical Brewer*) cited the use of the thermometer, recommending that the instrument bulb should be immersed in the mash. The writer gave quite extensive details on mashing temperatures in various examples but made no mention of the hydrometer. On the other hand, Robert Brakspear, a commercial brewer whose company still exists (although it no longer brews) was reported to be using both instruments as early as 1786 ("Focus on Brakspear & Sons Ltd.," *The Brewer*, August 1982). Further, a Scottish brewer, W. H. Roberts (*British Winemaker and Domestic Brewer*, 1835) was exhorting domestic brewers to use both the thermometer and the saccharometer (as Richardson's hydrometer was designated). Joseph Coppinger (*The American Practical Brewer and Tanner*, 1815) stated "Attenuation can only be done properly with the use of the thermometer and hydrometer." Since he recommends use of the two instruments, it seems likely that they were available for use in America, if not already used by other brewers.

Coppinger was an ex-Englishman who, together with Peter Shiras, set up the Point Brewery in Pittsburgh. Interestingly, Coppinger had petitioned President Madison to set up a national brewery in Washington, but his plans never came to fruition (*Beer in America*, 1998, Gregg Smith).

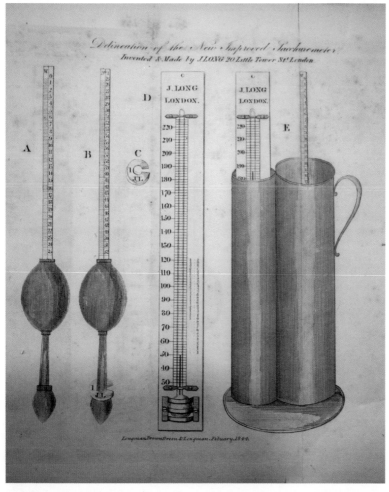

Long's hydrometer, a version produced commercially in the nineteenth century.

AMERICA INTO THE NINETEENTH CENTURY

So far, most of what I have written is concerned with brewing in Britain, and more specifically, England. You may be wondering why I have made little mention of what was going on in America, so let me take a little look at that. By 1800 the momentous separation of America from Britain had taken place, and the new nation was growing and expanding. But, at this point it was far behind Britain in terms of its economy and technical development. Britain had undergone the first stage of the industrial revolution and had become a manufacturing powerhouse. In particular its commercial breweries, especially those in London, had become hugely efficient enterprises, some of which were capable of producing up to 200,000 UK barrels of beer per annum. In contrast, American commercial brewers operated on a much smaller scale, mostly working on a purely local basis.

Of course, the art of brewing had been brought to America by its settlers, and since many of these were of English origin, Americans generally brewed in the English style. So, what do we know of American barley wines or strong beers? Well, not very much, it seems. It is reasonable to assume that there was some production of strong ales because of the English link. But it can also be argued that such beers were not widely brewed in America in its early days because of a shortage of ingredients, which often had to be imported from Britain at great expense. John Winthrop (Stanley Baron, *Brewed in America*, 1962) around 1629 had tried to introduce a bill to the House of Commons limiting the strength of beer and ale to 2½ bushels of malt per hogshead. His aim was to limit drunkenness, and he might have achieved his aim, for that would indicate the ale or beer was far from being strong, as it would have had an OG of only about 1.040 (10°P). However, Harvard apparently had its own brewhouse, and in 1667 it was brewing both single and double beer (Gregg Smith, *Beer in America*, 1998). Yet this does not seem to have led to the tradition of brewing audit ales as was practiced at Oxford and Cambridge in England. Smith opines that Benjamin Franklin, in a verse of a song he had written, referred to October beer, but Franklin could have been reminiscing about beer he had drunk when he lived in England, rather than to beer brewed in America. Then, Sanford C. Brown (*Wines and Beers of Old New England*, 1978) mentions "Double or Old or Strong beer," and stingo, but only in his glossary with no other details.

Baron quotes a Philadelphia brewery which was in operation from 1733 to 1735 as having for sale strong, or double (XX), which sold for somewhat less than stout. This tantalizing reference reveals nothing more about the beer and further confuses (me at least) by the mention of stout, since this term had not yet become common for strong porter in England. In 1767 it appears that Scottish brewers exporting to America included in the shipment instructions on how to keep bottled strong beer, although they gave no indication as to how strong it actually was. Baron also notes that Joseph Clarke, general treasurer of Rhode Island colony, gave, prior to 1775, a recipe for a brew yielding both strong ale and small beer. Clarke gives quite a bit of detail including the amount of malt used but does not say how much strong ale the recipe produced, so there is no way to calculate its actual strength. However, since he did say that only the first wort was taken for the strong ale, that would surely be of a pretty high OG, likely in the range for a barley wine.

There are few other references to strong beer as such, although it is well established that Robert Hare began brewing porter in Philadelphia in 1774 and that Washington himself was very fond of Hare's porter. As I have said it seems likely that strong beer was being produced both commercially and domestically, but the scale was surely very small. The first reason for this is that ingredients were expensive and relatively scarce—even imports of malt were small after the Revolution. Second, for many drinkers, beer took second place after spirits such as whiskey and rum. Third, the commercial breweries were still small by British standards—as late as 1810 the 132 breweries in the United States produced a total of 185,000 US barrels annually (see Baron). In contrast, Thrale, Barclay Perkins in that year brewed 235,100 UK barrels, and four other London brewers were turning out over 100,000 UK barrels in the same period (Mathias). One example was that of the brewery Coppinger had founded in Pittsburgh; owned by George Shiras Jr. in

1825, it was the largest in the city, but still produced only 4,000 US barrels annually (Baron). The larger part of this was porter, but at least some of the rest was strong beer. It should also be remembered that the US barrel was smaller, at 31½ gallons, than the British barrel at 36 gallons—I haven't allowed for this in the figures given above, since they more than adequately make the point as they stand.

You see, America had not yet experienced the full effect of an industrial revolution. By the time they were beginning to do so in the nineteenth century there was a definite trend away from very strong beers, and lager brewing was becoming the norm, rather than ale production. Yet it must not be thought that ale brewing disappeared entirely in the nineteenth century, for it remained popular throughout the century, especially in the Northeast. It was quite common for ale brewers who had decided to latch on to the new fashion of lager to keep brewing ale and porter as well. There were some who converted entirely to lagers and some who started as lager brewers and never produced anything else, but there are a few documented instances of brewers taking up lager and later ditching it in favor of ales. Some brewers continued to brew ale until well into the twentieth century.

In the nineteenth century, the term "strong beer" mainly went out of use, although in New Hampshire there were advertisement references to strong beer by John Bodger (1801), John G. Tilton (1827), and Mark Noble & Co. (1828). But a term that did see some fairly wide usage, especially in the second half of the nineteenth century, was "stock ale." Beers with this name were advertised (*Brewing in New Hampshire*, Glenn A. Knoblock and James T. Gunter, 2004) by John Swindell (1856), Cocheco Brewery (1869), Amoskeag Brewery (1877), C. E. Boynton (agent only, 1879), Frank Jones Brewing Company (1881), and the Portsmouth Brewing Company (ca. 1900). The latter also offered, around 1900, "Half Stock Ale," a designation whose meaning entirely escapes me. In Boston, Massachusetts, there were also references to stock ale (*Boston Beer*, Norman Miller, 2014) from McCormick Brewery (1885), The Star Brewery (1896), The Franklin Brewery (1897), and Hanley & Casey Brewery (1884). The last reference mentions not only the brewery's stock ale but also its old stock ale, which only serves to further confuse the terminology!

Details from other states are scant, although stock ale was reportedly brewed in Syracuse, New York, by Thomas Ryan's Consumer Brewing Co. around 1900 (*150 Years of Brewing*, H. S. Rich & Co.). And jumping ahead of myself here, Jules Kish (*Beer Cans of Connecticut Breweries 1935–2013*) shows examples of stock ale offered in Connecticut. These include Hull Brewing Co. in 1918 (they also offered a stock porter), Wehle Brewery Co. (1935), Cremo Brewing Co., who offered stock ale, half stock ale (1939), and old stock ale (undated). Stock ale was also certainly brewed in Providence, Rhode Island, by James Hanley around 1890 (see below). But none of these references give any clue to OG or abv of any of these beers. So, could they be seen as falling into the barley wine category?

One reference offers some indirect evidence (Robert Wahl and Max Henius, *American Handy Book of the Brewing, Malting and Auxiliary Trades*, 3rd edition, 1908). These gentlemen describe stock ales brewed in America as having OG 16–18°P (they actually used degrees Balling, which for our purposes are the same as degrees Plato). That range as SG is about 1.065–1.075 and means that these beers fall somewhat below that given in my definition of barley wine in chapter 1. So, they are out of contention, even though Wahl-Henius says they could be brewed not just from malt alone but with up to 25% sugar. But brewers deal in round numbers of "bags of malt" or "barrels of sugar" so that it could easily be that some brewers used somewhat more sugar and brewed to a slightly higher original gravity.

But I do have a piece of rather more solid evidence. Thanks to my good friend Jeff Browning, brewer and partner at Brewport Brewing Co., a brewpub in Bridgeport, Connecticut, I have in my possession copies of a series of letters written in the 1880s. They were addressed to James Hanley of Providence, Rhode Island, and were written by George Johnson, a brewer at Arnold & Co., in Ogdensburg, New York. The letters contained much specific brewing advice, plus several quite detailed accounts of his procedure for beers such as cream ale, IPA, and porter. Also included were accounts (and recipes) from his brewing logbook for three examples of stock ale. Two were brewed from pale malt alone and one used pale malt plus 25% sugar. The range of OG for the three was 1.060–1.065 (14.7–15.9°P), at or below the bottom of the range given by Wahl-Henius. So, it seems that American stock ales do not fit the barley wine category and that most nineteenth-century American brewers were likely not producing any beers that did so. But see under Burton ale below.

Perhaps that statement is not entirely true, for a 1904 advertisement in the *Plattsburgh Daily Press* lists an October ale, which if true to its name would surely be in the barley wine category. The beer was from Monroe Brewing Co. in Plattsburgh, New York, a brewery not listed in Plattsburgh, or anywhere else in New York State, in a very comprehensive directory (Dale P. van Wieren, *American Breweries II*, 1995). The ad is reproduced in an interesting article (G. Gillman, "The Arc of American Musty Ale," *Brewery History*, Winter 2016) which deals with an oddity, "musty ale," primarily a beer produced in the Northeast. The writer could not find any reference to the exact nature of the beer and suggests that it might have been some form of stock ale or even IPA which had been long stored in wood and whose flavor had been affected by bacteria and/or wild yeasts, such as *Brettanomyces*.

Taking a little diversion, there are some interesting points about Mr. Johnson. He was an Englishman who had learned to brew in both Burton and Nottingham, and as far as I can gather was an employee at Arnold's. He was, therefore, selling recipes from his employer, which seems to be a highly dubious practice to say the least! He also claims that the recipe for porter that he sold to Hanley actually came from his English master. The latter supposedly bought it in Dublin for what was then the enormous sum of five hundred pounds! We made a version of this porter at Brewport; it turned out to be a very nice, full-flavored, slightly roasty porter which we shall repeat at some stage.

Having said all that, there is a modern version of American stock ale, from North Coast Brewing Co. Inc. (Fort Bragg, California). It is called, appropriately, Old Stock Ale and weighs in at 11.8% abv, more than enough to make it match a barley wine. It was brewed in 2016, and the label says it will keep till 2032; it certainly drinks like a barley wine, with a little alcoholic heat, some oxidized notes, and just a hint of hop bitterness, but, though full-bodied, it is well-balanced and not too sweet.

Detail from a mural at Brewport Brewing Co., Bridgeport, Connecticut.

BURTON ALE

It seems likely that brewing started in Burton-on-Trent in medieval times, at Burton Abbey (William Molyneux, *Burton-on-Trent, Its History. Its Waters, and Its Breweries,* 1869). The Abbey and its holdings were purged by Henry VIII, but by the seventeenth century, commercial brewing was carried out to some extent. Molyneux reports that Burton ale was on sale in London around 1630, at the Peacock Inn. John Stevenson Bushnan (*Burton and its Bitter Beer,* 1853) asserts that Burton ale was popular in London in 1623, where it was actually known as Derby, since that was the town from which it reached London. It was quite difficult and expensive to carry beer over long distances by road in those days, so in 1698 the Trent Navigation Act was passed, which when implemented gave Burton brewers river access to Hull and the North Sea. They were thus able to build a relatively substantial trade with the Baltic countries, although it should not be forgotten that the most important part of that trade was imports from those countries and that often beer was just ballast for the outgoing ships.

Russia, via St. Petersburg, was the most important destination for Burton ales, and Molyneux says that both Peter the Great and Catherine the Great were very fond of this beer. In fact, C. C. Owen points out that when the Trent Navigation was opened in 1712, there is no evidence of any ale being exported from Hull to Baltic ports (*Burton upon Trent: The Development of Industry,* 1978). Therefore, any such ale going to Russia must "have been exported unofficially or sent to Petersburg via London." He further states that it was only by 1740 that exports to the Baltic from Hull were increasing, while those from London were decreasing. We cannot be sure, but this does throw some doubt on the story of Peter the Great liking Burton ales, especially as he died in 1725, just thirteen years after the Trent Navigation was opened. However, it is more likely that Catherine and her court did enjoy this beer, because she lived until 1796 and it seems likely that strong porter was being exported to Russia at this time. Samuel Allsopp of Burton added porter to his list in 1808 (Mathias), presumably to meet competition from London brewers in the Russian trade.

There are some interesting comments as to the nature of Burton ales at this time. Molyneux calls it "high coloured and sweet and of remarkable strength," while Owen refers to it as "sweet, nut-brown." It was also reported as being a "strong brown ale" ("The Breweries of England," *Brewery History*, no. 168, 2017). It is also reported that in 1808 Allsopp wrote to customers asking whether Pale Ale or "a darker colour" would suit them (Mathias). Apparently, Benjamin Wilson, answering complaints from customers that his ale was much darker than that of other brewers, said that strength was a greater virtue than color (Mathias). So where did this darker, nut-brown color come from? Roasted malts, such as chocolate and black malts, were not yet invented, so perhaps the darker color came from caramelization during a long (several hours) boil. It is difficult to be sure, because color is a very subjective aspect of beer, and in the eighteenth century pale malts were surely not as pale as those in modern times. Perhaps the Burton brewers used some amber and/or brown malt? What we do know is that Burton ales carried through even into the twentieth century as a very dark brown beer, suggesting that this was true of the original versions. For my part, this was a form of barley wine as we now know it.

Of some interest is Owen's comment that by 1740, Burton ale was still in demand "by those Londoners who could afford to pay the high price of seven shilling and sixpence per 12 bottles." That amounts to 37.5p (just under 50 cents) in today's money. That would obviously be much more today if inflation were accounted for. But some contemporary examples of earnings include 8 shillings (40p) per week for a skilled potter in Staffordshire (Maxine Berg, *Luxury and Pleasure in Eighteenth-Century Britain*, 2005) while legal clerks in London made only £50–60 per year (Jerry White, *London in the 18th Century*, 2012). Another source indicates that a skilled artisan needed £40 per year to support a family in London ("London History—Currency, Coinage and the Cost of Living," Old Bailey Proceedings Online www.oldbaileyonline.org). Clearly, a case of Burton ale would have been out of the reach of these people, particularly when porter could be had for just 3 pence a pot (a little over 1p a pot, or about 2 cents at today's exchange rates).

Indirectly, Burton ale had some responsibility for the rise of IPA, for by 1792 the Baltic trade had seriously declined. It had completely collapsed by 1807, caused by Napoleon's control of the North Sea ports. Russia had also become hostile to Britain, putting an embargo on British ships in 1800 and finally cutting the trade with Burton by imposing heavy tariffs in 1821. Consequently, the Burton brewers had to look elsewhere for their exports and looked particularly at India. The rest of that story does not form a part of this book, although, of course, the rise of IPA and pale ale did signal a move in public taste away from dark beers.

Yet Burton ale did not disappear as might have been expected, so let us look at what sort of beer it was. As far back as 1791 it was quoted as having an OG greatly exceeding 46 lb./barrel (George Blake, *Strictures on a New Mode of Brewing etc.*, 1791). That equates to in excess of 1.130 (30°P), which if the beer were well attenuated would indicate it could reach about 13% abv. Such a high OG could surely only have been achieved by long boiling of the wort, which is likely to have resulted in a high color due to caramelization and/or Maillard reactions in the kettle. At first glance, I thought that perhaps Blake's figure was far too high, but a later author gives a range of 46–56 lb./barrel (Anon., *The Young Brewer's Monitor*, 1824). The writer claims to have been a brewer "of thirty years practical experience" and offers the information that this ale attenuated to 20 lb./barrel. That is SG 1.055 (13.6°P), which at OG 1.130 (130°P) represents 58% attenuation and about 10% abv. That would surely have been a sweet-tasting beer with such a high finishing gravity, especially as the hop rate of around 5 lb./barrel would indicate only around 30–40 IBU.

In fact, later on George Blake (*Observations and Remarks on the Construction and Important Uses of Blake's Former and New Saccharometer*, 1822) wrote that Burton ale should be brewed at OG 38–40 lb./barrel. A later author gives a similar figure at 40 lb./barrel, 1.110 (26°P) (William Champion, *The Maltster's Guide*, 1832). Another author, William Chadwick, also quotes 40 lb./barrel (*A Practical Treatise on Brewing*, 1835). Chadwick's book was aimed at private families and is interesting in that even with such an audience it promoted the value of the thermometer and saccharometer to its readers. The same OG is quoted by Thomas Hitchcock (*A Practical Treatise on Brewing*, 1842), while a later book (James Herbert, *The Art of Brewing India Pale Ale & Export Ale, Stock & Mild Ales, Porter & Stout*, 1866) cites the range 35–40 lb./barrel, 1.097–1.110 (23–26°P). Herbert claimed to be a practical brewer at Burton-on-Trent, and states that Burton ales were attenuated to 14 lb./barrel, about 1.040 (10°P), a much lower figure than in the previous paragraph, about 64% attenuation, making for a less sweet beer. He also makes the comment that Burton strong worts were simmered for 1½–2 hours, not boiled, and makes a distinction between Burton ale and export bitter beer. Finally, he refers to stock ale, but without, apparently, defining it.

An earlier reference also mentions stock ale (A Brewer of 25 Years Standing, *Secrets of the Mash Tun*, 1847), stating that it has OG 31–40 lb./barrel (1.085–1.110, 21–26°P). He also says these are attenuated to 20–16 lb./barrel (1.055–1.045, 14–11°P), which amounts to an attenuation of 50% or less, so such beers would have been very sweet, unless they were vatted (stored) for a long time before bottling, thus permitting further attenuation. He does also mention ale meant for keeping 9–12 months as having OG 40 lb./barrel, and attenuated to 18 lb./barrel (1.110, 26°P to 1.050, 12°P) or 55% attenuation. Somewhat later in the century, E. R. Southby (*A Systematic Handbook of Practical Brewing*, 1889) reports that Burton export pale ale required 17 lb. hops per quarter of malt, while the corresponding figure for Burton strong ale was only 10–12 lb. per quarter. Trying to calculate IBU from such figures is a futile exercise, but it does show that Burton ale was less highly hopped than the pale ale. However, if we assume that the yield of the former from one quarter of pale malt would be 1½ barrels, then the hopping rate would be about 7-8 lb./barrel. This is a very high rate of hopping, much higher than anything we have seen above, so perhaps Southby's figures should be treated as suspect?

Burton ales were also produced by commercial brewers in other parts of England and even Scotland. Some of these may not have matched Burton ale such as we have seen so far, and some may even have been better termed simply "barley wine." Bass brewed no less than six Burton ales, numbered simply 1–6, in descending order of original gravity. There are few records of many of these commercial ales, but there is one record which is significant, that produced by George Stewart Amsinck (*Practical Brewing, A Series of Fifty Brewings in Extenso*, 1868). This book is important because Amsinck had been a brewer in London, at Combe Delafield and Joseph Carter Wood & Co., and he wrote the book for brewers, not for historians. It consists of nothing but a series of brewing records in very complete detail, including, for example, not only the separate worts and their specific gravities but also any return worts added from earlier brews. It is also an indication of just how efficient and science-based the commercial breweries had become.

Selected details of Amsinck's Burton Ales are given in Table 3 below; for comparison I have included numbers for his London Keeping Ale:

Table 3 Amsinck Burton Ales							
No.*	**OG (lb.)**	**FG (lb.)**	**OG (SG)**	**FG (OG)**	**Δ SG**	**ABV %**	**Hops** ** (lb./brl**
1 Burton	44.3	22.9***	1.121	1.064	57	7.5	5.5
2 Burton	30.6	13.5	1.085	1.038	47	6.2	5
3 Burton	31.1	11.5	1.086	1.032	54	7.1	3.6
4 Burton	27.9	11.5	1.078	1.032	46	6.0	2.3
5 Burton	29.8	12.5	1.082	1.035	47	6.2	2.2
6 London	40.0	14.0	1.110	1.039	71	9.4	3.2
8 London K/XXX	36.0	12.0	1.100	1.033	67	8.8	2.0

* These are Amsinck's brew numbers and do not correspond to those of Bass.

** This figure may be misleading; it is based on the total volume of wort produced. Apart from the first beer, all the others were parti-gyled (that is, two or more beers were taken from one mash), and it is not clear how the hops were split between the various worts, so it is not possible to estimate IBU.

*** This figure is somewhat questionable; it appears to have been measured after 10 days' fermentation when the beer was racked into delivery casks.

Except for No. 4 Burton ale, all these beers fit our barley wine designation in terms of OG, but in terms of alcohol content, only the two London brews do so. In short, all the Burton ales would have been very sweet, although the hopping rates were high by modern standards, so they probably had a high level of bitterness. They were also all dry-hopped in cask at the rate of 1 lb./barrel, again a fairly high rate of addition. There is a question as to how much these brewings match the original Burton ales, since all of them were brewed only from pale malt and might well have been pale in color. Was Amsinck confused about the term "Burton ale" and simply brewing a version of Burton IPA? Well, that can be categorically said not to be the case, for he also lists a series of brewing notes for East India pale ales at the level of 22–25 lb./barrel (1.060–1.070, 15–17°P). One other interesting fact that emerges from this is that, for No. 1 Burton ale at least, the mash water was boiled overnight, presumably to precipitate calcium carbonate, since London water contained a great deal of the ions from this salt, which would not have made it suitable for brewing from only pale malt. In short, Amsinck had a good idea of the effect of water quality in mashing.

I should point out that an earlier writer (Frederick Accum, *A Treatise on the Art of Brewing*, 1821) quotes numbers for London brewed ales. He states that the strongest London ales started at about OG 1.080 (19.2°P) and quotes a sample which exited the fermenters at 1.033 (8.3°P), which is about 54% attenuation. He further states the beer was at 1.022 (5.6°P), representing almost 73% attenuation after some unstated time of storage, and goes on to say that after 11 months' storage it was at SG 1.015 (3.8°P), so attenuation would have been as high as 81%. The latter would indicate that the finished ale contained 8.6% abv, and that it would have been relatively dry on the palate. Of course, this ale started at the bottom limit of the OG range I suggested for barley wines, which might partly account for the high attenuation achieved. However, do this and Amsinck's figures in Table 3 suggest that the London brewers had a better understanding as to how to manage fermentations than their Burton counterparts? The figures Accum quotes actually came from C. P. Ellis, an ale brewer in Knightsbridge in London, rather than from Accum himself, who was a chemist. It is possible there could have been some error in transcription, but these figures do tally with those of Amsinck, indicating that they were probably correct.

Whatever happened to Burton ale, in the sense of how it was originally brewed? Well, Bass No.1 continued through into the twenty-first century, and will be looked at again later under barley wine. Other English brewers kept their versions going, some even into the twentieth century—I remember in the 1950s Ind Coope & Allsopp bringing out a Burton ale each winter. I drank it and enjoyed it, but it could not have been anywhere near the high gravity of the original, because it came on draught, and I didn't fall over after drinking a pint of it! I suspect, as with so many other beers, brewers simply lowered the OG and alcohol content as time wore on, taxes rose according to alcohol content, and sales fell. Martyn Cornell and Antony Hayes ("Burton Ale," *Zymurgy*, January/February 2011) list some modern versions, but most of them are lower, some much lower, in strength than the original and do not fall into my barley wine category. This should all be put into the context of a steadily changing public palate as drinkers moved to pale, somewhat less alcoholic, beers, and the once-dominant porter was in decline itself in the latter half of the nineteenth century. This, of course, was a trend which would continue throughout the twentieth century, with porter virtually disappearing entirely in England before even mid-century.

However, Burton ales were brewed in the United States in the 1800s. Martyn Cornell ("Burton Ale," *Zymurgy*, January/February 2011) quotes four brewers who were doing so. The first of these was Amsdell Brothers of Albany, New York, who brewed under that name from 1857 to 1892, then under various names to 1916, when the brewery became Citizen's Corp., which closed in 1920. Second was C. H. Evans & Sons of Hudson, New York, who brewed under that name from 1888 to 1928, then opened again in 1934 but closed in that year, apparently without producing any beer. It seems that that brewery was actually founded in 1786 but only came into C. H. Evans's hands in 1865, before becoming C. H. Evans & Sons as above. Third was Grainger & Gregg, also of Hudson, New York, a company which brewed from 1886 to 1895, then as Grainger Brewing Co. from 1895 to 1902, when the company became bankrupt (all info is from Dale P. van Wieren, *American Breweries II*, 1995). I have no evidence as to exactly when and for how long any of the three brewed Burton ales. But there is more information available on the fourth, Peter Ballantine of Newark, New Jersey.

Ballantine, a Scot, had founded a brewery in Newark in 1840, brewing Burton-style ales, such as IPA, although I have seen no evidence that he produced any Burton ale as such at that time. The brewery company survived right through Prohibition, largely through malt syrup extract manufacture, and at this point it was still under control of Ballantine relations. But from there it underwent many changes of ownership, though retaining the name Ballantine right up to its closure in 1971. Even then the brand lived on under its Falstaff ownership, with its beers being brewed at several sites until being bought out by Pabst in 1985 (See *American Breweries II* and *P. Ballantine and Sons Brewing Company*). I remember the company well, since when I immigrated to the United States, Ballantine IPA was just about the only interesting American-brewed beer to be found in the Northeast. But for our present story the most important point about Ballantine was that they actually produced a Burton ale. This beer was first brewed in the 1930s (according to the label on the bottle discussed below) and was apparently aged for up to twenty years in American oak vats or barrels. It was never actually sold to the public, but simply given away to brewery executives and friends and reportedly also to the White House occupants. It is not clear when this beer ceased to be brewed, but the 1950s seem to be a likely cutoff point. Michael Jackson (*Beer Companion*, 1993) said he had sampled a 1950s version over twenty-five years later and found it to still be in good condition and described it as "a very aromatic, hoppy barley wine."

The outstanding point about Ballantine is that its Burton ale has been revived by Pabst and brewed at Cold Spring, Minnesota, in 2015, making it the only Burton ale true to the original still produced. It was produced for the Christmas season with abv 11.3%, 75 IBU from an OG of 26.5°P (about 1.112 SG); from the alcohol content the finishing gravity would be around 1.025 (6°P), so it would not be oversweet.

The brewmaster, Greg Deuhs, is reported to have said he wanted to bring out this beer "as the true Barley wine Style Ale that it was." I have a bottle of the 2015 version in front of me (I have not yet seen one from 2016), which I have been reluctant to taste as I would like to know how it would age. But, throwing caution to the winds, here goes (July 2017). It has a beautiful deep-red copper color, with a small but tight head and fine lacing. There is some ester and lemon character in the nose, and a full, toffee, raisin, date, nutty, and caramel flavor, with relatively slight sweetness and some slight sherry-like oxidation notes. The alcohol is not hot, and the bitterness is definite but not dominant, despite the 75 IBU. All in all, a very acceptable barley wine, and I still have another bottle left!

Close-up of a cherished and rare brand of barley wine.

STINGO

This is undoubtedly a name for a strong beer suited to the barley wine category, but the exact nature of stingo has proved to be quite elusive for me. It is often referred to as Yorkshire stingo (Michael Jackson, *The*

New World Guide to Beer, 1988; Martyn Cornell, "Only the Strong Survive," *Beer*, 2007). In *South Yorkshire Stingo* (David Lloyd Parry, 1997), a directory of South Yorkshire brewers from 1758 to 1995, only the title mentions stingo, suggesting that this was not a name used much in this part of the county. Alfred Barnard quoted two examples of breweries producing stingo in 1890, namely Tetley's of Leeds and John Metcalf and Son of Pateley Bridge, both in West Yorkshire. Martyn Cornell's article quotes a stingo from Hammond's of Bradford in West Yorkshire, and from the same part of the county I have recently come across a sample of Samuel Smith's Yorkshire Stingo.

All this suggests that stingo is solely a West Yorkshire term for a very strong beer. But Michael Jackson says that Watney's, once one of England's major twentieth-century breweries, based in London, also offered a beer called simply Stingo. He also states that this beer was exported to the United States; I never saw it here, but do remember seeing it in England in the 1970s. Jackson said it was a dark barley wine, with OG 1.076 (18°P), which would put it just below the cutoff point for my barley wine definition. Michael Jackson also said that Hall & Woodhouse from Dorset in the West of England offered "Stingo Barley Wine." A 1969 sample of this (Ronald Pattinson, *Numbers!*, 2009) is said to have had OG 1.077 (18.7°P), and a surprisingly low finishing gravity of 1.010 (2.6°P), making for 87% attenuation and 8.8% abv. That would surely mean that it was not sweet at all, and that while it is a little on the low side for a barley wine as far as OG is concerned, it certainly makes the category in terms of alcoholic strength. I do not know when Hall & Woodhouse ceased to produce their stingo, but in 1977 they did produce a one-off beer with OG at 1.090 (21°P) which was called Bicentenary Ale because, of course, the firm had been founded in 1777 (Frank Pike, "Fifty Years On: Hall & Woodhouse Ltd, 1945–1995, Part 1," *Brewery History*, no. 142, 2011).

Hammond's brewing books have been researched by Dr. Keith Thomas (University of Sunderland), according to Martyn Cornell in the article referenced two paragraphs ago. The 1903 stingo was brewed at OG 1.100 (24°P), finished at 1.027 (6.8°P), to give 9.5% abv (9.7% according to my calculations). That would not be particularly sweet for this style of beer, especially as the article states that the beer may have had a bitterness level of 119 IBU. Bitterness levels were not measured in those days, so this number must be a calculation and would have to have involved assumptions as to hop alpha acid content, alpha acid utilization, and so on. Nevertheless, it seems that this was a very hoppy beer and would actually have fitted the BA definition of American-style barley wine, rather than their corresponding British category! Another look at Hammond's 1903 stingo puts the OG at 1.102 (24.4°P) and suggests that a re-created version of this beer should use about 1% black malt in the grist (Dr. John Harrison and the Durden Park Beer Circle, *Old British Beers and How to Make Them*, 2003). For the record, in 1898–1899 Hammond's stingo was sold on draught at 2 shillings (10p, 13c at today's exchange rate) per gallon, or 2 shillings and twopence (10.8p, 14c) per twelve half-pint bottles, the latter being at the same price for Bass India pale ale from Hammond's (Anthony Avis, "A Brewery's Price List a Century Ago," *Brewery History*, no. 107).

So to Samuel Smith Yorkshire Stingo, which, in April 2017, I bought for £12 and 60p (about $16) for a 550 mL (just short of an English pint) bottle in a London pub. It was a bottle-conditioned beer at 8% abv. The brewery claimed that it was fermented in Yorkshire stone squares and aged in oak casks for "over a year." Some of the casks date back more than a century, with individual staves being replaced over time. I would think that this would mean that the casks would not confer oak flavors to this beer, although the label says it has a slight oak character. It also says the beer absorbs some of the character of the ales the casks previously contained, which seems more likely. It was a dark brown (not black) color, slightly hazy when poured, and formed little head. I found it a little unbalanced as the alcohol was noticeable on the palate, and it was not as full-bodied as I expected it to be (some cane sugar was used in its brewing). Bitterness was muted, but it did have some oxidized, sherry-like character and some nutty, raisin-like notes. Interestingly, there was no sourness, and I did not find it to have any flavors produced by *Brettanomyces,* as might have been expected from a beer produced in this way.

SCOTCH ALES

The Scots, of course, produced a good deal of malt whisky, but also brewed much beer, which is not surprising since the processes for making both start with mashing barley malt then fermenting the wort. It appears that even before 1700 Edinburgh was the center for commercial brewing, but there was significant brewing trade in many other parts of the country (Ian Donnachie, *A History of the Brewing Industry in Scotland*, 1979). Donnachie points out that at that time hops were little used in Scots brewing, because they were not grown there and were therefore expensive imports. He also says that Scots ales were of poor quality at that time and not well regarded elsewhere.

That was certainly not the case by the late eighteenth century, when exports to England increased relatively substantially (P. Mathias, *The Brewing Industry in England, 1700–1830*, 1959). Donnachie also points out that the Scots, until the arrival of porter in the late eighteenth century, basically made only two sorts of beer, strong and small, and that the latter was poorly regarded even in its home country. Indeed, the export trade consisted largely of strong ale, which attained a very good reputation. In the 1820s in Bristol, a big English shipping port, Scotch ale was listed at 11 shillings (55p, about 72c at today's exchange rate) for 1 dozen quarts, while Burton ale fetched a lower price for the same quantity, namely 10 shillings, 50p, 65c today (P. Lynch and J. Vaizey, *Guinness's Brewery in the Irish Economy*, 1960). A significant amount of Scotch ale was exported to other areas, notably North America, but also to Australia and India.

But what was the nature of Scotch ale, and was the Scottish brewing practice any different from that used in England? And was this strong ale truly strong enough to warrant consideration as a barley wine? First, let's deal with practice, starting with hops. Scottish brewers used only English hops at relatively low rates because of their cost. It is notable that two Scottish authors (W. Black, *A Practical Treatise on Brewing*, 1844; W. H. Roberts, *The Scottish Ale Brewer and Practical Maltster*, 1847) give only very brief sections on hops, almost as though they considered hop usage of minor importance in brewing. The next point is that, according to Black, the Scots mashed in at higher temperatures, namely 168–170°F (75.6–76.6°C) than did their English counterparts, who favored a temperature around 150°F (65.6°C). Such a high mash temperature would cause rapid breakdown of ↔amylase, so that production of fermentable sugars would be limited, and the finishing gravity would be high, making the beer sweet and full on the palate. However, Black's account is somewhat confusing, and he may be referring to mashing-in temperature, rather than that of the actual mash, which would be significantly lower than the former. Another different Scottish approach was that of sparging the mash with hot water when collecting the wort, rather than carrying out two or more separate mashes as was English practice. This is merely a matter of ensuring efficient extraction from the malt, and is, of course, common practice today. Scottish brewers also fermented their worts at lower temperatures than did the English. Black quotes 50–53°F (10–11.7°C) in Scottish practice and about 65°F (18°C) in England. That might well result in a longer fermentation time and less attenuation, again leading to a full, sweet beer. Finally, the Scots were bottling beer long before their English competitors (T. R. Gourvish and R. G. Wilson, *The British Brewing Industry, 1830–1980*, 1994). I make this point simply to emphasize that Scottish brewers, even though their total production was much less than that of the English, were not behind the latter in terms of brewing innovations.

When it comes to strengths of Scotch ales, Barnard (ca. 1890) is his usual fulsome self, describing the Five Guinea Ale from J. Calder & Co. as being "a rich and full-flavoured beverage of considerable gravity." Also, the twelve-guinea Crown Ale brewed by John Fowler & Co. was described thus: "a tablespoonful was about as much as we dare tackle, so rich, strong and old, was this *seductive* drink." What the "guinea" designation signified I am not sure; later on, Scottish brewers used a system of nomenclature derived from tax paid and based on "shillings," but twelve guineas would have been much, much more than any tax paid at that time, so may have been related to the actual price of the beer.

However, we do have some numbers as far as OG is concerned, with Black quoting them generally at 1.111–1.125 (26-29°P), certainly high enough to be called barley wine. But Roberts gives us much more detailed information on both OG and final gravity (FG), using a distillation process he devised himself. He examined some seventy-four samples, apparently from eighteen different Edinburgh brewers, five other Scottish brewers, and two "home-brewed," by which I assume he meant a publican brewer. In order to simplify understanding of his data, I shall just give you the average values for those beers with OG above 1.080 (19.3°P), which make up no less than sixty-six of the seventy-four samples. Roberts gave alcohol content as proof spirit, which is a somewhat antiquated measure, and I have calculated it as alcohol by volume. He also gave attenuation as simply the difference in gravity points between OG* and FG*, that is (OG*–FG*), whereas I have used the more common apparent attenuation $100 \times (OG^*–FG^*)/OG^*$. Note that in this case OG* stands for (OG–1) × 1000, and FG* for (FG–1) × 1000. So, the average values I have derived from Roberts's tables are as follows:

OG = 1.113 (26.5°P), range 1.086–1.134 (20.5–30.9°P)
FG = 1.046 (11.4°P), range 1.009–1.064 (2.3–15.7°P)
ABV = 9.0%, range 7.3–10.6%
Apparent attenuation = 55%, range 50–90%

Note that Roberts's analyses were carried out about one month after brewing. I used rounded figures, those of Roberts going to two further decimal places, a remarkable and unnecessary level of accuracy! Also, there is one outlier starting at 1.086 (20.5°P) and finishing at 1.009 (2.3°P). The other figures show a general pattern of high starting gravity, low attenuation, and a relatively low level of alcohol, all fitting in with descriptions given in the preceding paragraphs. And, of course, as I have previously asserted, that means that we can consider Scotch ales as a variant of barley wine.

Roberts also gave two recipes for Scotch ale which provide some useful information. Sparging was commenced immediately after a long mash (almost four hours), and in each case the first runnings were taken for the strong ale, the second mash going to brew a table beer. Each wort was boiled with the hops for 1 hour and 25 minutes, the first yielding 36.5 barrels at a gravity of 1.1035 (23.3°P), the second 43 barrels at 1.105. Hops added were 160 lb. East Kents for the first wort, and 195 lb. Farnham hops for the second. That gives us some idea of hop bitterness levels. If we assume the hops contained 3% alpha acid (a reasonable assumption for hops in those days, not stored under refrigeration) and an alpha acid utilization of 15% (this is low by modern standards, but not unreasonable with such a high-gravity wort), then both these beers would have come in at around 55 IBU. That, as suggested above, is a quite modest figure for such a big beer.

Roberts calculates in the examples, adding in the yield from the table beer that he obtained 206.3 and 211 gravity points per quarter. That would calculate out to about 65% efficiency or 24°/lb./US gallon, a modest yield. He also gave fermentation temperatures over several days, starting at 50–51°F (10–10.6°C), with the highest temperature reached being 63–64°F (17.2–17.8°C), certainly a cool fermentation by English ale standards. The finishing gravity of the first beer was 1.043 (10.7°P), right in the range given by his analyses.

Note that Greg Noonan (*Scotch Ale*, 1993) asserts that Scotch ales were darker than their English counterparts, because they were brewed with darker malts than those used by the English. He also suggests that such beers used about 1% black malt in the grist, but I have seen nothing on this elsewhere, and Roberts did not use this malt in either of his examples, even though it was widely available by then.

Now, moving on, Scotch ales at this high strength continued to be produced throughout the nineteenth century, as we have seen from Barnard. Dr. John Harrison (*Old British Beers and How to Make Them*, 1991) also lists several such ales from Younger's in the latter half of the century and Ron Pattinson (*Numbers!*, 2009) lists Younger's No. 1 at OG 1.085 (20.5°P) in 1925, McEwan's Scotch Ale at 1.080 (19.3°P) in 1940 and 1.088 (22°P) in 1955. Sometime in the late nineteenth century, the "shilling" designation came into being, this being based on the invoice price of the beer per hogshead (54 UK gallons, 65 US gallons). The designation "heavy" for strong ales also crept in, and by the twentieth century, when such beers were sold in small bottles, or nips, this became "wee heavy." But the twentieth century was to see a decline in the production of these strong ales; apparently wartime restrictions (particularly on the supply of malt) hit the market for these beers very badly, according to Gourvish and Wilson. Certainly there are few examples to be found in Scotland today, though some still exist, such as Belhaven's Wee Heavy (though a little low at 7.4% abv), Traquair House Jacobite Ale (8% abv), and Harviestoun's oak-aged Ola Dubh series at 8% abv and up. These days if you want to drink a wee heavy, you are more likely to find one that has been produced by an American craft brewer.

Present-day Scotch Ales, American versions in the middle, Scottish on the outside.

BACK TO BARLEY WINE

It may appear that I have skipped about a little in time, but that was merely so I could maintain the narrative on each variant of the predecessors of barley wine. But before I go on, there is one other point I must make, and that is that brewing in the big country houses of England was a long-standing tradition. I have already referred to this (William Harrison, *The Description of England*, 1587; Gervase Markham

The Husbandman's Jewel, 1620; Edward Whitaker, *Directions for Brewing Malt Liquors*, 1700; A Country Gentleman, *A Guide to Gentlemen and Farmers for Brewing the Finest Malt Liquors*, 1724).

Such houses brewed both strong ale/beer and small beer, with probably the former being for the nobles and gentlemen and the latter for the servants. Indirect evidence of this comes from the fact that the strong beer was drunk out of specially designed ale glasses. These were small, containing perhaps only a third of a pint or less, and were often very decorative with fancy stems and hop and barley motifs etched on the bowl of the glass (L. M. Bickerton, *English Drinking Glasses 1675–1825*, 1984). This author lists several places in England with displays of such glasses; several times I have gazed spellbound at the collection in the Ashmolean Museum in Oxford, a city worth visiting in its own right. The point about these glasses is that they were expensive and so would have been only for the use of the gentry.

There was another tradition in such houses, which was brewing a beer on the birth of an heir (always male) and storing in cask until he came of age. Martyn Cornell lists a number of examples of these ("'A Glass of Something Very Treble Extra': Coming-of-Age Ale, a Long-Forgotten British Beer Style," *Brewery History*, no. 153, 2013). I have seen no numbers to confirm this, but these would surely have been very strong beers. And, of course, after such a long time in an oak cask, they would surely have developed some unusual flavors from bacteria in the wood and probably from wild yeasts such as *Brettanomyces*. Apparently, this tradition lasted into the early part of the twentieth century but died out after the First World War. However, in 1965 it is reported that a double-strength brew was made for the twenty-first birthday of the heir to Lord Halifax. It was so strong that after the party "there were bodies laid all over the place, of the unwise who thought they could drink beer" (Pamela Sambrook, *Country House Brewing in England 1500–1900*, 1996). Was that the same Lord Halifax who tried hard to persuade Churchill to sue for peace with Hitler?

In contrast, commercial brewing of strong ales in Britain continued throughout the second half of the eighteenth century. Barnard in his 1889–1891 list of brewery visits quotes quite a few, starting with

Charles Garton & Co.'s October beer, March and October stock ales from The Lion Brewery, Chester, XXXX old October from Hall & Woodhouse, and "S. B." old October strong beer brewed by Plews & Sons in Yorkshire. These designations were almost obsolete by that date since cooling techniques had become much more sophisticated, and there was no longer any need for a brewer to be limited to brewing only in cool weather. Barnard also reported that Henry Bentley & Co. brewed "Timothy," "a luscious, full-bodied and nourishing drink," as well as College ale, very similar to Timothy. The latter is an interesting brew, first produced by the founder of the company, Timothy Bentley, in 1795, and continued to be brewed right up to 1956. However, it was then being brewed at OG 1.075 (18°P) (Anthony Avis, "Timothy Bentley of Lockwood Brewery Huddersfield," *Brewery History*, no. 95, 1999), which would put it just outside my barley wine range.

Barnard also mentions a number of brewers producing stock ales, such as the Red Lion Brewery, London; the Dorchester brewery; The Brewery, Leeds; the Exchange Brewery, Sheffield; Thomas Rawson & Co., Sheffield; and T. Ford & Son, Tiverton. There is no data on these beers, apart from Barnard's palate, so I cannot say whether these stock ales were of high enough gravity to be accounted as barley wines. However, he quotes a brew from P. L. Hudson of Cambridgeshire as XXXX stock ale, a designation indicating a beer brewed above OG 1.090 (21°P).

Other beers referred to by Barnard include a two-year-old KKKK ale from Mann Crossman and Paulin "of a rich brown colour and with a Madeira odour . . . a full-bodied beer." This is of personal interest to me, since this company had a brewery in Putney, Southwest London, one hundred yards from my uncle's barbershop. I have often speculated that passing that brewery and inhaling its smells long before I was of legal drinking age may have been what instilled my lifelong love of beer. Barnard continues with Jacob Street Brewery's "Bristol Old Beer," which is aged for a minimum of eighteen months, and which he found to be "rather too heavy." Other references include special strong ales from Joule's Stone brewery; old ale from Groves and Whitnall, Salford; XXXX from Thomas Berry & Co., Sheffield. James Hole of Newark offered BB strong ale; Savill Brothers of Stratford plied him with KKK, an extra-strong ale; the City Brewery in Oxford had a strong old ale; the Hereford Brewery in the West of England offered him strong old Hereford ale, which he found to be too powerful; Benskin's of Watford treated him to their Colne Spring ale; Thomas Hardy of the brewery in Kimberley supplied an XXX strong ale; the City Brewery in Lichfield also had an XXX old ale; at Flower & Son, Shaftesbury, he was given XXXX ale; and finally, the Don Brewery, Sheffield provided him with a glass of "Old Tom" or XXXX ale.

You may have found it a little frustrating to trundle through this list and not find anything more than Barnard's descriptors instead of concrete facts. But there were a couple of instances when he gave us much more solid information. The first example was Old Strong Ale from Worthington & Co., Burton-on-Trent, for which he provided an analysis. This indicated the beer had OG 1.110 (26°P) and finished at 1.030 (7.6°P) and contained 8.7% alcohol by weight. That would give 11.3% abv or calculating directly from the gravity difference using Her Majesty's Revenue and Customs table, 10.7% abv. That indicates a slight error in Barnard's figures, but that is probably not important. What they also show is an apparent attenuation of 73%, which is quite good for a beer of this gravity and means that it would not have tasted overly sweet. But in that context, he also supplies an analysis of the solid residue after evaporation of the liquid, and this shows that just under one-third of this residue is "fermentable maltose," which would have had a sweeter taste than the other components such as dextrins. Finally, he shows that the beer's acidity was 0.47%, calculated as lactic acid. This is high enough to be noticeable on the palate as sourness (though balanced by the residual sweetness) and is what might be expected for a beer matured a long time in wood. Note that this figure is not too different from the 0.37% lactic acid obtained with an eighteen-month-old sample of Worthington Burton Ale tested in 1890 (R. Wahl and M. Henius, *American Handy Book of the Brewing, Malting and Auxiliary Trades*, 1908). For the record, these authors also give an analysis carried out in 1890 on a ninety-year-old bottle of Worthington Burton Ale, which gave a lactic acid level of 0.61%.

The second instance where Barnard quotes numbers is interesting because of the story around it. It is a story which has been told several times (Jeff Evans, *BEER*, July 2002; Brian Glover, "Antifreeze for the World's Frozen Wastes," *What's Brewing*, January 2004; Amahl Turczyn Scheppach, "Seasonal Brews, a Tale of Arctic Ale," *Zymurgy*, November/December 2006) but it is worth repeating because recently there has been another twist in the tale. It starts with the famous quest to find the Northwest Passage, a route to the East around the top of Canada, a quicker way than going south around Cape Horn. In 1845 Sir John Franklin set off to find this route with two ships and 129 men, and neither ships nor men ever returned, having presumably been trapped in the ice. Two further expeditions in 1852 and 1857 were sent, the first being unsuccessful and the second reportedly finding Franklin's remains (I am not sure how since the ships were not found). A third expedition in 1875 also failed to find the ships. But the intriguing point about these expeditions was that the first, led by Captain (not Admiral, that came later!) Belcher took with him a strong beer commissioned from Allsopp's of Burton. Belcher's report on the beer was extremely favorable, and a second brew was taken on the third expedition by Sir George Nares. Barnard could not taste Belcher's beer when he visited the brewery as none of it was left, but he was able to taste that made for the 1875 expedition, for which he was able to give us an analysis.

Barnard says the Arctic Ale had OG 1.130 (30°P) and 9% alcohol by weight, which would amount to 12.8% abv. The latter seems to be rather high and would calculate out to a final gravity of 1.031 (7.8°P); Turczyn Scheppach quotes a reference giving an analysis of this 1875 version, carried out in 1961 stating that the beer had an FG 1.053 (13.1°P) and 9.65% abv. Either Barnard was quoting the wrong units, or over eighty-six years the sample had lost 3% alcohol; we know by his own admission that Barnard was not a beer drinker, much less an expert brewer, so perhaps the first explanation is correct? Both Glover and Turczyn (but not Barnard) state that the Arctic Ale wort was so viscous that it could not be run off from the copper in the normal way but had to be "lifted out in buckets." This may be something of a myth, for viscosity is a function of temperature. While the wort was still hot, as would be expected at the end of the boil, it should still be able to flow fairly freely through the taps. That is exactly what I have found when handling such high-gravity worts in my own brewery. The real problem comes when the wort is cooled and needs to be transferred to the fermenters; it would be nice to know how Allsopp brewers handled that.

A coda to all this is that Franklin's ships were found in 2016, seventy miles apart, as though the first ship, HMS *Terror*, had been abandoned and all crew had sailed south on the other ship HMS *Erebus*, only to share the fate of the first ship. Further, thanks to climate change and much melting of Arctic ice, the Northwest Passage is now open to commercial traffic. Ships using it do not carry any Arctic Ale, although the beer continued to be brewed and sold by what was now Ind Coope & Allsopp. In fact, according to Martyn Cornell (*Zythophile*, January 10, 2010) at sometime in the 1930s Ind Coope renamed its No.1 Burton barley wine Arctic Ale. It got the axe in 1974, when the brewers replaced it with something with less strength and flavor. However, according to Scheppach, it had already been somewhat dumbed down, since a 1937 version weighed in at the lower gravity of 1.085 (21°P).

There have been attempts to revive Arctic Ale, by which I mean brewing a beer to the same sort of OG but using modern ingredients. Scheppach reports that Elveden Ales produced a version, Harwich Charter Ale, at 10% abv, to commemorate the four-hundredth anniversary of the receiving of a royal charter by Harwich, a town in Essex, eastern England. John Moore of the Teignworthy brewery in the county of Devon brewed such a beer for Tucker's Maltings (Jeff Evans, "What's Brewing," *Beer*, July 2002). Moore aimed for 9% abv, added a good deal of crystal malt to give a dark red color, and added 2½ lb./barrel of a mix of Bramling Cross, Goldings, and Challenger hops in the copper. I can't calculate IBU from such imprecise information, but 2½ lb./barrel, translates to 5.6 oz. in 5 US gallons, a fairly healthy amount, although alpha acid utilization could be pretty low for such a high-gravity beer. But, Moore boiled the wort for 6¼ hours, which would help utilization because that surely means he collected all the extract from the grain rather than taking just the first runnings.

Perhaps the most intriguing revival is that from Harpoon, Boston, Massachusetts. This was first brewed in 2014, and had 13% abv, 32 IBU, and 135 EBC color (about 68 SRM). I have not had the fortune to obtain a bottle or two of this beer, so I cannot comment too much, except to say that the alcohol level seems a little too high and the bitterness level a little too low to make this an authentic revival. But I very much like the idea that an American brewer should make the effort to revive an iconic English beer. Yes, yes, I know that has happened in spades with IPA, but, in contrast to IPA, Arctic Ale was very much a niche product which did not, and probably never will achieve the level of sales attained by IPA in the United States.

What happened in the twentieth century? One significant event was that in 1903 Bass officially labeled Bass No. 1 as a barley wine (Fal Allen and Dick Cantwell, *Barley Wine,* 1998). But, Bass No. 1 was actually a Burton ale, so this renaming implies that Burton ales, as I have suggested, were simply another form of what we now call barley wines. Bass No. 1 was a dark beer, although it was brewed solely with pale malt. It is claimed (Ted Bruning, "Prince of Ales Back on Its Throne," *What's Brewing,* December 1996) that the brew was in the kettle for twelve hours, and that during this time 5.5 barrels were reduced to just three. It would be expected that such a long boil would make the beer dark, probably mainly through Maillard reactions along with some caramelization. However, if it was as reported, the evaporation rate during the boil was very low, under 5% per hour, whereas I would have expected something more like 10% per hour. Since, presumably, the aim was to increase the wort gravity, this must be seen as a very inefficient way to go about it!

The same source quoted an OG of 1.105 (25°P) for the wort and 10.5% abv for the beer, which would make FG about 1.025 (6.3°P). That, coupled with the fact that it was hopped with 6 lb./barrel of Goldings and Fuggles hops, would have meant that the beer was not overly sweet. Indeed, if we assume an alpha acid level in the hops of 5%, and a utilization of 15%, then that would calculate out to about 125 IBU, a figure probably higher than would be achievable in practice. A 1902 brew of Bass No.1 Burton Ale was bottled as King's Ale, to commemorate the visit of King Edward VII to the brewery in that year. This beer continued to be brewed, surviving two world wars with their severe restrictions on grain supply, almost through the century until it was finally axed in 1995. Bass had by that time undergone a series of mergers to become Bass Charrington Ltd. and just five years later would disappear into the maw of Interbrew, the Belgian brewing company now part of Anheuser Busch Inbev.

Other brewers produced barley wines, some simply designated as strong ales, in the twentieth century. As brewing techniques became more sophisticated, there was a shift toward making these beers paler. The first pale barley wine on the market was produced in 1951 by Tennant Bros. of Sheffield. Just ten years later, the Tennants were bought out by Whitbread, who removed the Tennants' name and replaced it with their own. Whitbread Gold Label became the leading barley wine brand by the end of the century. By this time, it had OG 1.095 (23°P) and had 10.9% abv, but sales were only about 38,000 barrels, down somewhat from its peak production of 46,000 barrels in 1969 (Nicholas Redman, "Wise Man from North's Fine Ale," *What's Brewing*, December 1996). A famous advertising slogan used by Whitbread was "Strong as a double Scotch—less than half the price," presumably targeted at those drinkers more interested in getting a quick buzz than in enjoying the taste. In fact, this statement was not too far from the truth, for a nip (one-third of a pint) of barley wine, the normal size sold then at 10% abv would amount to 19 mL of alcohol by my reckoning. A double Scotch would be 50 mL at 40% abv and would contain 20 mL of alcohol. A small difference perhaps, but surely no self-respecting advertising person would be bothered by such a detail!

An interesting event took place in the early twentieth century when N. H. Claussen in 1903 in Denmark isolated "wild" yeast from a sample of English stock ale. He named it after the source as *Brettanomyces*, although other strains have since been isolated, particularly from certain Belgian beers. The significant point about this is first that it gives the beer a very characteristic flavor, sometimes described as "horse blanket," which most certainly is not a flavor I would like in my beer. Second, a strong beer containing a significant amount of unfermented extract, such as barley wine, matured in a wooden cask for a year or more would be very susceptible to the action of *Brettanomyces* or even other wild yeasts. It was therefore assumed by Claussen and Wahl & Henius that the contribution of this yeast was an essential part of the flavor of English stock ales. It is difficult to know whether this is true of all barley wines of the period, and if it were true it became less likely as the twentieth century wore on and wooden vessels and casks were gradually phased out in brewing. But one barley wine stands out in his respect, namely Benskin's (an obvious source for sexual innuendo) Colne Spring Ale. For, according to Martyn Cornell (*Amber, Gold and Black*, 2008), this beer was deliberately "infected" with *Brettanomyces* during production. I have certainly drunk this beer in the 1960s when I frequented an Ind Coope pub, this company having bought out Benskin's in 1957. However, I do not remember it having a *Brettanomyces* character, but that may be the fault of my memory, or that fact that I did not then know much about any kind of yeast.

Throughout the twentieth century, English average or "regular" beers declined in OG and alcohol level, perhaps due to changes in taste, but more likely driven by steep increases in beer duty, especially between the two world wars. That, and the English habit of going to the pub for a session where the drinker would consume several pints in an evening would seem to have made barley wines less popular on grounds of both cost and strength. There is certainly some truth in this argument, but, as we have already seen, there were some brewers who persisted in brewing barley wines. Notable among these were Fuller's Golden Pride at 8.5%, released as a bottle-conditioned beer called Fuller's Vintage Ale in 1997, which has run as a dated series up to 2016. Both beers are still available, but hard to find even in Fuller's pubs. An interesting aspect of the keeping of this beer is that at least one beer aficionado I know thinks the Vintage Ale has "no legs," that is, that it soon deteriorates and develops a flat, uninspiring flavor. On the other hand, other drinkers think that Vintage Ale actually goes through cycles, tasting disappointing at times, then later picking up to become a full-flavored, satisfying barley wine.

Another well-known strong ale was Gale's Prize Old Ale, at 9.0% abv. Since the term "old ale" has become so fuzzy, and barley wines in general are all old, I have no hesitation in including this in my barley wine category. According to the head brewer there, Gale were still using a cool ship into the twenty-first century, but they have now been bought out by Fuller's and the old Horndean brewery closed. Prize Ale itself has disappeared after the buyout. One of the oddities about this beer is that it was sold in bottles sealed with a cork, rather than being crown capped in the usual way. I never felt this was a good system, since you had to keep the bottle upright, which meant the cork was likely to dry out and allow contaminants into the beer.

I have already mentioned Harvey's Elizabethan ale (8.2% in 2003, 7.5% currently); others worth mentioning include Orkney Skullsplitter at 8.5%, apparently still being brewed. Harviestoun, another Scottish brewery, has Ola Dubh, a limited series brewed annually and aged in whisky casks. Then there is Elgood of Cambridgeshire with a 9% abv Scotch Ale, this being a brewery with the most beautiful copper cool ship I have ever seen. Fredric Robinson from Cheshire has Old Tom, brewed at 1.079 (19°P), but 8.5% abv, according to CAMRA (*Good Beer Guide*, 2013). However, looking at the customs table, that alcohol content indicates a finishing gravity of just under 1.015 (3.8°P), making it very dry and hardly at all sweet. An English craft brewer, Parish Brewery of Leicestershire, is notable for a very big barley wine, namely Baz's Bonce Blower, weighing in at OG 1.120 (28°P) and 12% abv. But perhaps the most important keeper of the flame is J. W. Lees of Manchester, with its 11.5% abv Harvest Ale brewed once a year, every year since 1986. In some twenty-first century years the beer has been matured in whisky, sherry, port, and even calvados casks. It has been reported (R. Protz, "Dawn Chorus Welcomes Ale Bubble-Brain," *What's Brewing*, December 1997) that the brew uses a small amount of crystal malt and is bittered with Goldings and Northdown hops. Adding crystal malt to this kind of brew is not uncommon, but brewers often avoid its use since it provides some unfermentables and tends to make the beer sweeter—I'll discuss that in the chapter on brewing barley wines. But then there's Thomas Hardy Ale, a brew first produced by Eldridge, Pope in Dorset to commemorate the fortieth anniversary of the author's death, much of his work having centered on the county of Dorset. This was brewed at OG 1.125 and 11.7% abv, and each bottled was numbered and labeled with the vintage, an unusual step at the time. Unfortunately, the brewery decided to stop brewing and to concentrate on its pubs, passing the brewing of Hardy Ale, as I remember, to a separate company, Thomas Hardy Brewing, which had the beer contract brewed at the Burtonwood brewery in Cheshire. That did not last, and George Saxon's Imports bought the brand and had the beer brewed at O'Hanlon's Brewing Co. in Devon. Some drinkers averred that this version was not as good as it had previously been; whether that is or is not the case, O'Hanlon's ceased to brew it in 2009. Just recently, the brand has been bought by an Italian company and is being brewed at Meantime Brewing Co in London. But note that Meantime was bought out in 2015 by SAB Miller, and then as part of the takeover of that company by Anheuser-Busch Inbev, it was passed onto to Asahi Breweries of Japan in 2016. Let us hope that they will continue to produce Hardy Ale.

Let me explain why I said so much about Hardy Ale. In 1977, when I came to the United States from England, I brought with me two bottles of the 1974 vintage of this beer, along with two bottles of Courage Russian Imperial Stout of the same age. These were sampled at a gathering of brewers and people in the beer business in 2003, when they were just short of being thirty years old. The Courage beer had not lasted well; it was lackluster, slightly sour, and tasted a little of cardboard. But the Hardy Ale was glorious, full-bodied, redolent of sherry, nuts, and raisins with the warming effect of alcohol in the background. The people present at that tasting still remember this beer with fondness!

At this point, it is probably pertinent to ask what the future may be for barley wine in England. After all, in a land where 5% abv pale yellow lager has the biggest share of the market, and most ale drinkers are looking for something at even lower strengths, can there be any hope for beers at 10% abv or more? Perhaps just as a niche beer, which makes it uneconomical for many brewers, especially craft brewers concentrating on cask-conditioned beers. With my friend Jeff Browning from Brewport, I visited the 2003 CAMRA National Winter Ale Festival, held in the brewing shrine of Burton upon Trent. By definition, you would expect winter ales to be stronger than those for the other seasons, would you not? By my count there were some seventy-five beers on offer, yet the only barley wines amounted to just four, Coors Museum, No. 1 Barley Wine, Harvey's Christmas Ale, Orkney Skullsplitter, and Robinson's Old Tom.

There is a big problem for barley wine brewers in England, and that is the excise duty. Beer has been taxed in Britain since the 1640s, and brewing has always been a generous contributor to the National Exchequer. Beer taxation in England has a convoluted history, since at various times duties have been paid on malt, hops, and beer. This was somewhat simplified in 1880, when basically duty was paid on the basis of the OG of the beer, albeit by a somewhat cumbersome formula which I won't bother to explain here. This had a double-edged effect in that the duty was due when the wort went into the fermenter so that the brewer had to fork out long before he received any payment for the beer. This finally changed in 1993 when the duty was charged as the beer left the brewery to go to the retailer, and the rate of duty was assessed according to the beer's abv. That of course meant duties were higher on barley wines than on the lower-strength average beers (around 4% abv).

This changed again in 2011, when, instead of duty being directly proportional to abv, a big step change between 7.5% and 8.0% abv was introduced. I don't want to get too complicated here as I am no tax lawyer, so let's look at what this means in terms of the price of a pint of beer (taking the figures from HM Revenue and Customs March 2017):

4.0% abv £0.44 per UK pint ($0.57 at current exchange rates)
7.5% abv £0.82 per UK pint ($1.07 at current exchange rates)
8.0% abv £1.13 per UK pint ($1.47 at current exchange rates)
11.0% abv £1.55 per UK pint ($2.02 at current exchange rates)

In other words, there is twice as much duty on an 11% abv beer as on one at 7.5%, and almost four times as much as would be paid for a "standard" 4% abv beer. This is the standard rate; a small craft brewer would pay less according to his barrelage but would still be subject to a big jump above 7.5% abv. Note that beer is also subject to a 20% value added tax, which I have not factored in in order to keep things simple.

To put this into perspective, the federal tax in the United States, regardless of alcohol content, is only $18/barrel (7c a US pint) for big brewers and only $7/barrel (3c a US pint) for those brewing 60,000 barrels or less. There are, of course, state taxes, which vary widely, but are nowhere near the English 20% VAT charge. Clearly the English duty is especially onerous for barley wine brewers and must inhibit, if not actually discourage, them. In contrast, the US system makes life much easier for anyone wanting to brew a beer above 8% abv.

BACK TO THE USA

There is little evidence of strong ales being brewed in the United States after Prohibition until the last quarter of the twentieth century. Perhaps some stock ales reappeared after Prohibition, but these were generally below barley wine strength, with the exception of Ballantine's Burton Ale, which I have already discussed. That was to change with the advent of the craft brewing revolution in the United States. In fact, the first modern American barley wine appeared before it could be called a revolution, since there was only one brewery that could be considered to be what we now call a craft brewery. That was the Anchor Steam Brewery in San Francisco, a brewery that had survived Prohibition but was rescued from its financial problems in 1965 by Fritz Maytag, who turned it into a company producing quality, flavorful ales. In 1975 Anchor launched Old Foghorn Barley wine, said to be brewed at OG 1.100, and now listed at 8–10% abv.

Not long after, craft brewing did become a revolution, as Jack McAuliffe opened the short-lived New Albion Brewery in 1976. It lasted just six years, but McAuliffe's efforts were to inspire others to start up, such as Sierra Nevada and Boulder Brewing, in 1980, Albany

Brewing (New York) in 1981, Red Hook in 1982, and Pyramid Brewing in 1984. Fueled in part by the explosion in home brewing after it became federally legal in 1978, the American craft brewing movement blossomed. And since it was America, it blossomed in a variety of ways, such as contract brewing, where an entrepreneur would get beer brewed to his recipe by an established brewery, the most notable example of that being Jim Koch's Boston Beer Co., which became so successful that it was later able to establish its own brewing facility. Others latched on to the idea of the brewpub, where the beer is sold only on the premises where it was brewed. The first is generally acknowledged to have been Bert Grant's Yakima Brewing Co., opened in 1982, which was very quickly followed by Mendocino Brewing Co. and Buffalo Bill's Brewpub in Hayward, California. Not long after that, in 1987, Northampton Brewery opened its brewpub up in Massachusetts, the second such establishment in New England after Commonwealth Brewing in Boston. A third came soon after in 1988, when Greg Noonan founded the Vermont Pub and Brewery in Burlington, Vermont.

Not all in the craft industry was sweetness and light, and a good few of the new boys failed, for one reason or another. Notably, Catamount Brewing Co., the first new brewery in Vermont, ceased business; that was because of financial reasons, not because there was anything wrong with their beer. Their second, larger brewery is now being run by Harpoon. William Newman's Albany Brewery also closed doors quite early on, as later did the Commonwealth Brewing brewpub. The Manhattan Brewing Co. in New York City also failed to make the grade; so too did Elm City in New Haven, Connecticut; and New England Brewing Co. in Norwalk, Connecticut, also ceased to brew, but was then revived by Rob Leonard and is now thriving in Amity, Connecticut. There was in fact a quite a dip in craft brewing in the 1990s, but as we all know it came roaring back in the twenty-first century, with establishments now numbering in the thousands (about 5,000 craft breweries and brewpubs, according to the *Brewery History Society Newsletter*, no. 77, July 2017). Connecticut was very slow to catch on to craft brewing, but in the last few years there has been a boom in the state. In fact, the joke now is that while I was writing this paragraph three new breweries have started up in the state.

But, I am not writing a history of craft brewing in America, I am writing that of barley wine. And American craft brewers have not been slow to latch on to this style of beer. I have already mentioned Anchor's Old Foghorn, and Sierra Nevada introduced Bigfoot in 1983. This is brewed at OG 23°P (1.096 SG), FG 6°P (1.024 SG) and 9.6% abv. It is brewed from two-row pale and caramel malts, bittered with Chinook, and finished with Chinook, Cascade, and Centennial hops. Crucially it has 90 IBU, which means that it was the first American company to brew a hoppy barley wine, and this, coupled with a 75% attenuation, results in a full-tasting beer that is not very sweet. But note my comments earlier on how hoppy Bass Burton Ale No.1 may have been. Another brew along these lines emerged around 1989, namely Rogue's Old Crustacean Barley wine, now prefixed with "XS." Brewed from Pale, Munich, and caramel malts to an OG of 24°P (1.100 SG), with a color of 50 SRM and 11.5% abv, which is something like a deep amber color, it is hopped with Rogue Newport and Freedom hops, to IBU 105, a level higher than even some double IPAs!

There are many more and I cannot list them all, for the simple reason that there are just too many to do that. *Beer Advocate* lists no fewer than 1,370 American barley wines and some 250 wheat wines. Some breweries have put out more than one barley wine, and some have offered versions of the same beer as sold in bottle but in various barrel-aged forms. Old bourbon barrels seem to be favored here, though some have used rye whiskey barrels and even Scotch whisky barrels; several used red wine barrels, two aged in white wine barrels, one a cognac barrel, another a tequila barrel, and even sherry, rum, and calvados barrels. In a few instances the beer was aged in a bourbon barrel with added *Brettanomyces* (Marin Brewing Company), which some might consider as authentic in an English-style barley wine; there are other sour versions listed. Other variations include pumpkin barley wine, those using rye, smoked versions, added cherries, blackberries, chocolate nibs. Some claim to have been dry-hopped, which could be seen as crossing the line between barley wine and double IPA. But I

Bigfoot may be a myth but this beer is for real!

visited Firefly Hollow Brewing Company in Bristol, Connecticut, and sampled their 10.2% abv double IPA, an excellent beer which both the head brewer, Dana Bourque, and I agreed could just as easily have been called a hoppy barley wine. There's also a couple of black barley wines, and one which apparently was called "Imperial Mild Barleywine," which as far as I am concerned is not imperial as it never had a royal warrant and is certainly not mild in the modern sense.

Similarly, wheat wine examples have been barrel-aged in various types of used spirit casks, brewed with various fruits, including lemon, blueberries, cranberries, boysenberries, ginger, blood orange, melon, and mango; several have used added honey. Chocolate, of course, has also been used, and one such beer was brewed with spruce tips. This list may not be complete, and I do not necessarily recommend any or all of them! I have put it together just to demonstrate that American craft brewers have used their ingenuity and inventiveness on this style of beer just as much as they have on other styles. However, I would counsel you to be careful about adding exotic flavors to your barley wines—properly made, this beer is already full of flavor and adding others might well muddy the palate, if not actually spoil the beer.

Of course, not all of these are widely available, and many of them are one-offs, or brewed just once a year, and may disappear quickly into the mouths of those in the know. So, as mentioned in the former section, I conducted an experiment and over two or three weeks bought samples of all the barley wines I could find, just from liquor stores within a radius of no more than five miles from my home in Stratford, Connecticut. I came up with no fewer than forty beers fitting my designation of this category. Some fourteen of these came from Great Britain, including a series from J. W. Lees, Thomas Hardy Ale, Harvey's Elizabethan, Meantime barley wine, Fuller's Vintage Ale, and a couple from Harviestoun. The rest are all from the United States, including samples from Long Trail (Vermont), Dogfish Head (Delaware), North Coast Brewing (California), Smuttynose Brewing (New Hampshire), Ballantine Burton Ale, Founders Brewing (Michigan), Alesmith (California), Boulevard Brewing (Missouri), Shipyard (Maine), Goose Island (Illinois), and Speakeasy (California). I came up with only one wheat wine, from The Bruery (California) (see chapter 1).

The first point about these is that they come in a variety of bottle sizes, ranging from 6.3 ounces (Hardy Ale), England's traditional "nip" at 9 ounces (J. W. Lees) through 12 ounces (Boulevard) to one pint (Goose Island) up to 22 ounces (Shipyard, Speakeasy, and others) and even 25 ounces (The Bruery). Those below 1 pint are ideal in my view, because one person can consume the whole bottle in one session (sipping it slowly of course, and maybe shared with a friend); perhaps even

1 pint is acceptable in this way. But I do not see the reasoning for using the very large bottles for such strong beers. They cannot be consumed in one sitting, except with the help of two or three friends; remember that the cost of such beers and the effort that went into brewing them means that you should drink every drop and waste nothing. That often means that you never quite get around to deciding when would be a suitable occasion to set up such a session, and a very expensive beer languishes in your beer cellar for decades!

Enough nit-picking; let me talk about these beers a little. I am not going to give detailed tasting notes for each one, but there are some interesting points to be made about some of the beers in this selection. The offering from Goose Island, aged in bourbon barrels, uses not only a little caramel malt along with the pale malt base, but also chocolate, black malt, and even roasted barley and comes in at the relatively high 13.6% abv. It is quite black and analyses at 60 IBU. I do not know the exact proportions of these malts, but just looking at the list it would seem that this beer might be better called an imperial stout! However, I find it drinks fairly smoothly, with some roast character yet without the bite you would expect from a stout, so I think we have to take the brewer's designation of barley wine at face value. Shipyard's version also uses chocolate malt, roasted barley, and caramel malt, though at the slightly lower 8.5% abv.

Boulevard Brewing Co. (Kansas) brews Scotch on Scotch and claims to use some amber malt, plus "a touch of smoked malt" and clocks in at 9.6% abv with only 25 IBU. It is certainly a very nice barley wine, full-bodied, smooth, and malty with just a hint of bitterness as a true Scotch ale should have. It is actually called an "imperial Scotch Ale," a designation I have not seen before and one which is a cavalier, even careless, use of the imperial tag. Founder's (Michigan) Curmudgeon Old Ale, at 9.8% abv, 50 IBU, is brewed with some molasses, while Olde School Barley wine from Dogfish Head (Delaware), at no less than 15% abv, is brewed with figs and dates. The former drinks well, with just a hint of the molasses, whereas the latter does give a little heat on the palate, as might be expected from so much alcohol (which, incidentally, takes it out of my barley wine category on a numerical basis). I was going to discuss Speakeasy's (California) Old Godfather, but I just found out the brewery has closed, so you are unlikely to get a sample to taste yourself.

Then there are a couple of other beers which like Founder's version, do not call themselves barley wine. The first is Triple Bag from Long Trail (Vermont), at 11% abv and 65 IBU, which is claimed to have been brewed from the first runnings from the mash. There is no question in mind or on my palate that this is a barley wine. And it is a full-bodied, well-balanced drink with a fine touch of hop bitterness at the end. North Coast Brewing (California) offers Old Stock Ale at 12% abv and 34 IBU, which is brewed with English malt and hops. Perhaps the name comes from the fact that they have also offered a barley wine in 2013 as part of a collaboration with Rogue and Deschutes. Whatever, it drinks as a barley wine, with plenty of body, although with something of a hot, alcohol finish. The one example of wheat wine I have, White Oak, from The Bruery (California) has 12.5% abv and 20 IBU, with a very low color of 6 SRM, and is actually a mixture of 50% wheat wine and 50% ale. It is, of course, much paler than most barley wines, largely due to the wheat, and is somewhat lighter in flavor than its cousins, but still quite complex with caramel, vanilla, and some bourbon flavor from the barrel aging.

Lastly, there two beers which to me are oddities. A beer I discussed in chapter 1 is Avery Brewing's Maharajah IPA at 10% abv from an OG of 1.090 (21°P) with an IBU of around 100; it is also heavily dry-hopped. I first sampled this beer at a lunchtime tasting at Brewport and was immediately struck with the thought that it was simply a hoppy barley wine. With such a big beer, the hop character and bitterness just do stand out in the way you expect from a "normal" IPA, which only underlines the fact there is a very fine line, if a line at all, between a double IPA and a barley wine. Which suggests we only need one description for both beers? Or do we say that double IPAs are simply American barley wines as defined by the BA or BJCP? Finally, I have a beer from The Atlantic Brewing Co. (Maine), which bears the title "Brother Adam's Bragget Honey Ale Barley Wine Style." It is brewed to 10.5% abv, using pale, Munich, and black malts, and the English hops

Pilgrim and Whitbread Goldings Variety (actually a Fuggles derivative). The honey is mainly a source of fermentable sugar, but does add some flavor, and Bragget is supposedly a Welsh Honey Ale. On Beer Advocate this beer is quoted (presumably from the brewers) as being a Belgian-style ale. The bottle label says it is brewed with equal amounts of barley and honey, so it is clearly also a form of mead. Putting all that together means that it covers a lot of categories in one beer! If it was entered in a competition I wonder in what category it should be put?

The reason for the discussions in the last paragraph is simply to illustrate the variety of barley wines and to give some idea of how American brewers are pushing its envelope. Like them, you should also be open to what is and is not a true barley wine. What at first sight seems to be an ancient and fairly simple beer has many dimensions and offers the craft and home brewer the opportunity for much further experimentation.

CHAPTER THREE

BARLEY WINE INGREDIENTS

Jack Cade: and I will make it felony to drink small beer. (William Shakespeare, *Henry VI*, part 4, scene 2)

An unusual sight—an ingredient retailer and its companion craft brewery, Veracious. Sadly it has now gone, a victim of the pandemic.

AS IS THE CASE FOR MOST OTHER BEERS, MALT IS THE WORK-horse for barley wine, perhaps more so, since it takes greater amounts of malt to brew it than is the case with "everyday" beers. Many all-grain brewers tend to look down on malt-extract-based beers, but in fact malt extracts offer the brewer more versatility and less effort than does using only grain malts. For that reason, I am going to start by considering the former first.

MALT EXTRACT

The first choice would be to use a pale extract, to correspond with the pale barley malt used in grain brewing, especially if you want your barley wine to be on the pale side. Indeed, it is much easier to make a pale barley wine using extract than with grain malt, because you do not have to boil the wort for the same length of time as in the latter case, as we shall see in the section on brewing. This is because it is straightforward to achieve the desired original gravity with extract. Straight liquid extracts will yield an OG of 1.033–1.037 (8.3–9.3°P) with 1 lb. (0.45 kg) dissolved in water and made up to a total of 1 gallon (3.78 L) of wort. More commonly, we forget the "1" and multiply the rest of the OG figure by 1,000 and say that the extract gives 33–37°/lb./ gallon. This makes calculating the amount of extract required quite simple. If we want to brew 5 gallons (19 L) of barley wine with OG 1.100 (23.8°P), and we assume the extract gives 35° (8.8°P) /lb. (0.45 kg)/gallon (3.78 L), then:

total gravity points required = 5 × 100 = 500
total malt extract required = 500 ÷ 35 = 14.3 lb. (6.5 kg)

Now, that is an awkward amount of liquid extract, and you might well want to use a more convenient amount and make up the difference with dried malt extract (DME), which is an easier substance to weigh out accurately and yields 45° (11.2°P)/lb. (0.45 kg)/gallon (3.78 L). Let's say that your liquid extract comes in 6 lb. (2.7 kg) lots, so we'll take two of them and the rest as DME, then:

Points yield from liquid extract = 12 × 35 = 420
Points needed from DME = 500 – 420 = 80.
Amount of DME required = 80 ÷ 45 = 1.8 lb. (0.8 kg)

You can do similar calculations using the Plato numbers, but I find the gravity points system simple and easy to use.

This is the simplest example, using only pale extracts, giving as pale a barley wine as possible. Any good-quality malt extract will be fine, but you should check with your supplier or the manufacturer as to exactly what yield a particular sample will give. Many brewers consider that Maris Otter grain malt is the best (and traditional) choice for barley wine, and there is a liquid extract available made only from this malt. But if you want something darker, perhaps more approaching Bass No. 1 in color, what do you do? You could, of course, steep a medium grade of caramel malt (say 80° L) in hot water at around 150°F (65.6°C) for twenty minutes or so, run the liquid into the boiler, rinse the grains again with hot water, add the rinses to the first running, then dissolve up the malt extract and make the wort up to boil volume. You probably ought to account for the gravity contribution of this malt, which will be around 22° (5.6°P)/lb. (0.45 kg)/gallon (3.78 L). Now, 2 lb. (0.9 kg) in a 5-gallon (19 L) brew length represents about 10% of the grist (based on the grain equivalent of the extract) and is as much as you should use, since caramel malts contribute unfermentables, and you want to minimize those as much as possible so that you can achieve good attenuation in fermentation. So, 2 lb. (0.9 kg) will contribute $2 \times 22 = 44$ gravity points in total, which amounts to $44 \div 5 = 9$ points (rounding up) in 5 gallons. That is not a huge number, so you can ignore it if you are not too fussy, but if you have a precise target in mind, such as brewing a clone of a commercial barley wine, then you should include it in your basic recipe calculation. Of course, this contribution becomes insignificant if you use only a pound or less of caramel malt.

You could make your barley wine darker if you wish by adding a small amount of a high-roasted malt, such as chocolate or black malt. In this case you would not want to use more than 1% of the grist (based on grain equivalent), which amounts to about ¼ lb. (0.11 kg). Clearly, the effect of this on the original gravity of the beer can be ignored. You should note that I have given no numbers for color here; you should look under "Color" in the first chapter of this book and see my comments at the beginning of the recipe chapter. But see the next paragraph, because while it is virtually impossible to calculate the color of the beer when brewed from grain malt and long boiled, it is possible to make some estimate of beer color in the case of malt extracts..

There are alternatives to steeping grains as described above, if you want your beer somewhat darker than can be obtained with just pale extracts. There are several darker malt extracts on the market which can in part be substituted for part of the pale extract indicated above. Amber malt extracts would be the first option, as these are generally made from base malt plus some caramel malt and/or Munich malt. Unfortunately, that seems to be about as much information as the manufacturers are willing to reveal. Color specifications for such extracts suggest that if used in the right amount to give a wort with specific gravity of 1.050 (12.4°P), this wort would have a color of 15 SRM. The same gravity achieved with a pale ale extract would come in at 9 SRM, so assuming them to be additive, a wort made from a 50:50 mix of pale ale and amber extracts at OG 1.100 (23.8°P) would have a color of 24 SRM. For a barley wine, this level of color would put the barley wine outside the BA and BJCP guidelines, although it would suit those for Scotch ales.

Also available are Munich malt extracts based on a 50:50 mixture of Munich malt and base malt (which latter may be a pilsner malt, rather than 2-row pale). If mixed on a 1:1 basis with a pale extract to give a wort of OG 1.100 (23.8°P), then the color would again be ± 24 SRM. If that is not dark enough for you, then there are porter malt extracts available, which are generally made from base malt, Munich or Victory malt, caramel malt, 60 or 80°L caramel malt, and black or chocolate malt. Such an extract would be ideal as part of the extract bill for brewing Scotch ales, which are often darker than barley wines and also have a slight roasted character as part of their palate. You would have to check with your supplier for full details, and I can't really recommend at what level you should substitute such an extract for a pale extract. A calculation such as I showed above says that a 1:1 mix of this malt with a pale extract would have a color, at OG 1.100 (23.8°P), of around 35 SRM. But those extra levels of flavor might be more than you wanted to achieve. You would have to experiment with it to adjust to the color you are targeting and the flavor you want. Remember that barley wines are going to have a lot of flavor anyway and adding more might spoil the balance of the beer or even muddy its palate. Even with the relatively short boil used for malt extract barley wines, because of their high wort gravities there will be some darkening of the wort through Maillard browning reactions. All in all, it may be best to just not worry about color and to concentrate (not a pun) on the taste of the beer alone.

There are two other types of extract which may be considered suitable for barley wine brewing. The first is a rye malt syrup, made with up to 25% rye malt and some light-colored caramel malt. Using this as part of the total extract bill can add a spicy rye character to the beer, although some might regard it as an unauthentic version of the style. That's up to you to decide, as is just how much of this extract you want to use—I would suggest that for a first shot you should replace only half of the pale extract with the rye extract, and adjust the amount in a second brew, according to your taste tests on the first one. A second extract of interest is one made with wheat malt and called variously German Weizenmalt or Bavarian Wheat malt. These are produced from a grist containing 50% or more of wheat malt—check with your supplier on the exact proportions. This extract can be used directly on its own to brew a wheat wine. The high proportion of wheat malt in this extract helps to give the barley wine hints of bread and honey flavors. You can also use it in smaller proportions along with pale barley malt syrup to introduce these flavors into a "regular" barley wine and to improve head retention, which is often a problem with barley wines.

At the start of this section I referred to the versatility of malt extract in brewing barley wine. The first advantage over grain malt is that you do not have to boil for long periods just to concentrate the wort to achieve your target OG. That, as I have shown above, can be achieved simply by using the appropriate amount of extract. A maximum of one hour will suffice, enough to extract and convert the alpha acids of the hops. Indeed, if you want to make a very hoppy version of the style you can hold back a portion of the extract and add the remainder just ten minutes or so before the end of the boil. A 50:50 split will be fine, and that way you will, for a wort of OG 1.100 (23.8°P) for example, be boiling most of the time a wort of around OG 1.050 (12.4°P) and hop usage will be more efficient than in a 1.100 OG wort. Another way of looking at that is that for a given level of bittering you will need less hops, saving money and decreasing wort losses to the mass of hops/hot break settling out at the end of the boil. However, you should know that there is a school of thought that one of the most important components of barley wine flavor lies in the compounds generated by Maillard reactions during wort boiling. Therefore, the thought goes, even when using only malt extract, boils should be long, say, as much as three hours so as to further such reactions.

A second advantage of malt extract is associated with brewing from grain malt. In the latter, hitting a target gravity can involve boiling over several hours in order to reach the required OG. However, especially if you are looking for an OG above 1.100 (23.8°P), you can simply take the first runnings, measure the gravity and add pale malt extract to reach that specific gravity. That can be done by a simple calculation as in the above examples and means that only a regular sixty- to ninety-minute boil will be required. Apart from the convenience and time-saving, this approach would be well suited to producing as pale a barley wine as possible.

There is a potential disadvantage in using only malt extract for this style of beer. That is that they can result in a wort low in free amino nitrogen (FAN), an essential food for yeast growth and fermentation. Therefore, it is, I think, mandatory to use a yeast nutrient (see below) when brewing barley wine from malt extract.

GRAIN MALTS

Pale malt is the predominant ingredient of barley wine; that from two-row barley is generally preferred. The higher nitrogen levels of six-row barley malt are of no advantage, since this is not a beer in which high levels of starch providing adjuncts are going to be used, and its high nitrogen content would likely cause haze problems in a beer which uses such a huge amount of malt. In any case, brewers prefer the flavor contribution of two-row malt; in particular, when it comes to malt-derived flavors many brewers swear by Maris Otter malt, especially if it has been floor- rather than drum-malted.

Some seem to think that the use of Maris Otter malt for barley wines is traditional and gives their beer the cachet of being true to the history of this beer. In fact, commercial farming of Maris Otter barley did not start until as recently as 1966, and its merits, perceived or otherwise, in brewing is what made it popular. Duplicated blind taste tests of malts made from different barleys by England's Brewing Research Institute in 2006 resulted in wins by Maris Otter malt in each case, and the panel described its flavor as "very clean, crisp, with biscuit and grain notes." The owner of one well-known brewery called it "the Rolls-Royce of brewing barleys," averring that his brewery used no other malt.

Others are not so complimentary about Maris Otter malt and say that it is no higher in quality than most other two-row malts, including those produced in America. One proponent of this view is none other than my friend Jeff Browning of Brewport Brewing Co., Bridgeport, Connecticut. However, there is one point about Maris Otter malt that is important, and that is that it hydrates very readily and gives good yield under a variety of mashing conditions. That means that for any craft or home brewer with relatively unsophisticated mashing systems this malt is ideal, and it will give good yields with the large grain bills required for barley wine brewing. If you want further information on Maris Otter malt, read "50 Years of Maris Otter" by Terry Foster (*Brew Your Own*, November 2015).

Another "named" malt from Britain is Golden Promise, which also has a high reputation among brewers, especially those producing Scotch ales. But it is mostly common practice by maltsters to use simple generic names, like "ale malt," simply because they may not be made entirely from one variety of barley. That does not mean that such malts are of inferior quality to Maris Otter or Golden Promise, it is simply that commercial brewers prize consistency. Barley varieties can vary in quality depending upon factors like weather, different soil conditions, and so on, and the maltster can only ensure consistency of quality by using a mix of barleys. So, two-row malts may be called by various names, such as "Ale malt," "Pale malt," "Brewer's malt," "Pale ale malt," or just "two-row."

It may occur to you that if you wanted to make the palest barley wine possible pilsner malt might be the base of choice. Such malts are certainly paler in color, at around 1.1–2.0°L, than say Maris Otter at 2–3°L, although Golden Promise malt can come in at anywhere from 1 to 3°L. However, the difference is small as far as color goes and might be considered insignificant compared to color from Maillard reactions during boiling (see under "pilsner malt" below). Some brewers think that use of pilsner malt might result in a blandness of flavor in the barley wine, as compared to one brewed from an ale malt. I do not think so, but I do think that a better route to a pale barley wine would be to limit wort boiling. This can be done by "gravity substitution," that is adding a fermentable such as malt extract or sugar to adjust the gravity to the required value, rather than by boiling a long time to achieve this value.

If you are not bothered about color, there is another base malt you might consider, namely mild ale malt. The only version of this available to home brewers, as far as I can discover, is Briess Ashburne® Mild Malt, at 5.3°L. As the name implies, it is produced as the foundation for what is an essentially malty beer, mild ale. It therefore gives the finished product, barley wine in this case, a more malty and full-bodied flavor. If you use this malt as your base, then there is no need to use specialty malts to bolster the beer's body (as some brewers consider necessary).

Munich malt comes in a variety of colors, depending upon the maltster, and is sometimes used as an addition to pale malt. It can also perform as a base malt in its own right, since those versions at 10°L or less carry sufficient enzymes to give good starch conversion. It generally gives a malty character to the beer, and if you are brewing a very hoppy barley wine, Munich malt can be regarded as lending a helping hand in balancing the beer's palate. I prefer to use it as a supplement to base pale malt, at the rate of 20–40% of the total grist. Much the same can be said for Vienna malt, although at 3°L it is lower in color than Munich malt and tends to give a toasty, rather than a malty, flavor.

With this malt, I generally go for using it at the rate of about 10–20% of the grist.

All the pale base malts, however they are designated and whether they are English or American, are of high and consistent quality, as maltsters have carefully refined their techniques over the years. You can therefore use them with confidence in brewing barley wines. As far as yield goes, such malts give a maximum of 80–82%, which corresponds to 1.037° (9.3°P)/lb. (0.45 kg)/gallon (3.78 L). But this potential yield is what is obtained on a fine grind basis in a laboratory test, and actual yields will be somewhat lower; exactly how much lower depends upon the efficiency of the operation. If we take this 1.037 (9.3°P) figure as 100% of what we could obtain, then an experienced craft brewer would get perhaps 80–85%. A more likely yield for a competent home brewer would be 70–75% of the maximum, corresponding to 1.026–28° (6.6.–7.1°P)/lb. (0.45 kg)/gallon (3.78 L). Indeed, at least one home brewing magazine bases all its grain yields on 65% of the maximum, which amounts to 1.024° (6.1°P)/lb. (0.45 kg)/gallon (3.78 L).

What this means is that you need to know exactly how efficient your system is in order to be able to calculate your grain bill. The simplest way to do that is to check back on a brew which was made with pale malt and little or no other specialty malts. Take your total OG points and divide by the weight of pale malt, and that will tell you how close you are to the figures quoted above. Then use that figure to calculate how much malt you need to brew your barley wine. That last bit seems simple, but it is not, because there are several methods for brewing such beers, and all will require you to think on your feet depending upon the measurements you take during the process. I shall deal with this in more detail in the fourth chapter, which will take you through these various brewing processes.

But let's look at an example here. Let's assume that you want your barley wine to have OG 1.110 (25.8°P), that you are going to sparge and collect a full 6–7 gallons (23–27 L) of wort, which you will boil down to 5 gallons (19 L), and that your brewhouse efficiency is 70%, so you will get a yield of 1.026° (6.6°P)/lb. (0.45 kg)/gallon (3.78 L). Then:

$$\text{Total points required} = 110 \times 5 = 550$$
$$\text{Weight of pale malt} = 550 \div 26 = 21.2 \text{ lb., or 21 lb. 3 oz. (9.6 kg)}$$

That is a lot of grain which has to fit in your mash tun, and it will be accompanied by, say, 1.25 qt. (0.6 L) mash water per lb. grain, or 21.2 × 1.25 = 26.5 qt., or 6.6 gallons (25 L). That means you had better be sure that all this will fit into your mash tun *before* you start the brew, but more of that later.

PILSNER MALT

I am dealing with this separately since it is certainly not a traditional malt in producing barley wines, and perhaps some would say that it has no place in ale brewing at all, as I mentioned above. However, there is really no reason why that should be the case in general or in barley wine production in particular. This is especially true if you are looking to brew a pale barley wine, although as suggested earlier it will probably not make much of a difference to the final color if your procedure involves a long boil. Just to put it into perspective, it may not seem that there is a big difference in color between pilsner and ale malts. If, however, you take the maximum specification difference of 3 for Maris Otter and the lowest for pilsner malt of 1.1, that is 1.9°L, or nearly twice that for pilsner malt, so it is a significant difference. And remember that you will have a lot of malt in this brew, perhaps 15–20 lb. (6.8-9.1 kg) in 5 gallons (19 L), and this will accentuate the final color (see more on color in the brewing chapter). There is an argument that this type of malt will give a lighter, less malty, biscuit or bready flavor than an ale malt. While this may be true, the difference may not be noticeable in a high-gravity barley wine where a huge amount of malt is used and where there will be significant amounts of Maillard products present.

Pilsner malt, despite its low color (1.1–2.0°L) compared to ale malts, is well modified and will give extract yields similar to those for ale malts at a maximum of 80–82%, which corresponds to 1.037° (9.3°P)/lb. (0.45 kg)/gallon (3.78 L). The same arguments as for ale malts applies in that you will not get a yield as high as that in practice. A more likely yield for a competent home brewer would be 70–75% of the maximum, corresponding to 1.026–28° (6.6.–7.1°P)/lb. (0.45 kg)/gallon (3.78 L). Calculations of grist requirements for a given original gravity are identical to those for ale malts as above. Personally, I have never used it to brew a barley wine, because I am not overconcerned about its color and really rather prefer the red-hued colors and flavors you can get with ale malts and Maillard reactions during boiling.

CARAMEL/CRYSTAL MALTS

These can be, and often are, included in a barley wine grain bill, although opinions differ about the wisdom or need to do so. The idea behind their use is to add some caramel, nutty flavors, and, depending upon the caramel malt used, some red color hints in the finished beer. But such malts also contribute sweetness and some unfermentable material, both of which can make the finishing gravity of the beer higher than is desirable. You need to get good attenuation of the wort during fermentation so that the finished beer does not taste sickly sweet. Now, as discussed under malt extract, 2 lb. (0.9 kg.), about 10% of the total malt for a 5-gallon (19 L) brew, would be the maximum I recommend using. Which one should you use, considering that there is a whole range of these malts available, all roasted or kilned to a different degree? They are designated by their color starting at 10°Lovibond and going up to as high as 160°L. Caramel malts above 80°L will be much redder in color but can also be harsher in flavor and are not, in my opinion. really suitable for barley wine. I would choose a 60° or 80°L caramel malt if I were adding one, but some brewers prefer to use those at the lighter end of the range, say, 20–40°L, since there is going to be significant color development due to Maillard reactions in a long boil, such as three hours or so as would be necessary in the example quoted above. Note that these malts contribute to wort gravity, with a maximum yield of about 1.034° (8.5°P)/lb. (0.45 kg)/gallon (3.78

L). At our notional 70% brewhouse efficiency that amounts to 1.024°
(8.5°P)/lb. (0.45 kg)/gallon (3.78 L). As explained under malt extracts
above, you should take this into account in recipe formulation, if you
plan to use 2 lb. or more in a 5-gallon (19 L) brew.

OTHER MALTS

Briess Victory® Malt is relatively highly colored (25°L) and is rated as a
toasted pale malt. As such it can add a toasty, nutty character to a barley wine, and we have used it for that purpose at Brewport with good
results. Our addition rate was just under 4% of the total grist, which
amounted to only 0.1 lb. (0.045 kg)/gallon (3.78 L) and in such an
amount its contribution to OG was negligible. I do not recommend
adding this malt in any greater proportion than 5% of the total. Look
on it as a "polishing" addition, that is to say it will add some pleasing
nuances to the beer's flavor, without being at all obvious.

In that same beer we also used about 7% rye malt, which is at the
rate of about 0.2 lb. (0.09 kg)/gallon (3.78 L), or 1 lb. (0.45 kg) per 5
gallons (19 L). Rye malt does contain some starch-converting enzymes
and is low in color (3.5°L) and can be used in larger proportions, up
to 50% in a regular rye beer. However, the spicy flavor of this malt
means that it should be used sparingly in a barley wine; again, its spicy
character should be there as a background, not a dominant note. That
means keeping the addition rate to a maximum 10% of the malt bill.

Highly roasted products, such as chocolate and black malt, are
used by some barley wine brewers, but in small amounts, 1% or less
of the total, as discussed under malt extracts. These malts are added
for their color effects only, and if used in larger proportions they can
make the barley wine taste somewhat harsh. An alternative would be
to use one of the debittered black malts, which will give color but not
harshness. I prefer not to use them at all in my barley wines. However,
do note that these may find some use in brewing Scotch Ales, where
a little more beer color is desired, but keep the amount down to 1%
of the total or less, since this is definitely not a style which should be
astringent in any way. Greg Noonan (*Scotch Ale*, 1993, BA Classic Beer

Style Series, no. 8) propounds the use of roasted barley in this style of beer, but only at the rate of about 1 oz. (28 g) in a 5-gallon (19 L) brew, or about 0.5 lb. (0.23 kg) per barrel (31 gallons, 117 L). Interestingly, Noonan also favors using amber malt in Scotch Ales at 7–10% of the total grist. This is a very traditional English malt, often used in the eighteenth and nineteenth centuries, that can add biscuit/bready notes to the beer. It seems that Simpson's in England still produce amber malt, and it appears to be available to home brewers from some suppliers. I have not yet tried to use it in either a barley wine or a Scotch ale, but it might be interesting to do so.

There are other malts that you might think would work well in brewing this style, such as honey malt, melanoidin malt, and even smoked malt. If you want to experiment with them, that's your prerogative, and I applaud your innovative thinking. However, you get so much flavor and color from the high amount of pale malt, Maillard reactions in boiling, alcohol content, and even esters from the fermentation that you should be very careful about adding any other malts. If you do so, you run the risk of spoiling what would otherwise have been a great beer!

WHEAT MALT AND WHEAT WINE

By definition this beer must be made with more than 50% of the grist being wheat malt. This malt gives a slightly higher maximum yield (up to 85% in the fine grind laboratory test) than does barley malt. At our posited 75% brewhouse efficiency this comes to 1.039° (9.8°P)/lb. (0.45 kg)/per gallon (3.78 L), or about 2 gravity points higher than pale malt. There are at least two distinct types available, German wheat malt (color 2°L) and an American-grown white wheat malt (color 3°L), so they pretty much match the color levels of pale barley malts. That may, perhaps, be misleading in that most of the wheat wines I have seen are quite pale in color. Wheat malt is generally used at no more than 60% of the grist, because higher levels can easily form stuck mashes. Wheat malt, unlike barley malt, has no husk, which makes it difficult to form a permeable grain bed during runoff and sparging. Therefore, it is common practice to add rice hulls when mashing this malt, usually at the rate of 5–10% of the malt bill, in order to ensure that a stuck mash will not occur.

You should account for the extra yield for this malt in your recipe formulation, which makes for a little more complicated calculation than for barley wine. For example, let's suppose we want to brew 5 gallons (19 L) of beer OG = 1.100 (23.8°P), and that will require a total weight of grain, W lb., and we have 70% brewhouse efficiency, and are going to use 60% wheat malt, 40% pale malt then:

$$\text{Gravity points required} = 5 \times 100 = 500$$
$$500 = (29 \times 0.6 \times W) + (27 \times 0.4 \times W)$$
$$500 = 17.4W + 10.8W = 28.2W$$
$$\text{So, } W = 500 \div 28.2 = 17.7 \text{ lb. (8.0 kg)}$$
$$\text{weight of wheat malt required} = 17.7 \times 0.6 = 10.6 \text{ lb. (4.8 kg)}$$
$$\text{weight of pale malt required} = 17.7 \times 0.4 = 7.1 \text{ lb. (3.2 kg)}$$

Now, wheat wine can be brewed with not just these two malts, but also any of the caramel and/or roasted malts at levels that I have discussed under barley wine. That can make the above calculation more complicated, depending upon how much of such malts you use, but I think by now you have got the general idea. And if your calculations or brewing efficiency don't quite match the predictions and the gravity is lower than you wanted, you can always adjust it with one of the wheat malt extracts as discussed under malt extracts at the beginning of this chapter.

HOPS

I have talked about this before, but it bears repeating, namely that hop aroma and character are not necessarily a part of barley wine flavor and aroma. Indeed, if you take the view that these beers are to be long matured, perhaps for a year or more, then any hop aroma and character will have largely dissipated by the time the beer is drunk. That means that all you want from the hops is bitterness. I know that is something of a sweeping statement, and that some brewers, especially commercial brewers, might not wish to keep the beer so long before selling it. In fact, at Brewport Brewing Co. we have matured a barley wine for just over a month before serving it on tap in the bar. That was partly because it was at the low end of the barley wine OG range (1.088, 21°P) and partly because of limitations on tank availability, and we did put some of it into a couple of casks for longer aging. The point is that in the case of short maturation time you can late-hop, or dry-hop, your barley wine if you so wish.

But first, let's deal with bittering hops, and a couple of basic points. First is that alpha acid extraction and isomerization are not very efficient processes in worts of very high specific gravity. Or to put it another way, hop utilization is low in barley wines. You can help that a little by using only pelletized hops, which give slightly higher utilization than hop flowers. I have already mentioned that in an all-extract barley wine you can improve utilization by adding a good part of the extract toward the end of the boil. The second is that hop residues hold up some of the wort after the trub settles out at the end of the boil, and again, hop flowers will hold up more wort than hop pellets. But this also means that you want to use as small an amount of hops as possible to avoid such losses. Therefore, for bittering you should use only hops high in alpha acid, say at 10% alpha and above. This limits your choice somewhat, but for bittering purposes you do not need to be too picky. Note that I am not saying that low alpha acid hops cannot be used in barley wines, because of course they have been, especially those brewed before the latter half of the twentieth century. No, I am simply saying that the most practical and efficient use of hops requires that they be high in alpha acid.

The varieties you might use then, include, in no particular order, American favorites such as Columbus (14–16% alpha), Centennial (9–12), Chinook (11–13%), Magnum (13–15%), Millennium (ca. 14%) and Citra (ca. 11%). Others you may consider are Galena (ca. 12%), Amarillo (ca, 11%), Mosaic (ca. 12%), Simcoe (ca. 11%), Bravo (ca. 13%), New Zealand Green Bullet (ca. 13%), Pacific Gem (ca. 14%), Australian Galaxy (12–14%), and so on. Perhaps of prime choice, especially if you are aiming at very high IBUs, are some of the newer hops coming in at even higher alpha acid levels, such as UK Admiral (ca. 15% alpha), US Warrior (ca. 15% and up), US Apollo (18%), US Summit (ca. 18%) and New Zealand Waimea (16–19%). There are some new products on the market which are concentrated pellets at very high alpha acid levels. These are CRYO® hops, including Ekuanot, Citra, and Mosaic, all at 24–26% alpha. However, it seems that these may have been developed more for their aroma properties and intended to be used as late-addition hops, rather than as conventional bittering hops. I have used their Ekuanot LupulLN2 pellets as a bittering hop in brewing an all-extract barley wine at OG 1.094 (22.4°P) with good results. At 22.8% alpha acid it took only 1 oz. (28 g) in 4.7 gallons (17.8 L) for a nominal 90 IBU, and gave a remarkably small amount of trub, minimizing wort loss on separation of the latter.

The golden rules about hop selection are that they should be as fresh as possible and that the alpha acid rating of your sample should come from an actual analysis, and not just be an average figure for that variety. You need this figure to be as accurate as possible to calculate just how much of the bittering hops you should use. And how do you do that? Well, let us start with the simple approach, which is based on the definition of IBU, namely that it is the concentration of iso-alpha acids in milligrams per liter (as determined by a photometric method under specified conditions). The details of the analytical method are not important here, what matters is that this definition can be used to develop an equation which enables us to calculate our required hop usage:

Equation 1

$$IBU = \frac{G \times U \times \uparrow \times 0.1}{V}$$

Where G = weight of hops in grams
U = percentage utilization of alpha acids (as a whole number)
↑ = percentage of alpha acids in the hops used (as a whole number)
V = final beer volume in liters

This can be expressed in US units, thus:

Equation 2

$$IBU = \frac{W \times U \times \uparrow \times 0.749}{BV}$$

Where W = weight of hops in ounces
   U = percentage utilization of alpha acids (as a whole number)
   ↑ = percentage of alpha acids in the hops used (as a whole number)
   BV = beer volume in US gallons

Now, the problem with this is that U varies according to a number of factors, such as boil temperature and wort gravity. The latter changes throughout the boil, especially in the case of a barley wine, where considerable wort concentration occurs. It can be determined by using the standard analytical method for IBU and working backward in the above equation. While the larger commercial brewers will perform this analysis on all their beers, it is not practical for smaller craft brewers and home brewers to do so. It is a common practice for the latter to assume a value for U and to calculate IBU from that. In the case of home-brewed beers with OG, say, 1.040–1.060 (10–14.7°P), IBUs are often calculated on the basis of U = 25%, and the above equation can be used, along with your taste tests, to predict how bitter such a beer may turn out. At the higher OGs we are talking about with barley wine, alpha acid utilization will be much lower, although boil times may be longer. You might also assume a utilization of, say, 15% for a high-gravity barley wine, and similarly use it for predicting the bitterness for a new brew. But, in neither case does this give you the *actual* value for IBU in a given beer.

   You might argue that this is not important, given that there is a deal of evidence in the literature that suggests there is more to perceived bitterness than just the IBU of a beer. If so, more power to you, and you can go on gaily using the above equations. However, others are not satisfied with this approach and there have been a number of attempts to come up with a more accurate equation for IBUs, which considers both wort gravity and boil time. The equation now accepted by most home brewers as applicable to full wort boils is due to Glenn Tinseth, who derived it from IBU analyses of a range of beers of known OG and boil times (see www.realbeer.com/hops/). For completeness, here is Tinseth's equation:

Equation 3

$$IBU = \left(1.65 \times 0.000125^G\right) \times \left| \frac{(1 - e^{-0.04t})}{4.15} \right| \psi \left(\frac{\left| \frac{\uparrow}{100} \right| \times W \times 7490}{V} \right)$$

Where G = gravity -1
t = boil time in minutes
↑ = hop alpha acid percentage
W = weight of hops in ounces
V = beer volume in gallons

If that looks complicated and not at all simple to use, don't worry. There are several sources which actually give a simple calculator based on this equation, where you just enter the relevant data and it spits out the IBU number. Tinseth's page referred to above has one, as does www.rooftopbrw.net, www.morebeer.com/articles/Brewing_Calculators. These are just examples, and there are more on the web if you are inclined to look into this further.

If you do not want to get involved with Tinseth's approach and prefer to use the simpler equation 2, then you still need to decide on a value for U, hop alpha acid utilization. It seems to me that you can usefully go with an approximation since there are still other unknowns in that equation. For example, the alpha acid value you have for your hops will be that measured at harvesttime and may be different at the time you actually use them. In order to make that approximation useful in a practical sense it must have some relation to Tinseth's more accurate numbers. For a ninety-minute boil, equation 3 gives a value of 17% at 1.090 (21.5°P). decreasing to 10% at 1.150 (34.2°P). Therefore, to a first approximation, all you need to do is to choose a number between, say, 10 and 15%, with the lower end applying to higher wort gravities, and vice versa for the lower end of the Barley wine gravity scale. If you think that is a somewhat cavalier approach, then go back to equation 3 to determine a more precise value of U for your particular brew.

I have not made any recommendations as to what level of IBU you should shoot for. As I discussed in the first section on definitions, barley wines have had a wide range of bitterness, from as little as 30 up 100 IBU. You can therefore choose whatever level suits you, but there are a couple of very general guidelines to follow. First, if the malty character of the beer is to be the predominant taste (such as in Scotch ales, and so-called English barley wines), then do not go any higher than about 60 IBU. Second, the higher the original gravity, the higher the bitterness level should be, in order to balance the sweetness of the beer. If your target gravity is to be much above 1.100 (23.8°P) then you would probably want to aim for 90–100 IBU. In any case, if you accept the term American barley wine and want to brew one, you will obviously opt for a similar order of bitterness.

Cascade hops growing in Connecticut, as they once did a century or two ago.

HOP AROMA AND CHARACTER

I have suggested that this is probably not desirable in barley wine, largely because these hop-derived characteristics will have disappeared by the time the beer is drunk. However, you may disagree, and, anyway, there may be times when the beer is drunk while still relatively young, such as in the example of Brewport quoted above. So, let me make a few comments on this topic.

First of all, I have concluded after many years of brewing that late-hopping at or toward the end of the boil is ineffective in providing that elusive hop character in a beer. Hop oils are steam-volatile, meaning that they will distill off at the boiling point of wort, even if their actual boiling points are higher than that. That means you can't expect much by just chucking a few hops into the wort while it is still at or close to the boiling point. Adding the aroma hops about halfway through the whirlpool procedure would be better, and some craft brewers do practice that approach. Home brewers may not have an effective whirlpool system, so allowing the wort to cool before adding the aroma hops would work but would run the risk of allowing infecting organisms to get into the wort. In either case, adding more hops at this stage will increase the mass of trub, resulting in wort losses. This can be more serious with barley wine worts than with lower-gravity beers, because the high viscosity of such worts, which will become more viscous with cooling, means that the wort can be more easily held up in the trub.

All of which comes down to the fact that I think the best way to get hop aroma and character into a barley wine is dry-hopping. This is best done in the secondary fermenter, or even in the cask if that is what you are going to use. Just suspend the hops, contained in a sanitized muslin bag, if possible using a string leading out of the top of the vessel, so that the bag can be easily recovered. You must, of course, ensure that you still have a seal if doing this; if you can't, just let the bag float in the beer—I find this works better than weighting down the bag, in terms of getting good hop aroma in the beer. If you cask the beer, then put in the bag of hops, splaying out the top of the bag, then bang in the bung to hold the bag in place.

How much hops you use is up to you, but 2–3 oz. generally works well for me. Again, the choice of hops is yours, but since citrus type flavors seem to be popular, any one of the hop varieties with citrus character will do. For example, you might like Citra, Centennial, Simcoe, or Falconer's Flight 7Cs (which combines seven varieties of "C" hops). However, you might want to consider more traditional, non-citrus types, such as Saaz, Goldings, or the new Hallertau hop, Hüell

Melon. Just be sure you like the character of the hop you choose, before you use it in your expensive and hard-won barley wine.

I remarked on the very high alpha acid CRYO hops and noted that they might be suitable for dry-hopping barley wine. In particular, their LupuLN2 hop powder pellets are slated to give twice the hop aroma of conventional pellets and are apparently specifically designed for use at the end of the boil. That would mean you need to add half the amount compared to traditional pellets, and therefore, you would lose less wort if adding late in the whirlpool, or less beer if used for dry-hopping. I have not tried them as aroma hops and cannot really comment, but I would suggest that you try them in a lower-gravity beer, say, your favorite IPA, before taking a chance on them with a barley wine, especially if the latter has OG above 1.100 (23.8°P).

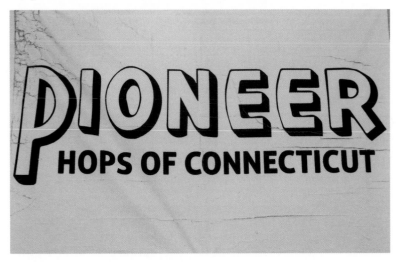

A 2017 poster for the hops shown in the previous photograph.

YEAST

This is not, to be precise, an ingredient as such, but it has a critical role in the case of barley wines. It can, of course, add flavors to the beer, depending upon the strain and on fermentation conditions. But the most important thing yeast must do in barley wine brewing is to give good attenuation. Basically, you need it to get the final gravity down to less than 1.035 (8.8°P), and preferably around 1.025, depending upon OG. That is because if you do not get it down to this level, the beer will be cloyingly sweet, and the sweetness will swamp all other flavors. This means you need it to ferment down to at least 70–75% of the OG. With most other beers and most yeast strains, this is not a problem, but in the case of barley wines the yeast is producing a lot of alcohol, to the extent that the alcohol can actually "poison" the yeast and inhibit it from forming more alcohol. That means that you need to pitch the wort with a lot of active yeast, and this should be a strain known to give good attenuation.

What exactly does "a lot of active yeast mean"? Well, a commonly accepted requirement is to pitch with 1 million cells/mL/°P, (see for instance Fal Allen and Dick Cantwell, *Barley Wine*, 1998, Brewers Publications). For high-gravity beers a rate of 1.4 million cells/mL/°P is suggested by Chris White with Jamil Zainasheff (*Yeast*, 2010, Brewers Publications), and I would agree with that. Now what that means is that for a barley wine at 1.100 (23.8°P) for a 5-gallon (19 L) brew you would need:

$$1.4 \times 10^6 \times 19 \times 23.8 \times 1000 = 600 \times 10^9 \text{ cells}$$

If you are not sure of the mathematical notation, that is 600 *billion* cells, and that is what I mean by "a lot of active yeast." The following table gives yeast requirement for different original gravities of barley wines:

Table 3.1

OG	OG as °P	Billion cells in 5 gallons*
1.090	21.5	570
1.100	23.8	600
1.110	25.9	690
1.120	28.0	750
1.130	30.0	800
1.140	32.1	850

*these numbers rounded for convenience

To put these numbers into context, a standard liquid yeast pack (Wyeast or White labs) contains about 100 billion yeast cells, so if you used only these you would have to pitch 6–8 packs to your barley wine wort. Other producers offer higher yeast counts in their standard packs, Omega Yeast Labs quote 150 billion cells, GIGA yeast is cited as containing 200 billion cells, and Imperial offers an organic yeast also rated at 200 billion cells, which would cut down on the number of packs you need to use. In practice, of course, you would not want to use so many packs and would probably prefer to make a starter, of which more later.

The beauty of liquid yeasts is that they are available in a wide variety of strains, and many brewers prefer them for that reason. But a problem with liquid yeasts is that they lose activity on storage, at the rate of about 10–20% a month. Therefore, the actual viability of the sample which reaches you depends very much on how old it is and how it has been stored, making it almost imperative to make a starter. Once, dried yeasts were considered to be much inferior to their liquid cousins and could actually be infected with wild yeasts. Many years ago, I lost two batches of beer to an infection before I realized the dried yeast I was using was contaminated. However, modern production techniques ensure that such yeasts are perfectly safe to use, and now a number of craft brewers (including Jeff Browning at Brewport) pitch only dried yeasts.

Dried yeasts have the advantage of being quite stable when stored for long periods, losing perhaps only 10% of their activity over a year if stored in a refrigerator. One standard packet (11.5 g) contains about 200 billion active cells so that you would need three or four packets for a 5-gallon (19 L) brew if you are pitching it directly. Dried yeasts are generally cheaper on a single-pack basis than liquid yeasts, so are even more economical on an active cell basis, so you may well be content to use four packs and not to bother with making a starter. The disadvantage of dried yeasts is that not all strains are suited to the drying process, so there is a narrower range of strains available than is the case with liquid yeasts.

How important is the choice of strain? As I have already indicated, you want a strain which will give you at least 70–75% attenuation, and for barley wine an ale yeast is pretty much mandated. Some would argue that the strain of choice should not flocculate too easily, since it might settle out before achieving the desired level of attenuation. That may not be too much of a problem, however, since a yeast that flocculates and settles out quickly in a medium gravity beer will be less likely to do so in the more viscous worts of high-gravity barley wines. There is also the question of yeast-produced flavors to be taken into consideration. If you want to minimize these, then the Chico yeast (For example, the liquid Wyeast 1056 American Ale, or the dried Fermentis US-05) is regarded as giving very clean fermentations, as does Lallemand Nottingham Ale dried yeast, which several brewers have told me works very well in barley wine fermentations. Just to be clear, what I mean by "clean fermentation" is one that gives little in the way of fruity esters and instead allows the malt and any hop aromatic character to stand out.

If you want a little fruitiness in your beer, then I very much like yeasts derived from the now-defunct Whitbread brewery (Wyeast 1098 British Ale, White Labs 002 English Ale, both liquid, or the dried yeast from Fermentis, Safale S-04). If you want even more estery fruitiness you could try White Labs 004 Irish Ale, or Wyeast 1084 Irish Ale. And if you want to go a little over the top with this kind of character, Wyeast 1187 Ringwood should do the trick as would Lallemand Windsor Ale yeast, although the Ringwood yeast can produce a fair bit of diacetyl; it is definitely a strain you either hate or love. Remember that, in general, higher fermentation temperatures tend to result in more ester formation. Barley wines generate quite a lot of heat during fermentation, so try to control the temperature as much as possible—maybe this is where it is worth investing in a jacketed fermenter? For myself, I like to ferment my barley wines at 68–70°F (20–21°C), so that the beers have a little fruitiness in the background behind all the strong malt flavors.

Now, there is some debate about how you should treat dried yeasts for pitching. Some recommend that it should be pitched directly into the wort. Others recommend that it should be rehydrated before pitching. The theory behind that is pitching directly into wort results in a severe osmotic shock to the yeast, which has essentially been dormant, and that it should be allowed to rehydrate by putting it into a little warm water for 15–20 minutes before pitching. To complete the record, here are the instructions for Safale dry yeasts: "Sprinkle the dry yeast in a minimum of 10 times its weight of sterile water or wort at 27°C (80.6°F) for Safbrew and Safale, leave to rest 30 minutes, gently stir for 30 minutes and pitch." I know craft and home brewers who do not bother to rehydrate and apparently still get good results, but I prefer to be cautious, as I am giving my yeast a hard job to do when it comes to fermenting barley wine, so I want to give it as gentle a treatment as possible before I put it to work.

At this point I should deal with a couple of topics which affect yeast health, starting with oxygen. This element is critical for the early growth stage of fermentation, producing among other compounds sterols, which are vital for ensuring the permeability of the yeast cell membrane. I cannot go into details here; suffice it to say that during fermentation many chemicals must pass to and fro through the cell membrane; if the latter is not fully permeable, then the yeast will not work in the way we want it to. White and Zainasheff (see above) recommend a minimum oxygen level in a high-gravity wort, that is above 1.090 (21.5°P), as being 8–10 ppm O2. Now, that is a higher concentration of oxygen than can be achieved by mere aeration, such as agitating or splashing the wort vigorously, which means you need to inject straight oxygen into the wort before pitching the yeast. About 1–2 minutes oxygenation should suffice, since, like so many other things, you can overdo it, and too much oxygen will cause too much yeast growth. White and Zainasheff also suggest that it is beneficial to the fermentation rate and helps to improve attenuation by adding another burst of oxygen 12 hours after pitching. If that it is correct, it is certainly worth doing with barley wines, because attenuation is everything! It is, however, not something I have tried myself as, with my brewing routine, 12 hours after pitching would be somewhere in the wee small hours.

If you have not yet practiced oxygenating your wort, then it is essential that you do so for your barley wines. It is not difficult but does require some expense to obtain a disposable oxygen cylinder, obtainable from hardware stores and containing enough oxygen to service many brews.

You will also need an oxygen regulator and a diffusion stone (preferably fitted onto the end of a stainless steel tube). A full kit, excluding the cylinder, can be obtained for around $60 from homebrew suppliers. Because of the limited use, it is probably not worth the home brewer purchasing the larger, refillable, more expensive oxygen cylinders.

A further point about yeast health is that of the use of a yeast nutrient. Some consider these unnecessary in all-malt beers, since these should contain most of the minerals, vitamins, and other essential yeast nutrients. But we want to give our yeast its best chance of achieving good attenuation, so I think it is a good insurance to add a yeast nutrient. Several commercial samples are available; these are usually based on diammonium phosphate, along with other minerals. They are not expensive, and only small amounts need to be added, say 5 g (1 tsp.) per 5 gallons (19 L) of wort (but read the instructions first). I have had better results with my barley wines using such nutrients, although I have not done a rigorous test (such as splitting a sample of wort, one without and one with nutrient, then duplicating on another wort) so other factors might be responsible for the difference. I do however, plan to continue using nutrients in all my future high-gravity beers.

Now, let me deal with making a yeast starter. There are several reasons for doing this, perhaps the first being that of economics, which becomes most important if you want to use a liquid yeast which would require using up to eight standard packs. The second is that making a starter ensures that the yeast sample you bought has not degraded substantially, say through an accident of shipping during hot weather. The third is more obvious in that a starter ensures an adequate supply of active yeast for pitching, whatever your source of yeast. The disadvantages are that you must plan carefully and begin starter preparation several days before brewing. The procedure for starters may require multiple transfers of the yeast into fresh wort samples, with the obvious risk of infection occurring during these transfers. You therefore need to keep things super clean and well-sanitized at each stage—I would not be surprised to find out that most infected beers have become so as the result of pitching a contaminated yeast sample.

You also need to do a bit of calculating to work out whether you have sufficient active cells in your starter, since you will be stepping up the amount of yeast at each of several stages. Let's say you start with one standard pack of liquid yeast, and assume there has been some degradation, so that it contains about 50 billion active cells, and you are going to pitch 5 gallons (19 L) of wort with OG 1.130 (30.0°P). That means, from Table 3.1, that you want around 800 billion active cells. If each stage doubles the amount of yeast, then starting with 50 billion you would need to step up four times to reach the required number of cells. Note that White and Zainasheff recommend that the starter volume should be at least 2 L (0.5 gallon) for the yeast count to double. If this seems a lot, do not worry, since it will be the yeast sediment that you pitch, not the liquid!

Start with a wort at about 1.040 (10°P), which can be made simply with malt extract. You do not want to start with a wort at the same high gravity as your barley wine because once the yeast has fermented wort of that strength it will be "tired out" and not capable of much more fermentation. To your starter vessel add yeast nutrient (as directed), oxygenate 1 minute, then pitch the yeast and cover the vessel. If all is well you should see active fermentation within 12 hours, and after 1–2 days, when significant sediment has formed, go to the next stage. In this case, you will need two worts of 2 L each prepared as before. Decant the liquid off the yeast sediment and split the latter into the two worts, oxygenating them just before pitching. Repeat this procedure until you have enough active cells for pitching the barley wine wort. Remember to pitch only the yeast sediment from this procedure and discard the liquid. You can do this with dry yeast as well, but the low cost of this product does not really make all the effort (and risk) of preparing a starter worthwhile.

You should also be aware that this is not an ideal procedure; if you use the same volume of wort each time you actually increase the starting concentration of yeast, and that reduces the amount of growth, so that you might not actually be doubling the number of active cells.

Commercial brewers have a different take when preparing a yeast sample for pitching and increase the volume of wort at each step-up stage by a factor of ten. That would not be practical for the home brewer, because the volumes involved would simply be too great. Now, the last three sentences might suggest that preparing a starter is not all that efficient and not worth the work involved. If nothing else, a starter will accustom the yeast to its work and have it straining at the leash to do its job when pitched in the barley wine wort. If you are thinking of re-pitching yeast from another brew (not a practice I favor for barley wines) then you should make a fresh starter with your harvested yeast, in order to reduce the concentration of dead cells before pitching.

Some brewers like to add a second dose of yeast, usually as they rack to the secondary. This yeast should be in the form of an active slurry from a starter, and the hope is that this will give some further attenuation. The strain can be the one you used for the primary fermentation, or another yeast, especially one known for its high alcohol tolerance. To some, this will suggest a champagne yeast, a strain that is well suited to this type of environment. This may produce some champagne-like tartness in the beer, and if overdone can result in too much attenuation, causing the beer to taste thin. I think it is better to concentrate on selecting the right yeast strain to begin with and pitching it in the wort with a sufficient number of active cells, an approach which should give you good attenuation of the final beer. However, if you consider that your barley wine is too sweet, then adding a champagne yeast might be worth trying.

If increasing attenuation (and, therefore alcohol content) is your target, other approaches can work. A possible approach would be freezing the beer until ice crystals form, then removing the crystals. This would have the benefit of concentrating the beer as well as increasing its alcohol content, so there would be no thinning of the beer. It has been done on a commercial scale—remember the "ice" beers of the later part of last century? However, it is not an easy technique for the small craft or home brewer to carry out. I have not tried it, so I cannot comment on the practicality of the method or give an idea as to how far you can take this in terms of increasing alcohol content.

It used to be a common practice in making country wines to feed the beer (after the main fermentation has finished) with small doses of sugar and yeast with high alcohol tolerance over a long period. As it stands this is not a very reliable method for producing more alcohol. If you add the sugar as a solution you can easily end up simply increasing the volume of the beer rather than its alcohol content. If you add the sugar as a solid, it will dissolve only slowly, making the whole process laborious—you must wait until each sugar addition has fermented out before adding the next. A more practical approach is to hold back some of the fermentable material and to add it later before fermentation is quite complete. Chris Colby tells you how to do this, complete with a suitable recipe in a series of articles ("'Feeding' the Biggest Beers," parts 1, 2 and 3; "JM 'Big Pig' Ale (a 14% ABV Barley Wine)," *Beer and Wine Journal*, April 23, 29, and 30 and May 14, 2015). Basically, this involves brewing, say, a 12% abv beer, then adding enough more fermentable material to take it up to 14% abv. Colby suggests doing this with a concentrated solution of malt extract, perhaps adding it in two stages. The whole idea is to avoid exposing the yeast to a wort of a higher gravity than it can handle. You have to allow for the increase in the final volume in the fermenter and calculate how much extra fermentable material you must add in order to reach your target alcohol content. Try it if you wish, but it may require some experimentation, and I do not know if it can be used to reach alcohol levels higher than 14% abv.

There is another way to improve attenuation during normal brewing procedures and that is to use the enzyme amyloglucosidase. Many craft brewers have used this enzyme to control finishing gravities in a variety of beers, and it seems to have now become fashionable to use it in brewing brut IPAs, so-called because they have a very dry finish. Amyloglucosidase breaks down some of the normally unfermentable complex carbohydrates to fermentable glucose, the sugar yeast most prefers to ferment. This enzyme, which is manufactured by a bacterial fermentation, can take the finishing gravity down as low as 1.000 (0°P). In other words it can convert all the dextrins and any other complex carbohydrates into fermentable glucose. While this extra glucose can be fermented in lower-gravity beers I have no evidence to say it will do the same with high-gravity barley wines; if it does not it may just end up making your barley wine sweeter. It can be added to the mash, but it is much more effective when added to the fermenter, usually after fermentation has passed its peak and begins to level off. But this has to be done with care, since it can easily take out all the dextrins and make your barley wine taste thin and over-alcoholic. In considering this approach I cannot help thinking that this is exactly how lite beers are produced and I, for one, do not wish to make lite barley wine! But try it if you want, bearing in mind that it will likely take some experimentation to get it right. Be cautious in such experiments, for barley wine is an expensive beer you do not want to have to throw away if your tests should not be successful.

To sum up these last few paragraphs, I do not think that chasing high levels of alcohol just for the sake of it is a good approach. A barley wine in which the taste and heat of alcohol stands out is not a good example of the style. Above all, you should aim for balance between alcohol, hop flavor, and bitterness and body or mouthfeel.

SUGARS

Various sugars have been used in brewing beers—I have had access to both pre- and post-Prohibition recipes that used significant amounts of sugar, and the use of brewing sugars (usually invert sugar) has been a common practice with English brewers since it was permanently allowed in brewing in 1880. White cane sugar (sucrose), corn sugar (dextrose or glucose), and Belgian Candi sugar (clear) have been used as gravity enhancers and could be used in that way for barley wines. In other words, if your wort has come out somewhat low in gravity, you can bump it up by dissolving one of these sugars in it. Sucrose will give a yield of 1.046° (11.4°P)/lb. (0.45 kg)/gallon (3.78 L). Dextrose gives less, because it contains water as a hydrate, at 1.037° (9.3°P)/lb. (0.45 kg)/gallon (3.78 L). None of these will add any color and should be used sparingly as they are fully fermentable and will tend to thin out the beer if overdone. Belgian Candi sugars, which give similar yields to dextrose, are available in a variety of colors and add to the beer's flavor spectrum. My limit for using such sugars would be no more than 10% of the total weight of the grist. Perhaps their best use would be if you wanted to make a very pale barley wine.

Invert sugars come in various colors and flavors and are commonly used by English brewers as colorants and flavorings, rather than just as gravity boosters although they will, of course do just that. Unfortunately, such sugars are not generally available in the United States, the only one of that description being Tate & Lyle's Golden Syrup, which is very low in both color and flavor, so I do not recommend its use. There is also a story attached to invert sugars, which are essentially produced by acid hydrolysis of sucrose. In the early part of the twentieth century, there was an epidemic of arsenic poisoning in the northwest of England, which was traced to certain beers. Further investigation revealed that the arsenic was contained in the invert sugar the brewers had used, and that the arsenic came from the acid used in the inversion of sucrose. That was sulfuric acid, which had been manufactured from pyrites, a standard procedure except in this case the pyrite contained some of the closely related mineral arsenopyrite!

There are other sugars which can confer flavor and/or color to a beer. These include brown sugar, 1.046° (11.4°P)/lb. (0.45 kg)/gallon (3.78 L), dark brown sugar, 1.046°(11.4°P), Demerara sugar,1.042°(10.5°P), and amber and dark Candi sugars, 1.036°(9.0°P) . Obviously, these will all provide some color, but since they should be used sparingly to avoid making the beer thin, they will not make a great deal of difference. After all, as I have repeatedly pointed out, most barley wines have significant color due to Maillard reactions during boiling. Other sugars that might contribute flavor are honey, about 1.032° (8°P)/lb. (0.45 kg)/gallon (3.78 L), and maple syrup, 1.030° (7.6°P/lb.(0.45kg)/gallon (3.78 L). Again, these are delicate flavors, which in my opinion will not really be noticeable in an already strong-flavored barley wine, when used in the low proportions of 10% of the total grist that I consider the limit for sugar usage in this style of beer.

Overall, the case for using sugars in barley wine brewing is not a good one. Perhaps I am a little biased since I have long favored all-malt beers. For that reason, I would use malt extract if I thought my brew needed a gravity boost, rather than using sugar. But if you want to try it, go ahead—it's your beer.

WATER

I have left this until last, but since it is the major ingredient of beer, perhaps I should have dealt with water first. Yet many brewers, especially those using only malt extract, do not think that water composition is all that important. A good deal of writing on the topic deals with the ionic content of water and its effect on mash pH and so is of concern only to all-grain brewers. But we must not forget that it also has an effect on flavor and so is important to extract brewers as well. Certain ions, most notably those of calcium, play a part in the brewing process itself, helping yeast flocculation for example.

Let's look first at how to measure pH, which is a measure of hydrogen ion concentration, and hence of acidity or alkalinity. The simplest and cheapest way to do this is by means of pH test strips, which are simply dipped into the wort and will change color according to pH. The strips are quite cheap, starting at as little as $3 for 12 strips. They do work, but it is not always easy to distinguish between the colors, something which I personally find difficult, but you may not. The more accurate and reproducible way of measuring pH is to use an instrument designed for the purpose, known appropriately as a pH meter. These were once quite expensive and difficult to use, but now are much cheaper and more convenient to handle. Typical prices of handheld meters range from $50 to $130, according to the degree of sophistication of the instrument. The best (and more expensive) types have what is known as automatic temperature compensation or ATC. This ability simply means that the instrument is self-correcting to allow inherent electrode errors as the temperature of the test solution varies. You will also buy some standard pH solutions (usually pH 4.0 and 7.0) as the instrument must be calibrated before use and must be carefully stored, according to the manufacturer's instructions. An extra expense will be that the electrode may need to be replaced annually, which can run you to another $45 or so. That extra effort and expense may be a little daunting, but, in my opinion, it is worth it all, and I recommend that you invest in such a meter.

I must point out here that the range of pH 5.2–5.5 given below for both pre-boil extract worts and for the mash are the readings obtained at the temperatures typical of a mash, that is ±150°F (65.6°C). These values will be higher at lower temperatures; by just how much seems to be a matter of some contention. A major reference (D. E Briggs, J. S. Hough, R. Stevens, and T. W. Young, *Malting and Brewing Science*, Vol 1, 1981, Chapman & Hall) states that at 65°F (18°C) pH is 0.35 units higher than at 149°F (65°C), which roughly translates into pH at mash temperature of 5.2–5.5 equaling 5.5–5.8 at room temperature. This is discussed by Ashton Lewis ("Help Me Mr. Wizard," *Brew Your Own*, December 2017), who points out that John Palmer has empirically determined that the lowering of pH should be 0.25 units in the case of an actual mash because of the effects of the mash itself. Strangely, quite a few other brewing texts I looked at had nothing to say on this matter and said nothing about the temperatures at which their recommended pH levels were measured. So, keep it simple and measure pH only at typical mash temperatures, and you won't have to worry about that!

Let me now deal with extract brewing; I am doing so now in case you should skip it if it comes at the end of the discussion on mashing. It is often said, and I have done so myself on occasion, that it is not necessary to check or adjust pH for an extract wort. This, prior to the boil, should be in the range pH 5.2–5.5; if it is higher than that, due to residual alkalinity (see below), then you have a problem. High pH, as defined in the last sentence, will affect beer color, hop utilization, and flavor, as well as the overall mouthfeel or body of the beer. The problem with color is that Maillard reactions proceed more readily at pH > 5.5, so that during the boil the beer becomes darker. In one sense, that may not be a bad thing in the case of barley wine as Maillard products are common components of such beers. However, this can be overdone, and would not be desirable if you were trying to make a pale barley wine. High pH will actually give higher hop utilization rates, which may be regarded as a bonus with a very-high-gravity beer, where utilization is normally quite low. But that may just make the beer taste more bitter than you intended and throw it out of balance. You may think that is fine if you are aiming for a so-called American barley-wine style, where you want a lot of bitterness. The difficulty is that high pH is well documented as causing the bitterness to be harsh and unpleasant, rather than sharp and clean.

You see, the pH drops during boiling and again during fermentation, and the beer should fall within the pH range 4.0–4.7 (see John J. Palmer, *How to Brew*, 2017, Brewers Publications). For pale beers—that is, other than those such as porters and stouts—the beer will taste cleaner with more distinct flavors and a pleasant mouthfeel. In contrast, if it is above that range the beer will be what is sometimes described as flabby or muddy. In short, even if you are brewing with extract you must take steps to ensure that your beer is not high in residual alkalinity. The definition of residual alkalinity is quite complicated, but for our purposes we can look at it as the concentration of bicarbonate ions. You can see this from an analysis of your water (see below). And you will see it if you measure pH of your wort and find it to be pH > 5.5.

If you know your water is high in bicarbonate, a relatively simple method of lowering this level is to boil the water and convert bicarbonate to carbon dioxide which is then expelled, leaving a residue of insoluble calcium carbonate behind. Let the water cool and decant it from the precipitate before use in brewing. This approach cannot remove all the bicarbonate, so it is a good idea to use it in a lesser brew than a high gravity barley wine and check wort pH prior to the boil. If that gives satisfactory results then it should also work well for your barley wine.

An alternative, if you know from analysis that your water is not much above 100ppm CaCO3 (how bicarbonate is measured—don't ask), is simply to dilute your water with distilled water. It will take quite a volume of distilled water (about the same amount as your own supply), so it seems to me that you might as well go the whole hog and use only distilled water, or even water produced by reverse osmosis. I have not had a need to use it, but, for the record, it seems that more and more brewing writers are recommending the use of water treated by reverse osmosis; it is, apparently, more expensive than distilled water, but is more readily available. But, if you use either of these demineralized waters, be aware that they contain virtually no ions, and that is not good for our barley wines, which will taste somewhat bland, if not actually unpleasant. So, in those cases you have to add back some ions, specifically as far as style is concerned, calcium and sulfate. Of course, you can't add ions as such, and have to add a salt, in this case, gypsum, a form of calcium sulfate. I would aim to add 1 teaspoon of gypsum which should nicely bring the pH of the brewing water to the desired level, as well as enhancing the beer's flavors, especially helping to ensure a good clean, crisp hop bitterness. You will find more on this in the discussion on mash pH that follows. There is one more method you can use to adjust the ionic content of your water, and that is acidification. I shall deal with that below, under mash pH.

A point about remedying your water supply is that you do not want to use a household water softener to do this. That is because it will not remove bicarbonate, but it will remove calcium and other cations such as magnesium and replace them with sodium, to the extent that it can have an undesirable, salty flavor. And do not expect an activated carbon filter to do the job; it is great for removing chlorine from city water and improving the flavor of your morning coffee, but it takes out no dissolved ions such as bicarbonate.

Let's deal with mash pH next, and how you can adjust the ionic content of your water supply to achieve the right range. You can get lucky of course, just like I have. The water supplies I have used at home, and at Brewport, Bridgeport, Connecticut, and BrüRm@BAR in New Haven, Connecticut, have all been very similar in ionic content. In fact, I am now supplied at home by the same utility as Brewport. The defining character of these waters is that they have a low ionic content with virtually no residual alkalinity. Therefore, I have only to add a little gypsum (calcium sulfate dihydrate, $CaSO_4.2H_2O$) and the pH of the mash will come out in the range of 5.2–5.5, which is where I want it to be. That's because this is the range that results in optimum activity for the starch degrading enzymes α- and β-amylase. How much gypsum do I use? For a normal brew, including barley wines, I add 5 g (about 1 tsp., if you prefer, but you should really weigh it) for a brew length of 5 gallons (19 L). For the record this will add 61 ppm Ca^{2+} and 147 ppm SO_4^{2-} to the ionic content of the water.

All well and good, but what if you do not have such a "simple" water supply? Well, providing it is clean and free of bacteria, then the likely problem will be that you have significant residual alkalinity. You should get a water analysis either from your supplier or, if you use well water, from a local laboratory (the cost is usually quite reasonable); you can also buy a kit from your brewing supplier and do the analysis yourself. That will give you the residual alkalinity in terms of calcium carbonate (CaCO3), although it is actually the bicarbonate ion (HCO3⁻) that immediately puts the thought in your mind that this is a very complicated chemical subject. It can indeed be so, but it need not be, and I shall endeavor to keep it as simple as possible. For that reason, I shall ignore the fact that "bicarbonate" actually represents an equilibrium between different species, and just refer to it as bicarbonate).

If bicarbonate is present in your water at levels of 100 ppm and above, it will act on mash pH as a buffer. Calcium ions in the mash (from calcium sulfate) react with phosphates in the malt to release hydrogen ions, which tend to bring down the pH, being acidic by definition. Bicarbonate ions tend to resist this acidification or buffer its effects and bring the pH back up. While this can be good if you are brewing a beer with roasted malts, it is definitely not so for one based almost entirely on pale malt. This means that you need to look at reducing the bicarbonate content of your brewing water.

That can be done by those methods already described, boiling off CO2, diluting with distilled or reverse-osmosis water, or starting from scratch with one of those last two waters. There is also the possibility of actually acidifying the mash (or wort in the case of extract brewing). This has the advantage that it is done directly with whatever beer you are brewing and requires no prior preparation of the brewing water or testing whatever treated water you have on a lesser beer, before you attempt it on your prize barley wine. Various acids would work, including sulfuric and hydrochloric acids, but these are very corrosive and therefore need very careful handling and proper safety equipment, so I cannot recommend their use.

In fact, those commonly used by brewers are phosphoric and lactic acids, both of which can be obtained quite readily as food-grade products. The residues they leave are phosphates and lactates, both of which are quite flavor neutral, and in the case of phosphates are already present in malt. Use the higher concentrations (85%, and 88% respectively); remember that although they are much less corrosive than mineral acids, they still need to be handled with care—gloves and safety glasses are recommended. All you have to do is to dough in the grain, and add the acid in small portions, stirring well after each addition and checking the pH after addition, until the mash is in the pH range 5.2–5.5. You will have to experiment a little, depending upon how much bicarbonate is present in your water, but I find using an eyedropper is a good way to ensure that you do not overshoot and take the pH below this range, which you definitely do not want. It is best to start with a known volume, such as in a small measuring cylinder, and measure the volume remaining when you have finished addition, then, of course, make a note of it for the next brew.

Phosphoric acid, in particular, will strip out some calcium and magnesium ions, which may not be a problem if the water has a lot of permanent hardness (basically calcium, magnesium, and sulfate ions). But, if you have had to use a lot of phosphoric acid to get the pH down, you will be well advised to add calcium ions back, by addition of gypsum as described above. Have an already weighed (or measured) amount (5 g should be good), so that you can add it immediately after finishing acidification. Note that gypsum will cause no significant change in mash pH, and that these operations must be done fairly quickly to avoid a drop in the temperature of the mash.

I have discussed only adding gypsum to achieve the required level of calcium and sulfate, and pointed out that, apart from pH adjustment, these are also added for reasons of flavor improvement. But, many brewers also like to add salt, NaCl, because this can add a soft luscious flavor to the beer, without making it flabby. That would be especially good for something like a Scotch ale, a beer that should be luscious rather than sharp and at least somewhat bitter as is barley wine. You would probably want to add a maximum of 5 g (1 tsp.) in a 5-gallon (19 L) brew, which would give concentrations of 100 ppm Na^+, and 160 ppm Cl^-. For a barley wine, you should perhaps go to the lower level of 2.5 g (½ tsp.), giving 50 ppm Na^+ and 80 ppm Cl^-. This does not need to be added in the mash as it will have little effect on mash pH, so is best added at the wort boil stage.

Well, I have said quite a lot about treating brewing water, and thought I was finished with it. But I have just checked the only other book I know which deals specifically with brewing barley wines (Fal Allen and Dick Cantwell, *Barley Wine*, 1998, Brewers Publications). These authors make the point that England is the home of barley wine, and high-gravity beers have been successfully brewed all over that country in areas in areas very different water chemistry. These range from London and the Southeast, which have soft waters, high in bicarbonate from the underlying chalk strata to places like Burton and Tadcaster, which have very high permanent hardness, mainly from calcium, magnesium, and sulfate ions. They consider that virtually any potable water is suitable for brewing such beers. If you take that view also, you can use water straight from your faucet. Nevertheless, I will continue to make what I see as necessary adjustments.

OTHER BREWING SUBSTANCES

There are other materials which you might use in brewing barley wines, and I am not going to deal with cleaning materials here. If you do not yet know how to properly clean and sanitize brewing equipment, do not even think of attempting to brew barley wine. All I will do is to emphasize the importance of cleaning and sanitizing in brewing this style, because you are usually going to have this beer mature for long periods. If your beer is infected with wild yeast and/or bacteria, remember that it still contains plenty of nutrients after fermentation, and leaving it for a long time gives them a good chance to multiply and ruin the beer.

I suppose the most important materials to discuss here are those used to help clarify the beer and to prevent haze formation. The first to consider is so-called Irish moss, a form of seaweed, which contains carrageenan, that, unusually for a naturally occurring product, is a molecule which contains sulfate groups. That makes it capable of reacting with protein residues to form a floc that will readily settle out. Proteins, as amino acids, are amphoteric, which means they can carry both a positive charge and a negative charge. At the pH of wort, proteins and protein residues are largely positively charged and can therefore react with the negatively charged sulfate groups of carrageenan.

The theory held by many brewers is that carrageenan flocculates these proteinaceous materials, forming a compact mass with the rest of the trub (largely hop residues), which is especially compact after whirlpooling, thus minimizing the loss of wort with the trub. That, as I have said elsewhere, is very desirable in brewing barley wines, where wort, because of its viscosity, is easily retained by trub. But what this would mean is that it is the hot break which is flocculated by carrageenan. In fact, there is evidence that this is not actually the case and that it is the cold break which is flocculated (Ian L. Ward, *Clear Beer through Finings Technology*, Brewers Supply catalog). As a result, the carrageenan-flocculated material comes down with the yeast in the fermenter. But that means that what the carrageenan actually does is to remove potential beer haze–forming species, which not only helps beer clarity but also helps to improve the stability of the beer. Whether you consider that carrageenan flocculates the hot or the cold break, it is worth using in barley wine brewing.

This product is available as the raw seaweed, or as a processed form of carrageenan under various tradenames, such as Whirlfloc, Koppaclear, Protofloc, and so on. I have found the raw seaweed products to be inconsistent in their performance; on one occasion a gel formed in the wort, which resulted in loss of wort in my efforts to remove the gel, quite the opposite effect from what I was looking for! So, I use the processed types, which come in tablet form and consist of carrageenan plus other constituents, namely a dispersant such as sodium bicarbonate and an acid, such as citric acid, so that the tablet effervesces and rapidly disperses when added to the hot wort. I recommend you use one of these products at the dosage recommended by the supplier. The addition rate is about ¼ tablet in the case of Koppaclear, or around 0.6 g (30 ppm) per 5 gallons (19 L) of wort. Measure this out as carefully as you can; just like other flocculants, more is definitely not better. Indeed, using too much carrageenan can actually strip out the proteins

Jeff Browning, brewer and partner at Brewport and a lover of barley wines.

responsible for head retention and reduce free amino nitrogen, an essential yeast nutrient. For this reason, John Palmer (*How to Brew*, 2017, Brewers Publications) for one does not recommend its use for all extract worts, because these tend to be somewhat low in free amino nitrogen to start with.

There are other polymers for treating beer, such as isinglass for flocculating yeast, polyvinyl polypyrrolidone (Polyclar®) for absorbing haze-forming proteins. Now, there are also silica gels which can remove both yeast and proteins. Strictly, neither of these last two products are flocculants, for they are both insoluble in beer. However, none of these products are necessary for barley wines, for the yeast should settle out over the time frame of aging. Haze formation should not be a problem, either, if you have used Irish moss and never kept the beer too cold. Remember that barley wines should not really be cooled before drinking, like most other beers, because you want to drink them at no less than about 50°F (10°C) so as to enjoy all of the multitude of flavors which make barley wine such an interesting beer.

CHAPTER FOUR

BREWING BARLEY WINE

Sir Toby Belch: Dost thou think, because thou art virtuous, there shall be no more cakes and ale? (William Shakespeare, *Twelfth Night*, act 2, scene 3)

I HAVE ALREADY DEALT WITH FERMENTATION, AND WE MUST now consider how we get the very strong worts we need in order to make a barley wine. It is not an easy process, unless you brew with only malt extract. If you are brewing from grain malt, there is difficulty in obtaining a wort with OG much above ± 1.090 (21.5°P). At least, that is true of a "standard" mash using mash water at the rate of about 1–1.5 quarts (1–1.4 L) per lb. (0.45 kg). If you have only ever brewed lower-strength beers, you may think that all you have to do for a barley wine is to step up the amount of grain and water in the mash, and the wort will run off at the gravity you want. I have never found it to be the case, and, judging from the brewing literature, neither has anyone else! It would seem that, since wort sugars are extremely soluble in water, this should not be the case, and I am not sure why it is so. It presumably has to do with the ratio of grain to water, which you cannot change much. Obviously, using more mash water would simply dilute the wort concentration, which you do not want. Decreasing the amount of water does make for a more concentrated wort; however, it would also reduce the volume of wort and would also make for a stiff mash which would be much harder to stir efficiently and may well result in a slower starch conversion rate and possibly even a lower extract yield. Apparently, you can achieve higher wort gravities (up to 1.130, 30°P) using a mash filter, rather than a lauter tun (Garrett Oliver, ed., "Malt Syrup," *The Oxford Companion to Beer*, 2012, Oxford University Press). However, I shall assume that home brewers and most craft brewers are unlikely to have this expensive piece of equipment.

Enough of the why, let's look and the what and consider a couple of actual examples from my own brewing of a barley wine. The first mash used 20 lb. (9.1 kg) pale malt and 22 qt. (5.5 gallons, 21 L) of water, or 1.1 qt. water/lb. of malt. The second used 18 lb. (8.2 kg) pale malt and 22 qt. (5.5 gallons, 21 L) of water, or 1.2 qt. water/lb. of malt. In each of them I collected 3 gallons (11 L) of wort, with no sparging. The first brew gave me a gravity of 1.093 (22.1°P), and the second was at 1.092 (22°P), so were virtually identical. Since my target in each case was ±1.125 (29°P), each of those brews would have to be treated somehow so as to get to where I wanted, and that is what I shall deal with here.

Note that for convenience I am assuming in what follows that you are operating on a 5-gallon (19 L) scale and that you are looking for a finishing volume of 3–5 gallons (11.4–19 L), at the OG you want. Obviously, if you have a 10-gallon (38 L) system and still want to produce 5 gallons (19 L) or less, you may well want to take a different approach to the methods described below, but they apply just as much to a 10-gallon (38 L) scale as to a 5-gallon (19 L) one, if you want to double up your finished volume of wort.

There are at least five methods you can use to reach very high OG:

Method 1: Use only malt extract.

Method 2: Straight grain mash, collecting all extract with sparging, then boil down to desired OG.

Method 3: Straight grain mash but collect only first runnings as in above example, then boil down to desired OG, *or* adjust gravity with extract or sugar to target value.

Method 4: Do two concurrent straight grain mashes, collect only first runnings from each, combine them, and boil down or adjust with extract/sugar as required to reach target gravity.

Method 5: Do a straight grain mash of medium target gravity, collect all wort, and use as mash water for a second straight grain mash, collecting all runoff with no sparging.

METHOD 1

Method 1 is the simplest approach, of course, especially in terms of time of boiling. You simply have to work out how much extract you need to reach a certain gravity at a given volume, dissolve it in hot water (at a volume according to where you want to finish), and carry out the boil and hopping in the normal manner. You do not need to boil for more than sixty minutes; longer boil times will cause loss of proteins and protein residues which can adversely affect head retention. Indeed, since the extract has already been boiled by the manufacturer, you really want to minimize further boiling to avoid removing enough proteinaceous material to make the beer thin and lacking in mouthfeel. Of course, you need to boil long enough to extract and isomerize the hop alpha acids, for which sixty minutes will be sufficient.

As mentioned earlier under "Ingredients," an advantage of all extract brewing is that not all the extract needs to be boiled for the full sixty minutes. You can simply do this by dissolving half the extract in hot water (enough to match the final volume), adding the hops, and boiling for sixty minutes. The remaining extract is then added and mixed into the hot wort before cooling. Do be careful when doing this—use a long-handled spoon and wear insulating gloves as well as safety glasses or even goggles. The plus of this approach is that, as discussed under hops in the previous chapter, hop utilization is improved compared to a boil at the full wort gravity, so this is a good way to get a high level of bitterness (if that's what you want), and to reduce wort losses to the hops residue, since there will be less of that as you will need fewer hops for the same bittering level. This approach also means half of the extract does not get boiled at all, so there is no risk of "over-boiling" the wort as mentioned in the previous paragraph.

A variation of this, touted by some for brewers who are short on vessel space and/or heating capacity, is to boil half the extract with half the final volume of water, adding the remainder of the extract at the end of the boil. That means you would be boiling at full gravity and would get no gain in hop utilization as with a full volume/half extract boil. But you would save on space, and cooling would be simpler, because the hot wort would be added to the remainder of the cold water (but be careful of pouring hot water into a glass fermenter; do it in the boiler or another stainless steel vessel!). I much prefer a full boil, and it could be argued that if you are pushed for space you are better off waiting until you can find more vessel space before attempting to brew an expensive beer like a barley wine. However, that applies if you want to brew a full 5 gallons (19 L) of the beer; if you are happy to brew only 2–3 gallons (7.6–11.4 L) and that will fit your vessel volumes, then this is a good method to use.

Now, there is a point which I should raise here, and that is the question of Maillard reactions. If you do a short boil with only part of the extract, then you very much limit the formation of Maillard products, because the tendency to form these increases with increasing wort gravity and boil time. Does that matter? You may well ask that and perhaps if you want a pale, crisp tasting barley wine, then no, it does not matter. But most people want their barley wines to have the rich, malty flavors that these products can give and so want to encourage formation of these products, although that makes for a darker color in the finished beer. If this is what you want then you should probably go for a full gravity boil, adding all the extract to the full final volume of water (plus some allowance for evaporation, depending upon your system). Clearly, the same effect can be achieved by adding half the wort to half the water, if you are pushed for space. If you want to really pack your beer with Maillard reaction products, then you will want to boil the wort for longer than sixty minutes, perhaps ninety minutes to two hours or so. John Palmer asserts that extended boiling can produce Maillard reaction products that are actually somewhat unpleasant and advises against doing so. However, Jeremy Cowan's Best of Show recipe for barley wine (*Brew Your Own*, July/August 2017) gives a grain version in which the wort is boiled for three hours, and an extract version (with steeped specialty malts and added brown sugar) which is also boiled for three hours; this suggests the latter is done only to match the levels of Maillard reaction compounds produced. My own experience suggests that such a long boil does not seem to result in unpleasant or "off" flavors. I have, however, only carried out long boils with a view to concentrating the wort and have never done so with the intention of increasing the levels of Maillard reaction products in the finished beer.

There is another alternative to achieving Maillard-type flavors without long boiling, and that is to use some caramel malt. This needs to be steeped in hot water for twenty to thirty minutes, and the resulting solution then forms the base of the wort, as noted in the section on ingredients. In that section I suggested that you use no more than 10% of the total grist of a medium grade caramel malt, say with a color of around 80°L. As discussed then, you could also use an amber malt extract for this purpose, and even more highly kilned caramel malts (although these are not my personal preference in barley wine brewing).

I shall leave the discussion on long boiling at this point and come back to it in discussing the next method.

METHOD 2

In this procedure you simply calculate the amount of grain needed, mill it if not already ground, then mash in the normal way at 148–150°F (64.4–65.6°C). Then run off the wort and sparge as usual; if you are doing a 5-gallon brew that means you would collect about 6–7 gallons (23–27 L) of wort. You must, of course, measure the gravity of this wort and should then calculate how much water you need to evaporate during the boil, so as to reach the OG you want. Let's look at an example:

If you used 20 lb. (9.1 kg) of pale malt and collected 7 (27 L) gallons of wort at a gravity of 1.075 (18.2°P), assuming you had a 70% brewhouse efficiency. What you want to finish up with is OG 1.130 (30°P) and to get that you need to boil down to:

$$(7 \times 75) \div FV = 130$$

where FV is the final wort volume in gallons.

then, FV = (7 × 75) ÷ 130 = 4 gallons (15.1 L)

That means you have to "lose" 3 gallons (11.4 L) of water in the boil, which will take well over the traditional sixty- to ninety-minute boil for "regular beers," making for an extended brew day. Just how much time this will take depends upon your system's heating efficiency but removing 1 gallon (3.8 L) per hour is a pretty good rate of evaporation, so you can expect the boil to take at least three hours.

A few points about this example, the first being that with that amount of grain and a water to grain ratio of 1.2 qt. (1.1 L) per lb., you need 24 qt. (23 L) of water. Yes, that is 6 gallons of water in addition to the 20 lb. of grain, and you will not get that into a mash tun designed to hold only 5 gallons (19 L). In fact, your tun should have a capacity of at least 8 gallons (30 L) and 10 gallons (38 L) would be preferable; at any rate, do make sure that it is big enough *before* starting to brew!

A second point is that you would be pushing your system so your brewhouse efficiency may be lower than 70%, or whatever is your "normal" figure. Therefore, your total yield of extract may be lower than suggested above, so your final wort volume going to fermentation will also be lower. That brings me to the second point, which is that your target parameters cannot be both beer volume and OG. Like Heisenberg's Uncertainty Principle (at least I think so) you can fix only one of these. Therefore, if your total extract is lower than that quoted in the example then you either have to go for the same 4-gallon (15.1 L) volume and accept a lower OG or stick to your original OG target and accept a lesser volume. In the latter case, that would mean carrying out an even longer boil. The only way out if you want both high gravity and full volume is to adjust the gravity by adding malt extract or sugar.

One point I have not made about boiling is that browning and caramel flavors can develop through actual caramelization rather than only from Maillard reactions (a) if you are using an external burner and have hot spots, or (b) if you are using an electrically fired boiler with the heating element directly immersed in the wort. I mention this here because electric boilers have become more popular among home brewers; indeed, I have used these myself for years. Quite significant caramelization can occur on the heating element, given that we are talking about very long boils and highly concentrated wort on the surface of the element. Inspection of the element after boiling has shown

English versions of the style. Note that only the Fuller's beer is dated and numbered.

me that such effects do take place; however, it is my opinion that such caramelization is a positive for a barley wine, adding a little lusciousness to the finished beer.

In this case, unlike the long boil discussed under method 1, the purpose of which was to facilitate Maillard reactions, we have to boil a long time purely to reach the required OG. That brings us back to the question as to whether a long boil, as described above, causes excessive, even detrimental formation of Maillard products. I am not convinced that this is the case, for barley wines were traditionally brewed with long boiling times, and certainly since the late nineteenth and into the twentieth century I have seen no evidence to suggest that odd or "off" flavors from this cause were apparent. My own tastings of English barley wines in the twentieth and twenty-first century have not found any such flavors to be present. However, in such a complicated beer as barley wine, lack of direct evidence does not mean that a problem of this nature cannot and has not ever occurred. If you are concerned enough about this to make you reluctant to use the approach of method 2, then you should think about adopting one of the following methods, although these are all more complicated and time-consuming.

METHOD 3

This is the classical method of brewing strong beers, in which two or more worts, or "gyles" are collected and used to produce different beers. This is the technique known as parti-gyling; it has been used for centuries. Before sparging became common practice in the nineteenth century, brewers would drain the mash to collect the first wort, then re-mash to collect a second, and sometimes even repeat the process to collect a third and even a fourth wort. This was the technique used to produce strong October and March Ales in the eighteenth and nineteenth centuries, and many commercial brewers still use it to produce very strong beers. Fuller's do so for their Vintage Ale, Woodforde's of Norwich in England do so to produce their barley wine (which is only at 7% abv—see the section on history re: beer taxation in England). If memory serves me correctly, Harpoon in Boston, Massachusetts, also used it in their 100-barrel series. Do note that though it is a technique well suited to barley wine production, it is not limited to that. By varying the volume of each gyle, you can produce two or more different beers of more modest gravity from the same mash, such as a 6% abv stout and a 4.5% abv porter, or a 5% abv ESB and a 3.8% English bitter.

But that last note is a digression, now back to barley wine. In essence, you simply conduct a "monster mash," that is one with more malt than normally used, then draw off part of the wort as the base of the barley wine. The remaining wort is collected, accompanied by sparging in the normal manner, and used to produce a second, lower-gravity beer. For the home brewer, working on a 5-gallon (19 L) scale, what this means is that you would collect the first 3 gallons (11.4 L) of wort, which would have a gravity of around 1.090 (21.5°P), and then sparge to collect a second wort, which might typically be about 4 gallons at 1.055 (13.6°P). Those are numbers taken from an actual brew of mine at an extract yield of 71%; your numbers will be different according to your own brewhouse efficiency. What you would then do is to take the first gyle for the barley wine and concentrate it by boiling to give the required original gravity. The second gyle can then be taken and used to produce another beer—if it ran at the gravity of the above example it would nicely fit for a pale ale, for example, but that choice would be up to you.

An example of this procedure is that of chancellor ale, brewed at Queen's College, Oxford for centuries, right up to 1937, using medieval methods right up to the end. The first wort runnings were collected and boiled for three hours to give wort with OG 1.135 (31°P), while the second wort went to make the "regular" college ale at OG 1.070 (17.1°P). To complete the picture, at Queen's College for the college ale they normally produced about 10 UK barrels (about 14 US barrels) of wort before the boil. In the case of brewing chancellor ale, they would collect 2½ UK barrels (3 US barrels) of the first wort, or 25% of the total. That compares with the example above in which we took 3 gallons out of 7, or about 43% of the total. The reason for doing this greater proportion of the total is that we are working only on a 5-gallon (19 L) scale, and if we had taken only 25% of the total that would have amounted to only 1.5 gallons (5.7 L), which would be an inconveniently small amount to handle on this scale. But, do be aware that the 3-gallon (11.4 L) collection would still be at the same specific gravity as the 1.5 (5.7 L) would have been had we opted to do that.

Let's look at our 3-gallon (11.4 L) collection and see what that would mean if you targeted an OG of 1.120 (28°P) for your barley wine. Total gravity points are (3 × 90) = 270. And you want (120 × FV), using the notation I employed previously. Therefore, FV = 270 ÷ 120 = 2¼ gallons (8.5 L), which is a relatively small volume. But now you only have to lose ¾ gallon (2.8 L) of water in the boil, which you should be able to do comfortably in sixty to ninety minutes. Note that you have to calculate the hop rate according to the actual volume you produce. So, this means that the brewing of the barley wine takes a much shorter time than method 1, although you still, of course, have to brew the second beer, so your overall brew day will still be fairly long.

You could adjust the gravity by adding malt extract so that you produce a large volume, say 3 gallons (11.4 L). Just remember in this case to add back water to allow for that lost in boiling. Let's look at what that entails: You have (3 × 90) = 270 gravity points, but you want to have (3 × 120) = 360 points. So, the extract has to give you (360–270) = 90 points. DME provides 1.045° (11.2°P) per lb. (0.45 kg) per gallons (3.8 L), so 2 lb. DME will nicely give us the 90 points we want. It will be convenient to dissolve it in the cold water used to replace evaporation losses—that's because it will not clump up when mixed with cold water but will do so in hot wort.

So, this method will enable you to achieve very high wort gravities without long boils, which would readily permit you to make a pale barley wine if you wish. It has the disadvantage of still taking a lot of time, because of the need to boil a second wort, which you may find difficult if you are short on space and/or number of suitable vessels. It also has the disadvantage that you can produce only a small volume of barley wine, although you may consider that 2–3 gallons (7.6–11.4

L) is enough for such a strong beer and like the idea that you will also have a second "drinking" beer from this effort. This method works well if you are someone who has a 10-gallon (38 L) setup, but if you want to produce a bigger volume while working only on a 5-gallon scale you will have to use one of the next two methods.

METHOD 4

Let's suppose you want to make a bigger volume of barley wine than the 2¼–3 gallons (8.5–11.4 L) given by method 3 above. That is easy enough if you have a 10-gallon brewery, but I am assuming you do not. So, you simply do a double mash, parti-gyle each one, and combine the two first collections before boiling, using the two second collections to make one or more lesser beers. It is possible to do these mashes sequentially in the same mash tun, but it does become something of a logistical nightmare to do so. You would have to keep the two worts from the first mash aside in separate vessels while you clean the tun, do the second mash, then run off the second two worts. A better way is to do the two mashes and wort collections more or less concurrently, assuming, of course, that you actually have two mash tuns. You probably only have one boiler, so you would have to heat the water for the second mash, after you have mashed in the first, so the two would not be exactly concurrent. You would also have to ensure that you have sufficient sparge water for the two second wort collections, as well as suitable collection vessels.

That sounds more complicated than it really is, but I have actually brewed a barley wine in this manner, as I do have two mash tuns. It turned out not to be too difficult, and the brew day was not more than an hour longer than it would have been for a regular beer, although I did have more work to do the next day with the second worts (see later). So, let's see how that actually worked out:

I used all electrical heating and switched on sparge water in the hot liquor tank and mash water in the boiler at 8:00 a.m. First mash was at 148°F (64.4°C), starting at 9:10 a.m.; after ninety minutes (10:40 a.m.) and a negative iodine test indicating conversion was complete, I ran off 3 gallons (11.4 L) of wort (11:00 a.m.). This gave an SG reading of 1.093 (22.2°P) at 60°F (15.6°C). The residual grain was then sparged with 5 gallons (19 L) of hot water to collect a second wort at 11:25 a.m.—see below.

After graining-in the first mash, I heated more water in the boiler and started the second mash at 9:40 a.m. at 150°F (65.6°C). After sixty minutes (10:40 a.m.) this gave a negative starch-iodine test, and I ran off 3 gallons (11.4 L) of wort (11:15 a.m.) with SG 1.092 (22.0°P) at 60°F (15.6°C). The grain in the tun was then sparged with 5 gallons (19 L) of hot water to collect the second wort at 11:50 a.m.—see below.

So, in four hours I had a combined 6 gallons (23 L) of barley wine wort at 1.093 (22.2°P). I boiled that for ninety minutes, using enough Simcoe hop pellets (13% alpha acid) for a nominal 95 IBU. Final volume, after cooling, was 4.25 gallons (16 L) at SG 1.128 (29.7°P), and I was able to pitch with SAFALE US-05 yeast (using 46 g, about 800 billion cells, oxygenating the wort at pitching and adding Servomyces yeast nutrient) at 5:00 p.m. For the record, finishing gravity was 1.028 (7.1°P), making for 13.1% abv.

So my brew day was nine hours from start to finish, not so bad at all. Ah, you say, but what about the second worts? Did I just throw them away? Of course I didn't; I used them to brew more beer. In classic parti-gyling, I would have made two separate beers, which would have made for a good deal more time-consuming effort. So, I made them into one beer, and what else should that be but another barley wine? I also decided to cheat a little and to conduct the boil the next day as my evening was committed on the first day. That meant there was a risk of infection of the wort, but it was in the winter and my basement was quite cool, so I took the risk.

I had collected 4.5 gallons (17 L) of wort from the first mash at a gravity of 1.069 (16.8°P), and 4 gallons (15.1 L) at 1.053 (13.1°P). Therefore, I had 8.5 gallons (32 L) at a gravity of ((4.5 × 69) + (4 × 53)) ÷ 8.5 = 1.061 (15°P). I boiled this for ninety minutes to reduce the volume to about 6 gallons (23 L), added Simcoe hop pellets (13% alpha acid) for a nominal 95 IBU, and boiled for another ninety minutes.

After cooling I had 4 gallons (15.1 L) at OG 1.124 (28.8°P), which I pitched with yeast in the same way as the first beer. Finishing gravity was 1.025 (6.3°P), so it had 13.0% abv.

This last stage took another four hours or so; if I had done everything on the same day it would indeed have been a long day. But, if I had used a second boiler and started this boil on the first day, while the other wort was boiling, I could have reduced the overall time quite a bit. But, for a first shot, the procedure went remarkably well, and I finished with 4-plus gallons of each barley wine. Obviously, quite a bit of effort and equipment is needed for this method, and it is probably not something for the fainthearted or inexperienced brewer to try. The best solution is to do this with a brewing friend who helps with the extra equipment as well as with the work!

METHOD 5

This, too, requires a double mash, but requires only one mash tun. That is because it involves one mash, collecting the wort and using this as the mash liquor in a second mash. It is by no means a new technique, although to my knowledge it is not practiced commercially today. It was first mentioned, as far as I can determine, by William Ellis (*The New Art of Brewing and Improving Malt Liquors*, 1741, which appeared in *The Complete Confectioner,* Hannah Glasse, 1762). Ellis quotes a publican who used the small beer wort from a first mash as the liquor for a second mash. He also cites an innkeeper who used the wort from a third mash of the first batch of malt as the liquor for the mashing of a second batch of grain.

A variant of this approach is to mash the malt, and sparge to collect a strong wort, which is then used to mash a subsequent batch of grain. The disadvantages of this procedure are that you only get one beer from two mashes, and that it is very time-consuming since you have to do one mash, collect the wort, clean out the mash tun, do the second mash, collect that wort, and boil and cool it. But the big advantage is that it allows you to produce a good volume of wort at very high gravity, 1.140 (32°P) and above, without doing a long boil.

The logic behind this approach is that the gravities from the two mashes will be additive. Therefore, looking at a simplistic example, if you expected each mash to yield worts at 1.090 (21.6°P), then combining them would give a wort of 1.180, which might result in a beer with at least 15% abv (depending upon the finishing gravity). That is somewhat fanciful, since you probably will not get the efficiency in the second mash as you would normally do with a one-off mash, especially as you are not going to be sparging the second mash, since that would dilute the concentration of that wort. In fact, John Blichmann and John J. Palmer ("Sequential Mashing," *Brew Your Own*, September 2017) quote the results from such a procedure where Blichmann got only 53% extract yield in the second mash.

I think the value (or otherwise) of this approach is best explained by looking at my own attempt to use this procedure so as to obtain a final wort OG of 1.140 (32°P) or above, in a reasonable volume, by which I was hoping for a finished 5 gallons (19 L) of barley wine. Note that although I brew on an overall 5-gallon (19 L) scale, my mash tun actually has a 10-gallon (38 L) capacity, and you would need a similar capacity to handle the amounts of grain involved. This approach may seem a little long-winded, but I think it should be instructive as to the problems inevitably involved in brewing very big barley wines.

First stage: I decided that I would do two big mashes in order to see how far I could go with this method, Accordingly, the first mash was carried out with 20 lb. (9.1 kg) Simpson's Best Pale, at a temperature of 150°F (65.6°C), using 6.25 gallons (23.7 L) of water. That is a ratio of 1.25 qt. (1.2 L) water per lb. (0.45 kg) lb. of malt, pretty much as I would normally use for mashing. I had decided that I would carry out the second mash at a slightly higher ratio of 1.4 qt. (1.3 L) of wort per lb. (0.45 kg) of malt, so as to keep down the viscosity of the final wort a little. That meant I needed to collect 7 gallons (26.5 L) of wort from this first mash.

Now, 20 lb. (9.1 kg) of spent grain will (usually) hold about 2 gallons (7.6 L) of wort, so I was going to have to sparge with a further 3 gallons (11.4 L) of hot water. In fact, in order to be sure that I achieved the predicted numbers, I actually decided to use 5 gallons (19 L) of sparge water; if the numbers did work out as planned for 7 gallons (26.5 L) I could just discard the last couple of gallons. But further, I decided not to sparge at all! That was because I wanted to run off 4 gallons (15.1 L) of wort to check its gravity, and to show some of the fundamental facts about mashing, which are seldom discussed in the literature. So, this is what happened:

First collection: 3 gallons (11.4 L) wort SG 1.096 (22.8°P)
Second collection: 1 gallon (3.8 L) wort SG 1.095 (22.7°P)

That meant that the mash was pretty homogeneous, as might be expected, and that I had got a pretty good extract yield and had been able to collect a full 4 gallons (15.1 L) of wort, leaving just over 2 gallons (7.6 L) in the grain bed. I then added 5 gallons (19 L) of hot water, through my sparge arm, so as not to disturb the grain bed. Further to that aim, I did not stir this second mash, largely because I did not want any significant number of fine particles to carry over to the second mash. As a matter of interest, this was the standard way of brewing in England until sparging came into use in the nineteenth century, except that the old brewers would have stirred this second mash. Again, out of interest I collected two worts, in order to see how SG varied during the runoff. What I got was:

Third collection: 2 gallons (7.6 L) wort at SG 1.082 (19.8°P)
Fourth collection: 1 gallon (3.8 L) wort at SG 1.052 (12.9°P)

This shows a relatively small decrease in SG for the third collection, and a much steeper drop for the last collection, as would be expected. Putting all those together, I had 7 gallons (26.5 L) of wort at 1.086 (20.6°P). This amounted to an extract efficiency of 81%, a pretty good number, but remember that this is for the wort prior to boiling. After boiling, a significant volume of wort would be lost to the trub and in transfers, so the actual brewhouse efficiency would have been lower in a more normal brew.

Second stage: As before, the second mash was carried out with 20 lb. (9.1 kg) Simpson's Best Pale, with the 7 gallons of wort (26.5 L) at a temperature of 148°F (64.4°C). As indicated above, this was a liquor to grain ratio of 1.4 qt. (1.3 L) per lb. (0.45 kg) of malt. Note that by the time I came to do the mash it was necessary to reheat this wort to get it up to strike temperature. At the end of ninety minutes a starch-iodine test gave a significant blue color, indicating the presence of unconverted starch, so I let the mash sit a further thirty minutes. Runoff was as follows, with no sparging:

> First collection: 2 gallons (7.6 L) wort at SG 1.153 (34.6°P)
> Second collection: 2 gallon (7.6 L) wort at SG 1.154 (34.8°P)
> Third collection: 0.8 gallon (3 L) wort at SG 1.152 (34.4°P)

Therefore, I had 4.8 gallons (18.2 L) at SG 1.153 (34.6°P). The runoff was quite slow due to the high viscosity of the wort and was a little less than the 5 gallons (19 L) I had calculated it would be. I added Simcoe hops (13% alpha acid) to a nominal 70 IBU (based on 10% utilization) at the start of the boil. I lost a little wort to the trub in the boil, finishing up with 4.5 gallons (17 L) at 1.150 (34.1°P); the slight loss in OG occurring because of a slight dilution as I kept the wort topped up with water during the boil. If I had not done this, evaporation during the boil would probably have given a final volume of around 4 gallons (15.1 L) at gravity close to 1.170 (37°P).

On the face of it I achieved my target of a high original gravity and a reasonable volume. But what did I really get out of what amounted to an extremely long brew day of almost sixteen hours? It is a little bit complicated to calculate exactly what was added in the second stage, because with no sparging somewhat over 2 gallons (7.6 L) was lost to the spent grain. Let's look at it this way:

> Final pre-boil wort had OG 1.153, so total points (153 × 4.8) = 734
> First pre-boil wort had OG 1.085, so points are (4.8 × 86) = 413
> So, points contributed by second mash are (743 – 413) = 321
> and second mash efficiency = (321 ÷ (20 × 37)) × 100 = 43%

This is the efficiency based on the wort only and normal practice is to calculate on the basis of the wort in the fermenter and if we do this:

Total points ex fermenter are $(4.5 \times 150) = 675$
points from first pre-boil wort $(4.5 \times 86) = 387$
And points contributed by second mash are $(675 — 387) = 288$
then second mash efficiency $= (288 \div (20 \times 37)) \times 100 = 39\%$

Whichever way you approach this number from, it is not a good one, when you consider that on a wort basis I got 81% efficiency with the same amount of grain! Further, this is lower than the 53% quoted by Blichmann above, although his approach was not identical to mine, as he went for a lower wort OG (1.094, 22.6°P) and used a higher water to grain ratio of 2.4 qt. (2.3 L) liquor per lb. (0.45 kg) of malt.

Looking at it yet another way, if I had taken that first wort of 7 gallons (26.5 L) at 1.086 (20.6°P) and concentrated it by boiling to give a post boil wort at a gravity of 1.150 (34.1°P), I would have had:

Total points $= (86 \times 7) = 602$
Wort volume at 1.150 SG $= (602 \div 150) = 4.0$ gallons (15.1 L)

In other words, I would have had the same gravity with under a gallon (3.78 L) less in volume, and it would have taken me much less time than the laborious sequential mash approach! In fact, if I could have squeezed in a bit more malt in that first mash I could have come even closer to the sequential approach in terms of both volume and gravity. That is pure speculation as my mash tun won't take any more than 20 lb. (9.1 kg) of malt. There is a question here, though; it would have taken perhaps two or three hours to boil down that first mash, whereas the second required only one hour or so. Would that mean that the former would have undergone more Maillard reactions than the latter? Probably so, in which case, all other brewing steps being equal, these would not have been identical beers. As I said, this is all speculation, and I have not tried to validate this hypothesis, but it is an interesting thought. It further suggests that it should come as no surprise that barley wines can be very different from one another, and that such differences may be due just as much to differences in brewing procedures, and not just to variations in hopping rates and yeast-produced flavors.

Now, it is clear that sequential mashing is not directly additive as I first suggested. I can't be sure as to why the second mash was so inefficient, and perhaps it could be improved by further experimentation, but, looking at Blichmann's results it does not seem that any improvement would be really significant. In any case, I do not propose to try it again in a hurry as it was just too much work, and there are other, simpler ways to reach that kind of very high gravity. But perhaps you may be sufficiently intrigued to try it for yourself?

There is one other point I should mention about this beer, and about the precaution you should take in producing it. I pitched it with SAFALE SO-4 yeast (60 g, about 1000 billion cells, oxygenated the wort and added 2 tablets Servomyces nutrient). The fermentation got under way in no more than five or six hours; I had made sure that it did so by pitching a sufficiency of yeast. In about twelve hours it was throwing up a huge yeast head, too much for my original 7-gallon (26.5 L) fermenter. I therefore had to quickly transfer it to a much bigger vessel, one capable of holding 12 gallons (45 L), that is a headspace of 7.5 gallons (28.4 L) above the fermenting wort. Even then, the yeast head just about filled this vessel, so be warned that these high-gravity worts must be given sufficient space so that your hard-won wort does not flow all over the floor!

Note that after a week the fermentation had (apparently) finished and the beer was at SG 1.038 (9.5°P). This was somewhat higher than I had wanted but represented almost 75% attenuation. This meant it contained 14.5% abv, and to my taste the residual sweetness is nicely balanced by the body and alcohol content.

SUMMARY AND RECOMMENDATIONS

In Table 4.1 I have attempted to summarize the merits, or otherwise of these five methods:

Table 4.1					
Method	Base*	Time hrs.**	Ease***	Achievable volume, gallons	Reach high OG ****
1	Extract	2	5	5	5
2	Grain	4	2	3-5	2
3	Grain	3	3	3	3
4	Grain	13	1	5	3
5	Grain	16	1	4-5	5

Notes: * If desired, all the grain-based methods can be augmented with extract or sugar, which would change the numbers in column 6
** approximate estimates from my own brewing
***relative numbers, with 1 being difficult, 5 being straightforward
****these are also relative; 5 means OG 1.140 (32°P) or higher inherently obtainable; lower numbers indicate very high OG only obtainable with extract or sugar augmentation.

My own suggestions are that method 1 is obviously the best method if you are new to barley wine brewing or are an extract brewer anyway. Method 2, though not complicated, is tedious because of the long boil required and is limited as to the final volume of wort by the extract efficiency you achieve. Method 3, the traditional parti-gyle system, is quite simple and a good approach for the less-experienced brewer; note that the time listed in Table 4.1 is for brewing the barley wine only and it will take longer than that to brew the smaller beer as well. Methods 4 and 5 are both much more complicated and time-consuming and should only be tackled by experienced brewers. Of the two, I would recommend Method 4 over Method 5, as it is more controllable in terms of reaching a good final volume and can be manipulated to actually produce two different barley wines. Method 5 does achieve very high gravities, but it is inefficient, wasteful, and expensive in terms of the amount of grain required.

Formation of the "rocky head" in the early stages of barley wine fermentation.

OTHER BARLEY WINE BREWING CONSIDERATIONS

There are a few points about brewing these beers that I have not specifically mentioned, or if I have, are worth repeating:

1. In all-grain brews, mash at 148–150°F (64.4–65.6°C), and no higher. That is because you want your wort to be highly fermentable so that you do not finish at too high a gravity and have the beer taste too sweet. In general, you want fermentation to cease at around 1.030 (7.6°P) or lower. That will not make the beer taste thin, I can assure you, because it will still have plenty of body and mouthfeel. Of course, in the case of Scotch ales, you do want it to taste somewhat sweet, and in that case would mash at the higher range of 152–154°F (66.7–67.8) and might look to finish at around 1.030–1.040 (7.6–10°P).

2. If you can, it is a good idea to control fermentation temperature at 65–70°F (18–21°C). That is because the early stages of barley wine fermentations can be extremely vigorous and can generate enough heat to raise the fermenting wort temperature considerably. If this is allowed to get out of hand, it may cause the production of high amounts of both higher alcohols (the so-called fusel oils) and esters, to the extent that the finished beer may actually taste unpleasant. Also, as alluded to under Method 5, this very vigorous fermentation can result in the formation of a huge head in its early stages (see below).

3. Do calibrate all vessel volumes, especially collection vessels and fermenters. This is very important in determining yields and brewhouse efficiency, especially if you are deciding when to make a split in parti-gyling or just how much wort you can collect without sparging. I know many brewing vessel suppliers do have volumes marked on them, but the accuracy of these is not always reliable. Get yourself a big (1 L) graduated measuring cylinder from a scientific supplier if necessary and fill it with water then empty it into the vessels as many times as necessary to check the volumes of your vessels. That way you can mark off the vessel wall at ¼-gallon levels and be sure you are working sufficiently accurately in your measurements and calculations.

4. Make sure that your vessels can hold the volume required for each particular step in the process. As I have indicated above, it is particularly important that you have a sufficient headspace in your fermenter to prevent the yeast head from overflowing. That means that once the big head has ceased to form, perhaps only after two or three days, you might want to rack to a second fermenter with a much smaller headspace and fitted with an airlock. It is also extremely important that grain brewers check that their mash tun can hold the amount of grain and water that brewing these big beers requires. If you are making a wheat wine, remember you will require a little more capacity

than for an equivalent barley wine because in addition to the grain you will have rice hulls present.

5. Do check gravities very carefully throughout the procedure; use an accurate hydrometer and thermometer, preferably from a scientific house, and check the calibration on them. At least do so at the low end, in ice water for the thermometer and water at 60°F for the zero on the hydrometer. When taking hydrometer readings, it is best to cool the liquid to that temperature first. There are correction tables available for readings taken at higher temperatures, but these should be regarded as being no more than approximations. It is a good idea, especially on your first attempt at a barley wine from grain, to collect intermediate samples from the mash and determine their SG, as this will show you how the process is going and allow you to make any necessary adjustments if everything does not go quite according to plan.

6. Be very careful about stages after the primary fermentation. Even after racking there will be a significant amount of yeast still suspended in the beer, because it will be slow to clear at the relatively high finishing gravities of these beers. Because of the latter there will still be a significant amount of fermentable material remaining, and this can cause a continuing slow fermentation. So be sure that fermentation has ceased before putting the beer into its final container, especially if you are bottling it. It is a good idea to keg it, even if you do plan to bottle it. That way, by checking the relief valve occasionally you can determine whether there has been any buildup of pressure. When you are sure all is done, check the gravity on successive weeks, and if it remains constant then you can bottle it with safety.

7. Always use the freshest ingredients possible—that is a good approach in all your brews but is particularly important in brewing barley wines, which take such effort and expense to produce. This applies first to malt extract syrups, which tend to darken and develop off-flavors on storage (DME, on the other

hand, will keep for several years without deteriorating). It used to be easy to tell when a beer was brewed from syrup extract because of a certain tang given by such off-flavors. That is no longer so common as it once was as suppliers are now more careful about ensuring that their extracts are in good shape. But you should buy it just before you brew your barley wine— do not use something that has sat in the back of a cupboard for the last two years! In the case of grain malt, you should use only freshly ground malt, because ground malt stored for any length of time readily picks up moisture and becomes what is known as "slack," with a resulting loss of extract potential, and possibly even mold formation which would be disastrous in barley wine! Either grind the whole grain yourself, or buy it ground by the supplier just a few days before brewing the beer.

Hops, as always, should be as fresh as you can get. Before you use them, rub a sample in your hand and inhale the aroma. If it is at all stale, or cheesy, do not use them. If it smells clean, sharp, and spicy go ahead and brew with them.

And as to yeast, with all that I have said about pitching a sufficient number of active cells, you should be just as discriminating in your choice. Dry yeasts keep pretty well and should present no great problems, but liquid yeasts do deteriorate relatively rapidly, so make sure you get samples which have recently been prepared and are a long way away from their sell by date, even if you are going to prepare a starter for pitching.

8. Color. There is a simple approach to determining what the color of a beer will be, known as malt color units (MCU), determined as follows:

$$\text{MCU} = \frac{(\text{lb. grain}) \times (\text{grain color in } °L)}{(\text{beer volume in gallons})}$$

This is by no means an absolute method, and MCU is usually regarded as being in units of SRM (see below). There have been various attempts by home brewers to improve this simple approach using relatively complicated equations relating MCU to SRM (see below), such as those by Ray Daniels (*Designing Great Beers,* 1996, Brewers Publications).

If you are wondering, SRM stands for standard reference method, as defined by the American Society of Brewing Chemists, and is the light absorbance of the beer at a given wavelength of light (430 nanometers), determined spectrophotometrically. As such, it is measured on the finished beer and is used by commercial brewers as a control method. It is also not really an absolute method since the true color of a beer comes from absorbance of light from the visible spectrum, that is at several wavelengths. For reference, the European Brewery Convention uses a similar method, at the same light wavelength, but a difference in the actual methodology means that their approach gives a different number from that obtained by the ASBC method.

It should then be clear that determination of beer color is very difficult by any means other than the human eye. Beer color in the case of barley wine will consist of amber, yellow, red, and even black hues when inspected by a drinker, yet most of those hues will not be detected by the SRM approach. Perhaps that is just as well since it is unlikely that the average home brewer has access to a spectrophotometer! That leaves us with the simpler approach of calculating MCU. The problem with that is that it is a measure of what goes into a beer, not of the beer itself. As I have discussed, darkening occurs during wort boiling, due to Maillard reactions plus, perhaps, some caramelization. In general, the colors produced by these reactions are mainly brown and reddish brown. The extent to which these reactions occur is much greater for high-gravity barley wines than for beers brewed at more "normal" gravity levels. That means that the color of your barley wine will depend not on just what goes into the starting grist, but on how the beer is treated during brewing. In particular, some of the methods for brewing barley wines that I have outlined involve long boiling times which will result in significant production of Maillard products. In addition to that, you may have opted to use some caramel or even roasted malts, which will also affect the final color. Also, methods such as parti-gyling involve splitting the wort from the mash, making it impossible to calculate beer color merely from the contribution of the ingredients.

Which raises the question that if beer color is hard to determine, why should we bother to do so? Why don't we just put our recipes together on the grounds of how the beer will taste and accept whatever color we get? It's a simplistic, subjective approach I know, but it is one of which Occam would have been proud. Therefore, in the recipe section I shall make no attempt at calculation of the color to be expected, and will use only descriptive terms, such as "pale," "gold," "reddish hue," "deep brown," or even "black."

STORAGE AND FLAVOR

I have mentioned several times that barley wines are beers meant to be kept for long periods, from many months to perhaps several years. When I say "meant" that is, of course, not written in stone, and you can drink your own example just as soon as it has clarified and is suitably carbonated. But it is the experience of brewers in general and myself in particular that such beers improve in flavor as they age. Hop character and aroma, if present right after brewing, will tend to simply disappear in just a few months, and for that reason it is probably not worth carrying out late- or dry-hopping unless you intend to drink the beer while it is still young. Hop bitterness does not so much diminish as ameliorate, becoming less harsh and blending into the overall palate of the beer.

Hot flavors due to the high alcohol content of barley wines do not so much disappear but should no longer dominate as other flavors emerge, as we shall see below. But do be aware that hot alcohol flavor in a barley wine is a fault as it will tend to mask other flavors by the burning effect on the palate. It should not really be a problem with a properly attenuated all-malt-based beer, but it may well be if you are using some sugar as a malt substitute. Purified sugars such as sucrose and dextrose (corn sugar) are fully fermentable and produce alcohol without adding any flavor so should be used with reserve. My limit would be 10% or less of the total weight of malt used. Of course, you might want to use colored sugars for a little extra flavor, but remember that they are still highly fermentable and, I think, they should also be subject to my 10% "rule."

But just how else does a barley wine alter in flavor as it ages? Remember the comments in chapter 2 on Fuller's Vintage Ale, actually made by Fuller's Head Brewer, that this beer seemed to go through cycles as it aged, and it might taste not so good now, yet be excellent a few months later. I have labored under the assumption that this was not true, and that this was a beer which would tend to deteriorate with keeping. Yet, I have just drunk the bottle-conditioned 1998 version, now a full twenty years old, and with a statement on the label "Best before 2001." It was delicious, nicely carbonated, with a beautiful deep, red-copper color and all the aspects I would look for in a barley wine, nutty, fruity, sherry-like, and full-bodied. I was astonished by its gorgeous taste and forced to discard my previous opinions of this beer. There is in the brewing literature much on the ways in which beers, especially those relatively low in alcohol, can deteriorate and develop unacceptable flavors. But I do not think we have any real understanding of the way in which very strong beers can alter and improve in flavor during long maturation. So, without any knowledge of chemical mechanisms involved, we can only assess the effect of long storage on these beers by means of describing the flavors we look for in a mature barley wine.

That is a problem for me as I do not like to use fanciful flavor descriptors as they are merely subjective, and in far too many cases are used only to impress the drinker rather than to inform them. However, I shall try to describe what happens using as few adjectives as possible! It seems likely that a certain amount of oxidation occurs during aging, resulting in the formation of flavors often described as sherry-like (sherry being a wine that is known to be subject to oxidation). To me, that means a full-bodied flavor (we are definitely not talking about dry sherries here), with caramel and perhaps nutty nuances. I can best sum it up by saying that I find a mouthful of a well-matured barley wine rolled around my palate to be a very satisfying experience. A good barley wine has a variety of flavors generated not only by oxidation but also by the presence of dextrins, some unfermented sugars, hop bitterness, and Maillard products. It is therefore probably fruitless (not a pun) to try to distinguish all these one from another and to just sit back and enjoy the complexity of a great beer. Just be warned that if oxidation is a mechanism in this aging process it comes from the presence of only a small amount of oxygen in the beer. Do not be tempted to add any more, or to be careless in bottling and kegging, as an excess of oxygen will result in over-oxidation and some unpleasant flavors, such as those often described as "wet cardboard."

How you should mature your barley wine is an open question. Clearly, many craft brewers prefer to do this in barrels, which have previously contained bourbon, whisky and whiskey, various wines, and so on. In such cases an extra layer of complexity is added to the beer as compared to aging it in a flavor-neutral container. Home brewers can also do this, although the volumes involved might make it impractical for them. If all you want is oak flavor, this can easily be added by soaking oak chips or spirals in the beer for a week or two. Keeping the beer in a stainless steel soda keg for a year or more might not be desirable if you have a limited number of kegs and want to brew some other beers. And given that you may take some time to drink several gallons of barley wine it would seem that bottling, rather than kegging, might be the best approach. Aging will certainly occur in the bottle, because no matter how careful you are during the bottling process, you will still have some oxygen present in the bottle. An advantage of bottling is that you can easily sample the beer at intervals to determine whether it has matured sufficiently for your taste; this would be a useful procedure if your own beer undergoes "flavor cycles" as described above for Fuller's Vintage Ale. My own approach would be to age it in a stainless steel keg for six months to a year, and then bottle it, so I can taste it over time. If you decide to prime the beer when bottling you need to add some fresh yeast along with the priming sugar, preferably from an active starter. A better approach would be to carbonate in keg and bottle using a counterpressure filler, since you cannot be sure at the high alcohol levels involved that you would get further fermentation on priming.

DRINKING BARLEY WINE

You should not need much education about this topic, but there are some points I should make. First of all, this is definitely not a beer which should be drunk cold, as near-freezing temperatures will simply suppress much of its flavor. It is best drunk at 45–50°F (7–10°C), a range in which all its flavor attributes will be evident. Since it is a sipping beer and will warm up during the time it takes to drink a glass, it may be best to serve it a tad colder, say, 40°F (4.5°C), which will allow it to come into the optimum range as the contents of the glass are consumed.

Which brings me to the topic of glasses for barley wine. I am a great believer in drinking from a glass and never, never directly from a can or bottle. Glass allows you to see and enjoy the color, and allows the aromas to emerge, both of which enhance your anticipation before you actually taste the beer. Which sort of glass you should use is up to you, and, as you can see in the photograph, brewers have touted quite a few different styles for their barley wines. I like the "brandy" snifters, although the

Not all barley wine glasses are created equal.

tulip types are also good. I also enjoy drinking from the almost straight but stemmed glasses such as those for Bass No. 1 and Harpoon Leviathan. It is your choice, but surely a beer which is so big and hard to brew deserves to be served in a vessel with more than a little class!

TAIL END

Brewing barley wines is a challenge, one which can be approached in many ways, all of them involving a deal of hard work and expense. But the results are very rewarding—your product will be unique, will last a long time, and, since it is a sipping rather than a quaffing beer, you can enjoy it over a long period. Some drinkers regard barley wine as an unimportant marginal beer, but as you do sip it, reflect on the fact that you are enjoying the ultimate in beers, and are keeping alive a long and honorable brewing tradition.

A varied array of J. W. Lees's Harvest Ales aged in different barrels.

CHAPTER FIVE

BARLEY WINE RECIPES

Mistress Ford: be ready hard by the brew-house. (William Shakespeare, *The Merry Wives of Windsor*, act 3, scene 3)

IN THE LAST CHAPTER I DETAILED THE BASIC APPROACHES TO brewing barley wines including preparations such as choosing the right equipment, so I do not intend to repeat these here. Each recipe will be designated 1–5 to indicate the brewing method as discussed in the last section. Since it is the most straightforward for all-grain brewing, method 2 will be the procedure of choice for most of the recipes. I shall, however, start out with recipes and directions for each of the five different procedures. There will be fairly specific directions for each recipe so there may be some repetition of the more important points. I will not give details of water treatment because your supply will probably not match mine. Be sure to follow the recommendations in chapter 3 as to how to adjust the salt content of your brewing water and mash pH where applicable. The brewing parameters should be regarded as being indicative, rather than definitive, especially when it comes to procedures such as parti-gyling and double mashing. For example, you may get slightly different original and finishing gravities than I quote, so alcohol levels will be somewhat different from mine. In most cases there is no standard finished volume, since this is decided by reaching the target OG in combination with mash tun capacity. IBUs are calculated values, based on assumed utilization factors of 10–15% (in most cases) depending upon the boil OG, and color, as I suggested, will be given only on a descriptive basis. Where appropriate, I shall include suggestions of suitable variations for each recipe.

STANDARD BARLEY WINES

KISS BARLEY WINE

METHOD 1 (all malt extract)

Malt: 12 lb. (5.4 kg) Pale Malt Extract syrup

Hops: 1.8 oz. (50 g) Simcoe pellets at 13.0% alpha acid

Yeast: Wyeast 1098 British Ale or White Labs 002 English Ale. You should aim to pitch 750 billion cells. This is best done as a starter—see below. Use a nutrient as recommended.

Procedure: Stir 6 lb. (2.7 kg) extract into 4 gallons (15.1 L) warm water, taking care to see that all of it is thoroughly dissolved before applying heat. Add the hops and boil for 60 minutes; turn off heat and carefully stir in 6 lb. (2.7 kg) of extract. Boil a further 20 minutes, cool to about 70°F (21°C), and pitch yeast. Ferment 7–10 days as close to 70°F (21°C) as possible, rack to secondary for 2 weeks, rack again, and leave for 3–4 months. Serve from stainless steel soda keg or bottle, force carbonating (keg) or priming if desired (bottles), preferably allowing the beer to age a further 6 months or more.

Projected parameters: 3.3 gallons (12.5 L) final volume
Original gravity: 1.127 (29.3°P)
Final gravity: 1.036 (9°P)
Apparent attenuation: 71.7%
Alcohol: 11.8% abv
Bitterness: 100+ IBU (calculated on 25% utilization and OG 1.053 (13.1°P) for first hour of boil)
Color: deep gold

Notes

As described above this would require seven to eight packets of fresh yeast. The best approach would be to prepare a starter from two packets of yeast, each in a separate vessel and doubling up twice. That means you would have to prepare the starter several days in advance of brewing.

Comments

I used Maris Otter extract, but any other pale syrup will do as well. In fact, although the apparent attenuation was reasonably good, the finishing gravity was a little high, so the beer was somewhat sweeter than I targeted. This might therefore be a good beer to add a champagne yeast to the secondary fermenter. But that could make the beer somewhat thinner, and the high hop bitterness would make the beer unbalanced. Personally, I would leave it alone; it is, and is meant to be, the simplest approach to brewing a barley wine imaginable.

ALL TOGETHER ALE

METHOD 2 (grain mash, collect all)

Malt: 17 lb. (7.7 kg) Maris Otter pale malt

Hops: 3.5 oz. (99 g) Target pellets at 11.6% alpha acid

Yeast: White Labs WLP007 Dry English Ale. You should aim to pitch 500 billion cells. This is best done as a starter as in the previous recipe, using two packets, starting each separately then doubling each twice. Use a nutrient and oxygenate as recommended for the main brew.

Procedure: Mash grain at 148–150°F (64.4–65.6°C), using 20 qt. (19 L) water (ratio 1.2 qt./lb., 2.5 L/kg). At 90 minutes perform a starch-iodine test and mash a further 30 minutes if positive for starch. If the test is negative and conversion is complete, run off and sparge with water at about 170°F (77°C) to collect 6 gallons (23 L) of wort. The specific gravity of this wort should be about 1.077 (18.7°P). Bring to a boil, add the bittering hops, and boil down to 3.3 gallons (12.5 L); this took about 3 hours in my case. Cool to about 70°F (21°C) and pitch the yeast starter. Ferment 10–14 days as close to 70°F (21°C) as possible, rack to secondary for 4 weeks, rack again, and leave for 6–8 months. Serve from stainless steel soda keg or bottle, force carbonating (keg) or priming if desired (bottles), preferably allowing the beer to age a further 6 months or more. This beer should keep well for several years, and I recommend that you do that with at least a portion of it.

Projected parameters: 3.3 gallons (12.5 L) final volume
Original gravity: 1.139 (32°P)
Final gravity: 1.038 (9.5°P)
Apparent attenuation: 72.7%
Alcohol: 13.2% abv
Bitterness: 92 IBU (calculated on 10% utilization at this high specific gravity)
Color: deep gold to light brown

Comments

This was my shot at brewing chancellor ale from Queen's College, Oxford, so I opted for a "traditional" English malt, and English hops. I would have preferred the older variety, East Kent Goldings, over Target, but the samples I had were low in alpha acid, and I wanted to limit the amount of hop debris in the boiler, so as not to lose too much of my valuable wort! I considered it essential to have a high bitterness in this beer, because of the high finishing gravity, so that there was balance to the brew. It also had a luscious flavor, probably due in part to the presence of many Maillard reaction products, which would have formed during the long boil at high specific gravity. Note, however, that apparent attenuation was quite good at 73%, so it would be difficult to get it much lower. Indeed, it would probably not be desirable to do so, or the beer would be thinner and higher in alcohol and quite unbalanced. Note also that at this level of bitterness this very traditional English brew is hopped at a rate which would make the BA and BJCP assess it as an American barley wine.

I brewed this beer for the wedding of Jeff Browning Sr. and Krista Nolan; none of it survived after the following celebrations.

PARTY TIME BARLEY WINE

METHOD 3 (parti-gyle approach)

Malt: 20 lb. (9.1 kg) Rahr 2-row pale malt

Hops: (i) 1 oz. (28 g) Waimea pellets at 17.8% alpha acid

(ii) 1.4 oz. (40 g) Goldings pellets at 5% alpha acid

Yeast: (i) 30 g SAFALE S-04 dry yeast (about 450 billion cells); use a nutrient and oxygenate as recommended

(ii) 11.5 g (1 pack) SAFALE S-04 dry yeast (about 200 billion cells)

Procedure: (i) Mash grain at 148–150°F (64.4–65.6°C), using 24 qt. (23 L) water (ratio 1.2 qt./lb., 2.5 L/kg). At 90 minutes perform a starch-iodine test and mash a further 30 minutes if positive for starch. If test is negative and starch conversion is complete, run off 4 gallons (15.1 L) of wort, with no sparge. That should have a specific gravity of ± 1.090 (21.5°P). Bring to a boil and add Waimea hops; boil down to 3 gallons (11.4 L), which should take 1–1½ hours. Cool to about 70°F (21°C) and pitch 40 g of yeast, rehydrating according to instructions on the packet. Ferment 7–10 days as close to 70°F (21°C) as possible, rack to secondary for 3 weeks, rack again, and leave for 4–6 months. Serve from stainless steel soda keg or bottle, force carbonating (keg) or priming if desired (bottles), preferably allowing the beer to age a further 6 months or more.

(ii) Sparge the residual grain from (i) above with hot water at about 170°F (77°C) to collect 4 gallons (15.1 L) of wort. Boil this for 90 minutes with Goldings hops added at the start; top it up with water as necessary to maintain 4 gallons. Cool to about 70°F (21°C) and pitch 11.5 g of yeast, rehydrating according to instructions on the packet. Ferment 7 days, transfer to secondary for 7 days, then keg or bottle by the usual procedures. Drink as soon as it is clear.

Projected parameters:
(i) 3 gallons (11.4 L) final volume
Original gravity: 1.120 (28°P)
Final gravity: 1.029 (7.3P)
Apparent attenuation: 75.8%
Alcohol: 11.9% abv
Bitterness: 66 IBU (calculated on 15% utilization)
Color: deep gold.

(ii) 4 gallons (15.1 L) final volume
Original gravity: 1.045 (11.2°P)
Final gravity: 1.010 (2.6°P)
Apparent attenuation: 77.8%
Alcohol: 4.5% abv
Bitterness: 33 IBU (calculated on 25% utilization)
Color: pale gold

Notes

Overall extract yield for both beers was 73%. The second beer was formulated as an English summer ale (which is really only a pale bitter ale). If you prefer, this beer could be dry-hopped in the secondary with, say, Styrian Goldings, or a citrussy American hop such as Citra.

Comments

This is an example which shows how simple a procedure parti-gyling can be. The downside of this method is that you have to perform two boils in one day, making for a long brew day. The upside, however, is that you finish with two beers from one mash and the second one you can drink while waiting for the first to mature.

The barley wine itself is only modestly hopped for its high OG, but is still quite full-flavored, though less rich than the All Together Ale. It is at the pale end of the barley wine color spectrum but will darken somewhat on aging. The hop rate makes it what some would call an English version of the style; you can, of course use a higher level of bitterness if you wish. Note that I used Waimea hops because of their high alpha acid level, which meant that there was only a small amount of trub to remove at the end of the boil.

TWOFER DOPPELGANGER

METHOD 4 (double mash)

Malt: 18 lb. (8.2 kg) Simpson Best Pale malt each mash

Hops: 2.1 oz. (60 g) Simcoe pellets at 13% alpha acid each boil

Yeast: 40 g SAFALE US-05 for each brew (700 billion cells); use a nutrient and oxygenate as recommended.

Mash Procedure: Do two mashes, preferably starting the second about halfway through the first. The method is identical for both mashes starting at 148–150°F (64.4–65.6°C), mixing the grain with 22 qt. (21 L) water (ratio 1.2 qt./lb., 2.5 L/kg). At 90 minutes perform a starch-iodine test and mash a further 30 minutes if positive for starch. If the test is negative and conversion is complete, run off and collect 3 gallons (11.4 L) of wort. The specific gravity of this wort should be about 1.090 (21.5°P). Put both 3-gallon collections in the boiler—see below.

The residual grain from each mash should then be sparged with 5 gallons (19 L) water at about 170°F (77°C) to collect 4 gallons (23 L) of wort from each. The specific gravity of these two worts should be about 1.065 (15.9°P); put them aside and proceed to boil 1.

Boil 1: Bring the combined first worts (6 gallons, 23 L) to a boil, add the Simcoe hops, and boil down to 4.25 gallons (16 L); this took about 1¾ hours in my case. Cool to about 70°F (21°C) and pitch the yeast. Ferment 10–14 days as close to 70°F (21°C) as possible, rack to secondary for 4 weeks, rack again, and leave for 6–8 months. Serve from stainless steel soda keg or bottle, force carbonating (keg) or priming if desired (bottles), preferably allowing the beer to age a further 6 months or more. This beer should keep well for several years, and I recommend that you do that with at least a portion of it.

Boil 2: Bring the combined second worts (8 gallons, 30.3 L) to a boil, add the Simcoe hops, and boil down to 4 gallons (15.1 L); this took about 2¼ hours in my case. Cool to about 70°F (21°C) and pitch the yeast. Ferment 10–14 days as close to 70°F (21°C) as possible, rack to secondary for 4 weeks, rack again, and leave for 6–8 months. Serve from stainless steel soda keg or bottle, force carbonating (keg) or priming if desired (bottles), preferably allowing the beer to age a further 6 months or more. This beer should keep well for several years, and I recommend that you do that with at least a portion of it.

Projected parameters:
(i) 4.25 gallons (16 L) final volume
Original gravity: 1.128 (29.7°P)
Final gravity: 1.032 (8.1°P)
Apparent attenuation: 75%
Alcohol: 12.6% abv
Bitterness: 55 IBU (calculated on 12% utilization)
Color: pale gold.

(ii) 4 gallons (15.1 L) final volume
Original gravity: 1.124 (28.9°P)
Final gravity: 1.027 (6.8°P)
Apparent attenuation: 78.2%
Alcohol: 12.7% abv
Bitterness: 62 IBU (calculated on 12% utilization)
Color: deep red-gold

Notes

Overall extract yield 78.1%, somewhat higher than I expected, which suggests that this double-mash approach might be the most efficient of methods 2–4. On the other hand, I brewed these beers one after the other, so perhaps it was just my technique that had improved? There was a slight difference in apparent attenuation which may simply illustrate the fact that brewing barley wine is not an easy matter and brewing it with absolute consistency is extremely difficult. Note also, as mentioned in the previous section this method requires two mash tuns, a luxury many of you may not have.

Comments

Clearly, this method involves a lot of work and it is no easy task to fit it all into a single day. But the positive result is that it yields good volumes of two quite big barley wines. I kept the hop rates relatively low, and on reflection might have liked to have gone nearer to 100 IBU but would have wanted to use a hop variety with a higher alpha acid level than that of the Simcoe I used. The big question, one I am sure you have asked, is whether there was any difference in these two beers as regards their flavors. Well, after one year both were rich in flavor, full-bodied, with every sip enjoyable. But the first brew was of a luscious, sumptuous character, while the second had a good deal of that but backed by the almost savory complexity coming from the presence of Maillard reaction products due to the somewhat longer boil the wort had undergone.

OVER THE GREEN MONSTER

METHOD 5 (wort as strike water for a second mash)

Mash 1

Malt: 20 lb. (9.1 kg) Simpson's Best Pale malt

Procedure: Mash grain at 148–150°F (64.4–65.6°C), using 24 qt. (23 L) water (ratio 1.2 qt./lb., 2.5 L/kg). At 90 minutes perform a starch-iodine test and mash a further 30 minutes if positive for starch. If the test is negative and conversion is complete, run off and sparge with water at about 170°F (77°C) to collect 7 gallons (26.5 L) of wort. The specific gravity of this wort should be about 1.080 (18.7°P), although in my case it was 1.085 (20.3°P).

Mash 2

Malt: 20 lb. (9.1 kg) Simpson's Best Pale malt

Hops: 4 oz. (113 g) Warrior at 15% alpha acid

Yeast: 60 g SAFALE S-04 (about 1000 billion cells); use a nutrient and oxygenate as recommended.

Procedure: Mash grain at 148–150°F (64.4–65.6°C), using 7 gallons (26.5 L) of the wort from the first mash (ratio 1.4 qt./lb., 2.9 L/kg). At 90 minutes perform a starch-iodine test and mash a further 30 minutes if positive for starch. Do not sparge, just run off wort and collect as much as possible, 4.75 gallons (18 L). Bring to a boil, add the hops, and boil 1 hour. Cool to about 70°F (21°C) and pitch the yeast. Ferment 10–14 days as close to 70°F (21°C) as possible, rack to secondary for 4 weeks, rack again, and leave for 6–8 months. Serve from stainless steel soda keg or bottle, force carbonating (keg) or priming if desired (bottles), preferably allowing the beer to age a further 6 months or more. This is a very big beer and should keep well for several years, and I recommend that you do so.

Projected parameters:

4.5 gallons (17 L) final volume
Original gravity: 1.149 (34°P)
Final gravity: 1.038 (9.5°P)
Apparent attenuation: 74.5%
Alcohol: 14.5% abv
Bitterness: 100 IBU (calculated on 10% utilization)
Color: pale red-brown

Notes

Yes, I know I detailed this brew in chapter 4, but I repeated it here in order to make the recipe clearer to follow.

Comments

The extract yield from the second mash was poor, being only around 40%, whereas for the first mash it was about 80%. This is therefore an inefficient procedure and the resultant beer was much more expensive to brew than most barley wines. It is also a time-consuming process involving an early start to the brew day and a late finish. It did, however, brew the biggest beer I have ever made and is potentially a route to beers of even higher gravity if you want to produce them by grain mashing only. Of course, you can reach OG up to and even beyond 1.150 (34.1°P) using only malt extract, or a mash boosted by addition of sugar or extract, both of which are simpler procedures than that given here. It can be argued that these alternative methods would not produce the same beer, and the one described above is very good, with a good balance between residual sweetness, high hop bitterness and high alcohol and lots and lots of mouth-filling body. I think, however, that my next attempt would be to reduce the gravity of the wort from the first mash to, say, 1.050–1.060 (12.4–14.7°P), in order to try and improve the extract yield of the second mash.

CUTTING-EDGE BARLEY WINE

METHOD 1 (all malt extract)

Malt: 12 lb. (5.4 kg) Maris Otter pale malt extract

Hops: 0.75 oz. (21 g) Ekuanot LupulLN2 at 22.8% alpha acid bittering; 0.5 oz. (14 g) dry-hopping.

Yeast: White Labs 004 Irish Ale. You should aim to pitch 600 billion cells. As described above this would require six packets of fresh yeast. The best approach would be to prepare a starter from two packets of yeast, each in a separate vessel and doubling up twice. That means you would have to prepare the starter several days in advance of brewing. Use a nutrient as recommended and oxygenate the wort at pitching.

Procedure: Stir 6 lb. (2.7 kg) extract into 4 gallons (15.1 L) warm water, taking care to see that all of it is thoroughly dissolved before applying heat. Add the hops and boil for 60 minutes; turn off heat and carefully stir in 6 lb. (2.7 kg) of extract. Boil a further 20 minutes, cool to about 70°F (21°C), and pitch yeast. Ferment 7–10 days as close to 70°F (21°C) as possible, rack to secondary for 2 weeks, dry-hopping with the second amount of hops, rack again, and leave for 3–4 months. Serve from stainless steel soda keg or bottle, force carbonating (keg) or priming if desired (bottles). This beer will improve on further aging but can be drunk after 4 months.

Projected parameters: 4.6 gallons (17.4 L) final volume
Original gravity: 1.091 (21.8°P)
Final gravity: 1.029 (7.3°P)
Apparent attenuation: 68%
Alcohol: 8.2% abv
Bitterness: 70 IBU (calculated on 25% utilization and OG 1.053 (13.1°P) for first hour of boil)
Color: yellow to gold

Note

The lowest OG beer so far in my list.

Comments

Apparent attenuation was somewhat low considering the starting gravity, suggesting that my choice of yeast may not have been the best! But the intention was to test out one of the LupulLN2 hops, and the first point is that only a small amount of trub was formed, so wort loss was very small. The second point was that bitterness was nice and clean and the hop character was pleasantly citrus-like, but not dominant. To me it is a barley wine, but would others see it as a double IPA?

GILDED AGE ALE

METHOD 2 (grain mash with additions; boil down)

Malt: 17 lb. (7.7 kg) 2-row pale malt
1 lb. (0.454 kg) Caramel 60°L (5.5% of total malt bill)
2 oz. (56 g) Black malt

Hops: 2.5 oz. (71 g) Millennium pellets at 14% alpha acid

Yeast: 40 g DANSTAR Nottingham Ale (700 billion cells); use a nutrient and oxygenate as recommended.

Procedure: Mash grain at 148–150°F (64.4–65.6°C), using 22 qt. (21 L) water (ratio 1.2 qt./lb., 2.5 L/kg). At 90 minutes perform a starch-iodine test and mash a further 30 minutes if positive for starch. If the test is negative and conversion is complete, run off and sparge with water at about 170°F (77°C) to collect 6 gallons (23 L) of wort. The specific gravity of this wort should be about 1.080 (19.3°P). Bring to a boil, add the Millennium hops, and boil down to 4 gallons (15.1 L); this took about 2 hours in my case. Cool to about 70°F (21°C) and pitch the yeast. Ferment 10–14 days as close to 70°F (21°C) as possible, rack to secondary for 4 weeks, rack again, and leave for 6–8 months. Serve from stainless steel soda keg or bottle, force carbonating (keg) or priming if desired (bottles), preferably allowing the beer to age a further 6 months or more. This beer should keep well for several years, and I recommend that you do that with at least a portion of it.

Projected parameters:
4 gallons (15.1 L) final volume
Original gravity: 1.121 (28.2°P)
Final gravity: 1.033 (8.3°P)
Apparent attenuation: 72.7%
Alcohol: 11.6% abv
Bitterness: 79 IBU (calculated on 12% utilization at this high specific gravity)
Color: deep red-brown

Notes

Exactly as All Together Ale, except for somewhat lower OG and the addition of caramel and black malts.

Comments

Slightly low in apparent attenuation, probably due to the use of caramel malt. This and the black malt yield a beer of darker color than any of the previous beers, but the caramel malt intensifies the nutty flavor, while the black malt adds just a hint of roast character to offset the extra sweetness form the caramel malt. It is a variation on the standard method 2 approach which some might regard as unnecessary, but I find the extra little bit of complexity makes for a very satisfying barley wine.

ALL NATIONS BARLEY WINE

METHOD 2 (grain mash and boil down)

Malt: 18.7 lb. (8.5 kg) 2-row pale malt

Hops: 2.5 oz. (70 g) Target pellets at 10% alpha acid
2.0 oz. (57 g) Amarillo pellets at 8.2% alpha acid

Yeast: White Labs WLP500 Monastery Ale yeast (billed as Trappist yeast when I brewed this beer).You should aim to pitch about 900 billion cells. This is best done as a starter as in the previous recipe, using two packets (or even three if you are not sure of the freshness of the yeast), starting each separately then doubling each twice. Use a nutrient as recommended and oxygenate for the main brew.

Procedure: Mash grain at 148–150°F (64.4–65.6°C), using 22 qt. (21 L) water (ratio 1.2 qt./lb., 2.5 L/kg). At 90 minutes perform a starch-iodine test and mash a further 30 minutes if positive for starch. If the test is negative and conversion is complete, run off and sparge with water at about 170°F (77°C) to collect 6 gallons (23 L) of wort. The specific gravity of this wort should be about 1.077 (18.7°P). Bring to a boil, add the Target and Amarillo hops, and boil down to 3.5 gallons (13.3 L); this took about 2 hours in my case. Cool to about 70°F (21°C) and pitch the yeast. Ferment 10–14 days as close to 70°F (21°C) as possible, rack to secondary for 4 weeks, rack again, and leave for 6–8 months. Serve from stainless steel soda keg or bottle, force carbonating (keg) or priming if desired (bottles), preferably allowing the beer to age a further 6 months or more. This beer should keep well for several years, and I recommend that you do that with at least a portion of it.

Projected parameters: 3.5 gallons (13.3 L) final volume
Original gravity: 1.140 (32.1°P)
Final gravity: 1.037 (9.3°P)
Apparent attenuation: 73.6%
Alcohol: 13.6% abv

Bitterness: 88 IBU (calculated on 10% utilization at this high specific gravity)
Color: deep gold

Notes

The process is exactly the same as for All Together Ale, but for the use of two hop varieties and a very different yeast.

Comments

Every now and then I go a little emotional and brew an "Anglo-American" beer, that is, one with ingredients from both England and America. In this case I went even further and used a Belgian Trappist yeast in order to see if I could get a low finishing gravity; at least I didn't go completely mad and add ingredients from some of the other brewing and hop-growing countries. In this case my extract yield was a little down, probably because of the large amount of hop residue in the trub as I used hops which were relatively low in alpha acid. Apparent attenuation was satisfactory, but the Trappist yeast showed no significant improvement over other yeasts I have tried. I could not discern any of that elusive "Belgian" character in the finished beers, perhaps because it was already too complex with high alcohol and Maillard reaction products from the quite long boil. It was certainly greeted with acclaim when it

A very new Connecticut brewery in Derby.

debuted at a beer festival in New Haven and was quickly consumed by the participants.

WHAT THE OCTOBER ALE

METHOD 3 (all-grain parti-gyle approach)

Malt: 16 lb. (7.3 kg) Simpson's Best Pale malt
1 lb. (0.454 kg) Amber malt (5.7% of total grist)
0.5 lb. (0.227 kg) Brown malt (2.9% of total grist)

Hops: (i) 1 oz. (28 g) Admiral pellets at 15% alpha acid
(ii) 0.5 oz. (14 g) First Gold pellets at 7.5% alpha acid

Yeast: (i) Wyeast 1056 American Ale. You should aim to pitch 600 billion cells. As described above this would require 6 packs of fresh yeast. The best approach would be to prepare a starter from two packets of yeast, each in a separate vessel and doubling up twice. That means you would have to prepare the starter several days in advance of brewing.

(ii) 11.5 g (1 pack) SAFALE S-04 dry yeast (about 200 billion cells)

Procedure:
(i) Mash grain at 152–154°F (66.7–67.8°C), using 21 qt. (20 L) water (ratio 1.2 qt./lb., 2.5 L/kg). At 90 minutes perform a starch-iodine test and mash a further 30 minutes if positive for starch. If test is negative for starch and conversion is complete, run off 3.5 gallons (13.3 L) of wort, with no sparge. That should have a specific gravity of ± 1.090 (21.5°P). Bring to a boil and add Admiral hops; boil down to 3 gallons (11.4 L), which should take 1 hour. Cool to about 70°F (21°C) and pitch yeast starter. Ferment 7–10 days as close to 70°F (21°C) as possible, rack to secondary for 3 weeks, rack again, and leave for 4–6 months. Serve from stainless steel soda keg or bottle, force carbonating (keg) or priming as appropriate. This beer can be drunk at this stage, although it should improve with further aging.

(ii) Sparge the residual grain from (i) above with hot water at about 170°F (77°C) to collect 4 gallons (15.1 L) of wort. Boil this for 90 minutes, or until reduced to 2.5 gallons (9.5 L) with First Gold hops added at the start. Cool to about 70°F (21°C) and pitch 11.5 g of yeast, rehydrating according to instructions on the packet. Ferment 7 days, transfer to secondary for 7 days, then keg or bottle by the usual procedures. Drink as soon as it is clear.

Projected parameters:
(i) 3 gallons (11.4 L) final volume
Original gravity: 1.105 (24.8°P)
Final gravity: 1.025 (6.3°P)
Apparent attenuation: 76.2%
Alcohol: 10.4% abv
Bitterness: 56 IBU (calculated on 15% utilization)
Color: deep red-brown.

(ii) 2.5 gallons (9.5 L) final volume
Original gravity: 1.056 (13.8°P)
Final gravity: 1.014 (3.6°P)
Apparent attenuation: 75%
Alcohol: 5.5% abv
Bitterness: 28 IBU (calculated on 25% utilization)
Color: ruby to brown

Notes

This was an experiment with some quite different specialty malts, a sort of tongue-in-cheek version of an eighteenth-century October ale from the first gyle. The second gyle was more like a table beer than a small beer, because that was what I preferred to drink. Overall extract yield was 70.3%.

Comments

In fact, this was by no means an authentic eighteenth-century October ale; such a beer might well have had some amber malt in the grist, but not brown malt, as the latter was used only in porter. And, of course, Admiral hops were not then available; what there would have been would probably have been quite low in alpha acid content. I could have used something like Goldings hops, but I opted for a high alpha variety to minimize wort losses in the trub. Also, it is quite probable that those early brews never reached the same level of apparent attenuation as did my recipe. Nevertheless, this was a really good beer with all the usual richness of a barley wine, overlain with some biscuit notes from the amber malt and licorice hints from the brown malt. This combination almost overlaps barley wine with imperial stout!

The beer from the second gyle was also interesting with a nice smooth and full flavor and light caramel and subdued licorice notes. It is, in fact, nothing less than a strong mild ale, or even a brown porter, if, indeed, it is possible to distinguish between the two!

BEYOND THE PALE

METHOD 2 (grain mash with added extract)

Malt: 20 lb. (8.2 kg) 2-row pale malt
1.5 lb. (0.68 kg) Briess Golden Light DME

Hops: 2 oz. (57 g) Waimea pellets at 17.8% alpha acid

Yeast: 40 g SAFALE US-05 (700 billion cells); use a nutrient and oxygenate as recommended.

Procedure: Mash at 148–150°F (64.4–65.6°C), mixing the grain with 24 qt. (23 L) water (ratio 1.2 qt./lb., 2.5 L/kg). At 90 minutes perform a starch-iodine test and mash a further 30 minutes if positive for starch. If the test is negative and conversion is complete, run off and collect 4.5 gallons (17 L) of wort, without sparging. The specific gravity of this wort should be about 1.090 (21.5°P). Transfer wort into boiler and stir in the DME making sure that it is all fully dissolved. Add the Waimea hops and boil for 60 minutes. Cool to about 70°F (21°C) and pitch yeast, rehydrating as instructed. Ferment 7–10 days as close to 70°F (21°C) as possible, rack to secondary for 3 weeks, rack again, and leave for 4–6 months. Serve from stainless steel soda keg or bottle, force carbonating (keg) or priming as appropriate. This beer can be drunk at this stage, although it should improve with further aging.

Projected parameters: 4.2 gallons (15.9 L) final volume
Original gravity: 1.106 (25°P)
Final gravity: 1.027 (6.8°P)
Apparent attenuation: 74.5%
Alcohol: 10.3% abv
Bitterness: 83 IBU (calculated on 13% utilization)
Color: pale yellow to gold

Notes

Standard grain mash, collecting only first runnings; you could sparge and collect wort for a lesser beer if you wished, but I opted not to do so in this case.

Comments

This demonstrates the approach of using extract to "fortify" a grain beer in order to reach a higher gravity. You could, in theory, add a greater amount of extract to reach an even higher OG, but, arguably, that could also be done using extract alone, which would be a simpler approach. You could also use a darker extract to produce a deeper-colored beer, but this recipe is specifically aimed at yielding about as pale a barley wine as you can get. It is still a beer with a lot of chewy character, with hops and alcohol nicely balancing its relatively modest sweetness. It might, in fact, be a good recipe to try if you are new to all-grain brewing and getting variable extract yields from the mash.

DARKNESS FALLS

METHOD 1 (all extract plus sugar)

Malt: 12 lb. (5.4 kg) pale malt extract
2 lb. (0.91 kg) Dark Muscovado sugar

Hops: 2 oz. (57 g) Whitbread Golding Variety at 8.5% alpha acid.

Yeast: Wyeast 1968 London ESB. You should aim to pitch 650 billion cells. As described above this would require six packets of fresh yeast. The best approach would be to prepare a starter from two packets of yeast, each in a separate vessel and doubling up twice. That means you would have to prepare the starter several days in advance of brewing. Use a nutrient as recommended and oxygenate the wort at pitching.

Procedure: Stir 12 lb. (5.4 kg) extract into 5 gallons (19 L) warm water, taking care to see that all of it is thoroughly dissolved before applying heat. Add the hops and boil for 60 minutes; turn off heat and carefully stir in 2 lb. (0.91 kg) of sugar—be sure this is fully dissolved before proceeding. Boil a further 5 minutes, cool to about 70°F (21°C), and pitch yeast. Ferment 7–10 days as close to 70°F (21°C) as possible, rack to secondary for 2 weeks, dry-hopping with the second amount of hops, rack again, and leave for 3–4 months. Serve from stainless steel soda keg or bottle, force carbonating (keg) or priming if desired (bottles). This beer will improve on further aging but can be drunk after 4 months.

Projected parameters: 4.6 gallons (17.4 L) final volume
Original gravity: 1.119 (27.8°P)
Final gravity: 1.039 (9.8°P)
Apparent attenuation: 67.2%
Alcohol: 10.4% abv
Bitterness: 42 IBU (calculated on 15% utilization)
Color: dark red-brown

Notes

Muscovado sugar seems to come in varying levels of color; the type I used was almost black.

Comments

I used a yeast which would give me a low attenuation, and kept the hop bitterness low, in order to ensure that this beer was sweeter than most of the others I have given recipes for. The reason for that is I wanted to make a beer which might look like a barley wine but could just as easily be called a 140 shilling Scotch Ale. I opted for Muscovado sugar, because I knew it would contain some unfermentable material and would add hints of molasses to this full, but sweetish beer. You could, of course, use corn sugar instead; if you did you would get a lighter-colored and somewhat drier beer, which would still have tasted sweet but without the extra complexity provided by the molasses character from the Muscovado sugar.

BREXIT BARLEY WINE

METHOD 1 (all extract plus sugar)

Malt: 3 lb. (1.4 kg) pale malt extract
6 lb. (2.7 kg) amber malt extract*
2 lb. (0.91 kg) corn sugar

Hops: 1.75 oz. (50 g) US Northern Brewer pellets at 6.5% alpha acid.

Yeast: White Labs WLP 002 English Ale yeast. You should aim to pitch 580 billion cells. As described above this would require six packets of fresh yeast. The best approach would be to prepare a starter from two packets of yeast, each in a separate vessel and doubling up twice. That means you would have to prepare the starter several days in advance of brewing. Use a nutrient as recommended and oxygenate the wort at pitching.

Procedure: Stir the two extracts into 5 gallons (19 L) warm water, taking care to see that all of it is thoroughly dissolved before applying heat. Add the hops and boil for 60 minutes; turn off heat and carefully stir in 2 lb. (0.91 kg) of corn sugar—be sure this is fully dissolved before proceeding. Boil a further 5 minutes, cool to about 70°F (21°C), and pitch yeast starter. Ferment 7–10 days as close to 70°F (21°C) as possible, rack to secondary for 2 weeks, dry-hopping with the second amount of hops, rack again, and leave for 3–4 months. Serve from stainless steel soda keg or bottle, force carbonating (keg) or priming if desired (bottles). This beer will improve on further aging but can be drunk after the first 4 months.

Projected parameters: 4.2 gallons (15.9 L) final volume
Original gravity: 1.093 (22.1°P)
Final gravity: 1.030 (7.6°P)
Apparent attenuation: 67.7%
Alcohol: 8.1% abv
Bitterness: 31 IBU (calculated on 15% utilization)
Color: red-brown

Notes

The amber malt extract I used was made with base malt, caramel and Munich malts; if your supplier does not offer something similar try to use one based on the Munich malt rather than on caramel malt only.

Comments

As in the previous example, I went for a yeast strain giving relatively low apparent attenuation. This would be offset by the use of corn sugar, making for a drier palate in the beer; in turn this would be offset by the Munich constituent of the extract, which would give the beer a more full-bodied, malty character than straight pale extract. The low hop bitterness takes it into the realm of a wee heavy Scotch ale, but it is really a little too dry in the finish for that style. So, in the end it is a beer that needs a referendum to make up its mind what it is!

HADRIAN'S CONTRABAND

METHOD 1 (all extract)

Malt: 6 lb. (2.7 kg) pale malt extract
6 lb. (2.7 kg) amber malt extract
3 lb. (141 kg) amber DME

Hops: 1.25 oz. (35 g) Admiral pellets at 15% alpha acid

Yeast: Wyeast 1728 Scottish Ale yeast. You should aim to pitch 700 billion cells. As described above this would require seven packets of fresh yeast. The best approach would be to prepare a starter from two packets of yeast, each in a separate vessel and doubling up twice. That means you would have to prepare the starter several days in advance of brewing. Use a nutrient as recommended and oxygenate the wort at pitching.

Procedure: Stir the extract syrups into 5 gallons (19 L) warm water, followed by the DME, taking care to see that all of these thoroughly dissolved before applying heat. Add the hops and boil for 60 minutes. Cool to about 70°F (21°C) and pitch yeast starter. Ferment 7–10 days as close to 70°F (21°C) as possible, rack to secondary for 2 weeks, and leave for 3–4 months. Serve from stainless steel soda keg or bottle, force carbonating (keg) or priming if desired (bottles). This beer will improve on further aging, and I would keep it for at least 6 more months.

Projected parameters: 4.5 gallons (17 L) final volume
Original gravity: 1.123 (27.6°P)
Final gravity: 1.041 (10.2°P)
Apparent attenuation: 66.7%
Alcohol: 10.7% abv
Bitterness: 37 IBU (calculated on 12% utilization)
Color: dark red-brown

Notes

The amber malt extract and DME I used were made with base malt, caramel, and Munich malts; if your supplier does not offer something similar try to use versions based on the Munich malt rather than on caramel malt only.

Comments

This is another variation on the theme of "maybe 140 shilling Scotch Ale, or English Barley Wine." But this yeast gives less apparent attenuation than the one in the previous example, and the total amount of Munich malt-based extract has been increased. The result is a sweetish, lightly-hopped brew, but very palate-filling thanks to the Munich and caramel malts. I find this a little too sweet for me to drink anything more than a one-third nip bottle, but others may find it a very satisfying brew.

STRONG-ARM TACTICS

METHOD 2 (grain mash, collect all)

Malt: 15 lb. (6.8 kg) Maris Otter pale malt
4 lb. (1.8 kg) Munich malt (10°L)
1 lb. (0.454 kg) Caramel malt (80°L)
0.5 lb. (0.227 kg) chocolate malt

Hops: 2 oz. (57 g) Magnum pellets at 14.5% alpha acid

Yeast: 46 g (1.4 oz., 4 × 11.5 g packages) SAFALE S-04. This is about 700 billion cells. Rehydrate according to instructions on packages. Use a nutrient as recommended and oxygenate when pitching.

Procedure: Mash grain at 152–154°F (66.7–67.8°C), using 25 qt. (24 L) water (ratio 1.2 qt./lb., 2.5 L/kg). At 90 minutes perform a starch-iodine test and mash a further 30 minutes if positive for starch. If the test is negative and conversion is complete, run off and sparge with water at about 170°F (77°C) to collect 6 gallons (23 L) of wort. The specific gravity of this wort should be about 1.080 (19.3°P). Bring to a boil, add the bittering hops, and boil down to 4.2 gallons (15.9 L); this took about 2 hours in my case. Cool to about 70°F (21°C) and pitch the yeast starter. Ferment 10–14 days as close to 70°F (21°C) as possible, rack to secondary for 4 weeks, rack again, and leave for 6–8 months. Serve from stainless steel soda keg or bottle, force carbonating (keg) or priming if desired (bottles), preferably allowing the beer to age a further 6 months or more. This beer should keep well for several years, and I recommend that you do that with at least a portion of it.

Projected parameters: 4.2 gallons (15.9 L) final volume
Original gravity: 1.130 (30°P)
Final gravity: 1.032 (8.1°P)
Apparent attenuation: 75.4%
Alcohol: 12.8% abv
Bitterness: 52 IBU (calculated on 10% utilization at this high specific gravity)
Color: deep red brown

Comments

This was simply meant to be a dark barley wine, but using a high mash temperature, Munich malts, and caramel malts so that the fullness of the beer is emphasized, with the dash of chocolate malt adding just a hint of roast character, and an intermediate level of hop bitterness to provide some balance to the sweetness, although the relatively low FG serves to distinguish it from a strong Scotch Ale.

SON OF CUTE FAT KID

METHOD 2 (grain mash, collect all)

Malt: 13 lb. (5.9 kg) Crisp pale malt
1.25 lb. (0.57 kg) Crystal malt (77°L)
1.25 lb. (0.57 kg) Weyermann Rye malt
1.25 lb. (0.57 kg) Vienna malt
0.6 lb. (0.27 kg) Victory malt

Hops: 2 oz. (57 g) Magnum pellets at 13.5% alpha acid

Yeast: 35 g (1.4 oz., 3 × 11.5 g packages) SAFALE S-04. This is about 600 billion cells. Rehydrate according to instructions on packages. Use a nutrient as recommended and oxygenate when pitching.

Procedure: Mash grain at 149°F (65°C), using 21 qt. (20 L) water (ratio 1.2 qt./lb., 2.5 L/kg). At 90 minutes perform a starch-iodine test and mash a further 30 minutes if positive for starch. If the test is negative and conversion is complete, run off and sparge with water at about 170°F (77°C) to collect 6 gallons (23 L) of wort. The specific gravity of this wort should be about 1.078 (18.9°P). Bring to a boil, add the bittering hops, and boil down to 5.0 gallons (15.9 L); this took about 90 minutes in my case. Cool to about 70°F (21°C) and pitch the yeast starter. Ferment 10–14 days as close to 70°F (21°C) as possible, rack to secondary for 4 weeks, rack again, and leave for 6–8 months. Serve from stainless steel soda keg or bottle, force carbonating (keg) or priming if desired (bottles), preferably allowing the beer to age a further 2–3 months.

Projected parameters: 5 gallons (19 L) final volume
Yield: 73%
Original gravity: 1.094 (22.3°P)
Final gravity: 1.020 (5.1°P)
Apparent attenuation: 78.7%
Alcohol: 9.8% abv
Bitterness: 61 IBU (calculated on 15% utilization)
Color: pale copper red

Comments

This is not my recipe, but I have calculated it down from a beer (Cute Fat Kid) produced by Jeff Browning at Brewport Brewing Co., Bridge-port, CT. Note the use of Vienna and Victory malt to boost the body of the beer, and the use of rye malt to add just a soupçon of spiciness to the finished beer. It is not the biggest of barley wines, in part due to equipment limitations, but it is a good example of the style, full bodied, nutty, chewy, with a little spice. But don't rush down to the brewpub to drink it, as it has already gone. No doubt it will be brewed again soon—check the website for the next version, which will have a different name!

YOU'RE LOOKING PALE

METHOD 3 (all-grain parti-gyle approach)

Malt: 20 lb. (9.1 kg) Premium Pilsner Malt

Hops: (i) 1 oz. (28 g) Warrior pellets at 16% alpha acid
(ii) 0.75 oz. (21 g) First Gold pellets at 7.5% alpha acid

Yeast: (i) 35 g (1.4 oz., 3 × 11.5 g packages) SAFALE US-05 Ale. This is about 600 billion cells. Rehydrate according to instructions on packages. Use a nutrient as recommended and oxygenate when pitching.

(ii) 11.5 g (1 pack) SAFALE US-05 dry yeast (about 200 billion cells)

Procedure:

(i) Mash grain at 150–152°F (65.6–66.7°C), using 24 qt. (23 L) water (ratio 1.2 qt./lb., 2.5 L/kg). At 90 minutes perform a starch-iodine test and mash a further 30 minutes if positive for starch. If test is negative for starch and conversion is complete, run off 4 gallons (15.1 L) of wort, with no sparge. That should have a specific gravity of ± 1.090 (21.5°P). Bring to a boil and add Warrior hops; boil down to 3.5 gallons (13.3 L), which should take 1 hour. Cool to about 70°F (21°C) and pitch yeast starter. Ferment 7–10 days as close to 70°F (21°C) as possible, rack to secondary for 3 weeks, rack again, and leave for 4–6 months. Serve from stainless steel soda keg or bottle, force carbonating (keg) or priming as appropriate. This beer can be drunk at this stage, although it should improve with further aging.

(ii) Sparge the residual grain from (i) above with hot water at about 170°F (77°C) to collect 4 gallons (15.1 L) of wort. Boil this for 90 minutes, or until reduced to 3.5 gallons (13.3 L) with First Gold hops added at the start. Cool to about 70°F (21°C) and pitch 11.5 g of yeast, rehydrating according to instructions on the packet. Ferment 7 days, transfer to secondary for 7 days, then keg or bottle by the usual procedures. Drink as soon as it is clear.

Projected parameters:
(i) 3.5 gallons (13.3 L) final volume
Original gravity: 1.103 (24.0°P)
Final gravity: 1.025 (6.3°P)
Apparent attenuation: 75.6%
Alcohol: 11.4% abv
Bitterness: 51 IBU (calculated on 15% utilization)
Color: deep red-brown.

(ii) 3.5 gallons (13.3 L) final volume
Original gravity: 1.045 (11.2°P)
Final gravity: 1.011 (2.8°P)
Apparent attenuation: 75.6%
Alcohol: 4.4% abv
Bitterness: 30 IBU (calculated on 25% utilization)
Color: pale gold

Notes
The aim was to brew a barley wine just as pale as possible, and this brew was just that, yet was still as mouth-filling and chewy as a barley wine should be. The second gyle was more like a table beer than a small beer, because that was what I preferred to drink. Overall extract yield was 70.3%.

Comments
The beer from the second gyle was also interesting with a nice smooth and full flavor, a good Ordinary Bitter Ale.

FADING AWAY BARLEY WINE

METHOD 1 (all malt extract)

Malt: 9 lb. (4.1 kg) Briess CBW® Pilsen Syrup
2 lb. (0.91 kg) Briess CBW® Pilsen DME

Hops: 1.5 oz. (43 g) Warrior pellets at 16.0% alpha acid

Yeast: 35 g (1.4 oz., 3 × 11.5 g packages) SAFALE US-05 Ale. This is about 600 billion cells. Rehydrate according to instructions on packages. Use a nutrient as recommended and oxygenate when pitching.

Procedure: Stir extracts into 4 gallons (15.1 L) warm water, taking care to see that all of it is thoroughly dissolved before applying heat. Add the hops and boil for 60 minutes; turn off heat, cool to about 70°F (21°C), and pitch yeast. Ferment 7–10 days as close to 70°F (21°C) as possible, rack to secondary for 2 weeks, rack again, and leave for 3–4 months. Serve from stainless steel soda keg or bottle, force carbonating (keg) or priming if desired (bottles), preferably allowing the beer to age a further 6 months or more.

Projected parameters: 3.3 gallons (12.5 L) final volume
Original gravity: 1.101 (22.8°P)
Final gravity: 1.028 (7.1°P)
Apparent attenuation: 72.3%
Alcohol: 9.7% abv
Bitterness: 55 IBU (calculated on 12% utilization)
Color: pale gold

Notes

Single addition of malt extracts for the sake of simplicity.

Comments

A match for the previous all-grain pale barley wine, but actually paler than that beer, because of the shorter boil time. But that means there was less opportunity for Maillard reactions to occur, and consequently the beer was not quite so full on the palate as its all-grain counterpart.

RED SUNSET

METHOD 2 (grain mash and boil down)

Malt: 20 lb. (9.1 kg) Briess Ashburne Mild Malt
1 lb. (0.45 kg) Weyermann Melanoidin Malt
3 lb. (1.4 kg) Briess Bonlander Munich Malt (10°L)

Hops: 2 oz. (56 g) Millennium pellets at 10% alpha acid

Yeast: White Labs WLP1968 London ESB yeast. You should aim to pitch about 800 billion cells. This is best done as a starter using two packets (or even three if you are not sure of the freshness of the yeast), starting each separately then doubling each twice. Use a nutrient as recommended and oxygenate for the main brew.

Procedure: Mash grain at 148–150°F (64.4–65.6°C), using 29 qt. (27 L) water (ratio 1.2 qt./lb., 2.5 L/kg). At 90 minutes perform a starch-iodine test and mash a further 30 minutes if positive for starch. If the test is negative and conversion is complete, run off and sparge with water at about 170°F (77°C) to collect 6 gallons (23 L) of wort at a specific gravity about ± 1.080. Bring to a boil, add the Millennium hops, and boil down to 5 gallons (19 L). Cool to about 70°F (21°C) and pitch the yeast. Ferment 10–14 days as close to 70°F (21°C) as possible, rack to secondary for 4 weeks, rack again, and leave for 6–8 months. Serve from stainless steel soda keg or bottle, force carbonating (keg) or priming if desired (bottles), preferably allowing the beer to age a further 6 months or more. This beer should keep well for several years, and I recommend that you do that with at least a portion of it.

Projected parameters: 3.5 gallons (13.3 L) final volume
Original gravity: 1.130 (30°P)
Final gravity: 1.039 (9.8°P)
Apparent attenuation: 70%
Alcohol: 11.8% abv
Bitterness: 41 IBU (calculated on 10% utilization)
Color: red-brown

Notes

Relatively low hop rates and use of Munich and Melanoidin malts in order to emphasize the malt character of this beer.

Comments

A very full palate, even somewhat sweetish, but with a distinct pale red hue, It is a beer that would age well in a used bourbon barrel.

CARDINAL'S HAT BARLEY WINE

METHOD 1 (all malt extract)

Malt: 12 lb. (5.4 kg) Briess CBW® Sparkling Amber syrup
6 lb. (2.7 kg) Munich malt extract syrup

Hops: 2 oz. (57 g) Millennium pellets at 14.0% alpha acid

Yeast: White Labs WLP1968 London ESB yeast. You should aim to pitch about 800 billion cells. This is best done as a starter using two packets (or even three if you are not sure of the freshness of the yeast), starting each separately then doubling each twice. Use a nutrient as recommended and oxygenate for the main brew.

Procedure: Stir extracts into 4 gallons (15.1 L) warm water, taking care to see that all of it is thoroughly dissolved before applying heat. Add the hops and boil for 60 minutes; turn off heat, cool to about 70°F (21°C), and pitch yeast. Ferment 7–10 days as close to 70°F (21°C) as possible, rack to secondary for 2 weeks, rack again, and leave for 3–4 months. Serve from stainless steel soda keg or bottle, force carbonating (keg) or priming if desired (bottles), preferably allowing the beer to age a further 6 months or more.

Projected parameters: 5 gallons (19 L) final volume
Original gravity: 1.126 (29.1°P)
Final gravity: 1.040 (7.1°P)
Apparent attenuation: 68.3%
Alcohol: 11.2% abv
Bitterness: 41 IBU (calculated on 10% utilization)
Color: pale gold

Notes

An extract version of the previous all-grain beer—not a very precise match since no melanoidin malt was used as I wanted to keep this brew easy to do.

Comments

This beer has a little less mouthfeel than the all-grain version, but is still a good chewy, warming drink.

EASY WRITER BARLEY WINE

METHOD 2 (grain mash and boil down)

Malt: 11 lb. (5.0 kg) Crisp Floor-malted Maris Otter Malt
1 lb. (0.45 kg) Briess Victory® Malt
0.25 lb. (0.11 kg) Simpson's Chocolate Malt

Hops: 2 oz. (56 g) Magnum pellets at 12% alpha acid

Yeast: Wyeast 1098 British Ale yeast. You should aim to pitch about 400 billion cells. This is best done as a starter using two packets, starting each separately then doubling each twice. Use a nutrient as recommended and oxygenate for the main brew.

Procedure: Mash grain at 148-150°F (64.4-65.6°C), using 15 qt. (14 L) water (ratio 1.2 qt./lb., 2.5 L/kg). At 90 minutes perform a starch-iodine test and mash a further 30 minutes if positive for starch. If the test is negative and conversion is complete, run off and sparge with water at about 170°F (77°C) to collect 6 gallons (23 L) of wort at a specific gravity about ± 1.050 (12.4°P). Bring to a boil, add the Magnum hops, and boil down to 3.5 gallons (13.3 L). Cool to about 70°F (21°C) and pitch the yeast. Ferment 10–14 days as close to 70°F (21°C) as possible, rack to secondary for 4 weeks, rack again, and leave for 6–8 months. Serve from stainless steel soda keg or bottle, force carbonating (keg) or priming if desired (bottles), preferably allowing the beer to age a further 6 months or so.

Projected parameters: 3.5 gallons (13.3 L) final volume
Original gravity: 1.088 (21.2°P)
Final gravity: 1.022 (5.6°P)
Apparent attenuation: 75%
Alcohol: 8.7% abv
Bitterness: 77 IBU (calculated on 10% utilization)
Color: dark brown, hints of red

Notes

Can be regarded as an American-style barley wine.

Comments

Definite bitterness from this beer, with hints of roast malt and biscuit.

BISHOP'S AMBITION BARLEY WINE

METHOD I (malt extract plus steeping)

Malt: 6 lb. (2.7 kg) Maris Otter malt syrup
1.7 lb. (0.77 kg) Amber DME
1 lb. (0.45 kg) Briess Victory® Malt
0.25 lb. (0.11 kg) Simpson's Chocolate malt

Hops: 1.5 oz. (57 g) Magnum pellets at 12.0% alpha acid

Yeast: Wyeast 1098 British Ale yeast. You should aim to pitch about 400 billion cells. This is best done as a starter using two packets, starting each separately then doubling each twice. Use a nutrient as recommended and oxygenate for the main brew.

Procedure: Steep the grains (using a muslin bag) in 1.5 qt. (1.4 L) water at about 160°F (71°C) for 30–45 minutes. Remove the liquid to the boiling pot, and rinse the grain in the bag twice, using 2 qt. (1.9 L) hot water. Collect the washings in the boil pot, stir in the DME and 3 lb. (1.4 kg) of the Maris Otter extract, adding warm water to a total volume of 4 gallons (15.1 L). Add the hops and boil for 60 minutes; turn off heat and carefully stir in 3 lb. (1.4 kg) of Maris Otter extract. Boil a further 20 minutes, cool to about 70°F (21°C), and pitch yeast. Ferment 7–10 days as close to 70°F (21°C) as possible, rack to secondary for 2 weeks, rack again, and leave for 3–4 months. Serve from stainless steel soda keg or bottle, force carbonating (keg) or priming if desired (bottles), preferably allowing the beer to age a further 6 months or more.

Projected parameters: 3.5 gallons (13.3 L) final volume
Original gravity: 1.088 (21.2°P)
Final gravity: 1.029 (7.3°P)
Apparent attenuation: 67%
Alcohol: 7.8% abv
Bitterness: 77 IBU (calculated on 20% utilization)
Color: deep brown with a red hue

Notes

An extract version of the previous all-grain beer.

Comments

As with the all-grain version, definite bitterness from this beer, with hints of roast malt and biscuit. Relatively light in alcohol but still a satisfying drink.

TIGER'S BACK BARLEY WINE

METHOD 2 (grain mash and boil down)

Malt: 8 lb. (3.6 kg) Briess Ashburne Mild Malt
11 lb. (5 kg) US 2-row Pale Malt
1 lb. (0.45 kg) Belgian Biscuit Malt

Hops: 1.75 oz. (50 g) Newport pellets at 15% alpha acid

Yeast: GIGA Yeast GY001 NorCal yeast. You should aim to pitch about 700 billion cells. This is best done as a starter using two packets, starting each separately then doubling each twice. Use a nutrient as recommended and oxygenate for the main brew.

Procedure: Mash grain at 148–150°F (64.4–65.6°C), using 24 qt. (23 L) water (ratio 1.2 qt./lb., 2.5 L/kg). At 90 minutes perform a starch-iodine test and mash a further 30 minutes if positive for starch. If the test is negative and conversion is complete, run off and sparge with water at about 170°F (77°C) to collect 6 gallons (23 L) of wort at a specific gravity about ± 1.090 (21.5°P). Bring to a boil, add the Newport hops, and boil down to 4 gallons (15.1 L). Cool to about 70°F (21°C) and pitch the yeast. Ferment 10–14 days as close to 70°F (21°C) as possible, rack to secondary for 4 weeks, rack again, and leave for 6–8 months. Serve from stainless steel soda keg or bottle, force carbonating (keg) or priming if desired (bottles), preferably allowing the beer to age a further 6 months or more. This beer should keep well for several years, and I recommend that you do that with at least a portion of it.

Projected parameters: 4 gallons (13.5 L) final volume
Original gravity: 1.139 (32.0°P)
Final gravity: 1.027 (6.8°P)
Apparent attenuation: 80.6%
Alcohol: 14.7% abv
Bitterness: 50 IBU (calculated on 10% utilization)
Color: red-gold

Notes

In the range of a British style barley wine, with a modest level of bittering.

Comments

Full-bodied, very malty, backed up by bready/biscuit flavors. Should barrel-age well.

MASTER'S BARLEY WINE

METHOD 1 (malt extract plus steeping)

Malt: 15 lb. (6.8 kg) Munich malt extract syrup
1 lb. (0.45 kg) Belgian Biscuit malt

Hops: 1 oz. (28 g) Newport pellets at 15.0% alpha acid

Yeast: GIGA Yeast GY001 NorCal yeast. You should aim to pitch about 700 billion cells. This is best done as a starter using two packets, starting each separately then doubling each twice. Use a nutrient as recommended and oxygenate for the main brew.

Procedure: Steep the grain (using a muslin bag) in 1.5 qt. (1.4 L) water at about 160°F (71°C) for 30–45 minutes. Remove the liquid to the boil pot, and rinse the grain in the bag twice, using 2 qt. (1.9 L) hot water. Collect the washings in the boil pot, stir in 9 lb. (4.1 kg) of the Munich extract, adding warm water to a total volume of 4.5 gallons (17 L). Add the hops and boil for 60 minutes; turn off heat, carefully stir in 6 lb. (2.7 kg) of the Munich extract. Boil a further 20 minutes, cool to about 70°F (21°C), and pitch yeast. Ferment 7–10 days as close to 70°F (21°C) as possible, rack to secondary for 2 weeks, rack again, and leave for 3–4 months. Serve from stainless steel soda keg or bottle, force carbonating (keg) or priming if desired (bottles), preferably allowing the beer to age a further 6 months or more.

Projected parameters: 4 gallons (15.1 L) final volume
Original gravity: 1.137 (31.5°P)
Final gravity: 1.031 (7.8°P)
Apparent attenuation: 77.3%
Alcohol: 13.9% abv
Bitterness: 56 IBU (calculated on 20% utilization)
Color: gold-brown

Notes

A sort of extract version of the previous all-grain beer, not quite a match because of using Munich extract instead of the Mild malt.

Comments

A "big" mouth-filling beer with a little biscuit complexity.

RED ROBIN BARLEY WINE

METHOD 2 (grain mash and boil down)

Malt: 10 lb. (4.5 kg) Maris Otter Malt
1.5 lb. (0.68 kg) Weyermann CaraAmber Malt
1.5 lb. (0.68 kg) Caramel 60°L Malt

Hops: 1.5 oz. (43 g) Admiral pellets at 16% alpha acid

Yeast: SAFALE S-04 English Ale yeast, 40 g, about 700 billion cells. Rehydrate according to instructions on package. Use a nutrient as recommended and oxygenate when pitching.

Procedure: Mash grain at 148–150°F (64.4–65.6°C), using 24 qt. (23 L) water (ratio 1.2 qt./lb., 2.5 L/kg). At 90 minutes perform a starch-iodine test and mash a further 30 minutes if positive for starch. If the test is negative and conversion is complete, run off and sparge with water at about 170°F (77°C) to collect 6 gallons (23 L) of wort at a specific gravity about ± 1.060 (14.7°P). Bring to a boil, add the Admiral hops, and boil down to 3 gallons (11.4 L). Cool to about 70°F (21°C) and pitch the yeast. Ferment 10–14 days as close to 70°F (21°C) as possible, rack to secondary for 4 weeks, rack again, and leave for 6–8 months. Serve from stainless steel soda keg or bottle, force carbonating (keg) or priming if desired (bottles), preferably allowing the beer to age a further 6 months or more.

Projected parameters: 3 gallons (11.4 L) final volume
Original gravity: 1.115 (26.9°P)
Final gravity: 1.022 (5.6°P)
Apparent attenuation: 80.1%
Alcohol: 12.2% abv
Bitterness: 72 IBU (calculated on 12% utilization)
Color: red to amber

Notes
Showcasing caramel-type malts in a barley wine.

Comments
A standard barley wine with some added nutty, toffee flavors.

REDTOP BARLEY WINE

METHOD I (malt extract plus steeping)

Malt: 12 lb. (5.4 kg) Maris Otter malt extract syrup
1.5 lb. (0.68 kg) Weyermann CaraAmber Malt
1.5 lb. (0.68 kg) Caramel 60°L Malt

Hops: 1.5 oz. (43 g) Admiral pellets at 16% alpha acid

Yeast: SAFALE S-04 English Ale yeast, 40 g, about 700 billion cells. Rehydrate according to instructions on package. Use a nutrient as recommended and oxygenate when pitching.

Procedure: Steep the grains (using a muslin bag) in 1.5 qt. (1.4 L) water at about 160°F (71°C) for 30–45 minutes. Remove the liquid to the boiling pot, and rinse the grain in the bag twice, using 2 qt. (1.9 L) hot water. Collect the washings in the boiling pot, stir in the Maris Otter extract, adding warm water to a total volume of 4.5 gallons (17 L). Add the hops and boil for 60 minutes; turn off heat, cool to about 70°F (21°C), and pitch yeast. Ferment 7–10 days as close to 70°F (21°C) as possible, rack to secondary for 2 weeks, rack again, and leave for 3–4 months. Serve from stainless steel soda keg or bottle, force carbonating (keg) or priming if desired (bottles), preferably allowing the beer to age a further 6 months or more.

Projected parameters: 4.2 gallons (15.9 L) final volume
Original gravity: 1.115 (27.9°P)
Final gravity: 1.031 (7.8°P)
Apparent attenuation: 75.7%
Alcohol: 11.5% abv
Bitterness: 72 IBU (calculated on 12% utilization)
Color: red-amber

Notes

An extract match for "Red Robin."

Comments

As expected, good body with some added nuttiness.

WRY SMILE BARLEY WINE

METHOD 2 (grain mash and boil down)

Malt: 10 lb. (4.5 kg) US 2-row pale malt
1.5 lb. (0.68 kg) Weyermann CaraAmber Malt
1.5 lb. (0.68 kg) Fawcett Crystal Rye Malt

Hops: 1 oz. (28 g) Magnum pellets at 12% alpha acid

Yeast: White Labs WLP 007 Dry English Ale yeast. You should aim to pitch about 700 billion cells. This is best done as a starter using two packets, starting each separately then doubling each twice. Use a nutrient as recommended and oxygenate for the main brew.

Procedure: Mash grain at 148–150°F (64.4–65.6°C), using 16 qt. (15.1 L) water (ratio 1.2 qt./lb., 2.5 L/kg). At 90 minutes perform a starch-iodine test and mash a further 30 minutes if positive for starch. If the test is negative and conversion is complete, run off and sparge with water at about 170°F (77°C) to collect 6 gallons (23 L) of wort at a specific gravity about ± 1.060 (14.7°P). Bring to a boil, add the Magnum hops, and boil down to 3.5 gallons (13.3 L). Cool to about 70°F (21°C) and pitch the yeast. Ferment 10–14 days as close to 70°F (21°C) as possible, rack to secondary for 4 weeks, rack again, and leave for 6–8 months. Serve from stainless steel soda keg or bottle, force carbonating (keg) or priming if desired (bottles), preferably allowing the beer to age a further 6 months or more.

Projected parameters: 4 gallons (15.1 L) final volume
Original gravity: 1.100 (23.8°P)
Final gravity: 1.025 (6.3°P)
Apparent attenuation: 75.0%
Alcohol: 10.0% abv
Bitterness: 72 IBU (calculated on 12% utilization)
Color: amber with a pale red tinge

Notes

A relatively modest barley wine, but with the unusual addition of rye crystal malt.

Comments

A standard barley wine with some added nutty, toffee flavors from the caramel malt and hints of the characteristic rye "spicy" flavor.

TRY RYE BARLEY WINE

METHOD 1 (malt extract plus steeping)

Malt: 9 lb. (4.1 kg) Amber malt extract syrup
1.5 lb. (0.68 kg) Fawcett Crystal Rye Malt

Hops: 0.75 oz. (21 g) Magnum pellets at 12% alpha acid

Yeast: White Labs WLP 007 Dry English Ale yeast. You should aim to pitch about 700 billion cells. This is best done as a starter using two packets, starting each separately then doubling each twice. Use a nutrient as recommended and oxygenate for the main brew.

Procedure: Steep the grain (using a muslin bag) in 2 qt. (2 L) water at about 160°F (71°C) for 30-45 minutes. Remove the liquid to the boil pot, and rinse the grain in the bag twice, using 2 qt. (1.9 L) hot water. Collect the washings in the boil pot, stir in the Amber extract, adding warm water to a total volume of 4 gallons (15.1 L). Add the hops and boil for 60 minutes; turn off heat, cool to about 70°F (21°C), and pitch yeast. Ferment 7–10 days as close to 70°F (21°C) as possible, rack to secondary for 2 weeks, rack again, and leave for 3–4 months. Serve from stainless steel soda keg or bottle, force carbonating (keg) or priming if desired (bottles), preferably allowing the beer to age a further 6 months or more.

Projected parameters: 3.5 gallons (13.3 L) final volume
Original gravity: 1.100 (23.8°P)
Final gravity: 1.029 (7.3°P)
Apparent attenuation: 71%
Alcohol: 9.4% abv
Bitterness: 72 IBU (calculated on 12% utilization)
Color: dark red-brown

Notes

A showcase for rye flavor in a barley wine

Comments

Lower in caramel flavors than "Wry Smile," but the rye character comes through a little more strongly than in that beer.

BEAUTY BARLEY WINE

METHOD 2 (grain mash and boil down)

Malt: 7 lb. (3.2 kg) Great Western American Pale Malt
5 lb. (2.3 kg) Briess Goldpils® Vienna Malt
1 lb. (0.45 kg) Dingeman Special B Malt
1 lb. (0.45 kg) Weyermann Melanoidin Malt

Hops: 1 oz. (28 g) Apollo pellets at 18% alpha acid

Yeast: Lallemand Nottingham Ale yeast, 33 g, about 600 billion cells. Rehydrate according to instructions on package. Use a nutrient as recommended and oxygenate when pitching.

Procedure: Mash grain at 148–150°F (64.4–65.6°C), using 24 qt. (23 L) water (ratio 1.2 qt./lb., 2.5 L/kg). At 90 minutes perform a starch-iodine test and mash a further 30 minutes if positive for starch. If the test is negative and conversion is complete, run off and sparge with water at about 170°F (77°C) to collect 6 gallons (23 L) of wort at a specific gravity about ± 1.060 (14.7°P). Bring to a boil, add the Apollo hops, and boil down to 4 gallons (15.1 L). Cool to about 70°F (21°C) and pitch the yeast. Ferment 10–14 days as close to 70°F (21°C) as possible, rack to secondary for 4 weeks, rack again, and leave for 6–8 months. Serve from stainless steel soda keg or bottle, force carbonating (keg) or priming if desired (bottles), preferably allowing the beer to age a further 6 months or more.

Projected parameters: 4 gallons (15.1 L) final volume
Original gravity: 1.095 (22.6°P)
Final gravity: 1.020 (5.1°P)
Apparent attenuation: 78.9%
Alcohol: 10.0% abv
Bitterness: 50 IBU (calculated on 15% utilization)
Color: deep red-brown

Notes

This uses Apollo, one of the newer high alpha acid hops, as well as a trio of specialty malts.

Comments

This beer is modest in alcohol but full of biscuit, bready malt flavors, with counterpoint from the hop bitterness.

UNITED NATIONS BARLEY WINE

METHOD 1 (malt extract plus partial mashing)

Malt: 9 lb. (4.1 kg) Golden Light malt extract syrup
1 lb. (0.45 kg) Pale 2-row Malt
1 lb. (0.45 kg) Dingeman Special B Malt
1 lb. Weyermann Melanoidin Malt

Hops: 1 oz. (28 g) Apollo pellets at 18% alpha acid

Yeast: Lallemand Nottingham Ale yeast, 33 g, about 600 billion cells. Rehydrate according to instructions on package. Use a nutrient as recommended and oxygenate when pitching.

Procedure: Mash the grains (using a muslin bag) in 4 qt. (3.8 L) water at about 150°F (65.6°C) for 45 minutes. Remove the liquid to the boil pot, and rinse the grain in the bag twice, using 2 qt. (1.9 L) hot water. Collect the washings in the boil pot, stir in the Golden Light extract, adding warm water as necessary to a total volume of 4.5 gallons (17 L). Add the hops and boil for 60 minutes; turn off heat, cool to about 70°F (21°C), and pitch yeast. Ferment 7–10 days as close to 70°F (21°C) as possible, rack to secondary for 2 weeks, rack again, and leave for 3–4 months. Serve from stainless steel soda keg or bottle, force carbonating (keg) or priming if desired (bottles), preferably allowing the beer to age a further 6 months or more.

Projected parameters: 4 gallons (15.1 L) final volume
Original gravity: 1.095 (22.6°P)
Final gravity: 1.025 (6.3°P)
Apparent attenuation: 73.6%
Alcohol: 9.3% abv
Bitterness: 50 IBU (calculated on 15% utilization)
Color: red-brown

Notes

Needs a partial mash with added 2-row malt because the melanoidin malt contains some starch.

Comments

Remarkably like the "soul food" flavors of the previous brew.

GOT 'EM? SMOKE 'EM!

METHOD 2 (grain mash and boil down)

Malt: 6.5 lb. (3 kg) Great Western American Pale Malt
6 lb. (2.7 kg) Briess Goldpils® Vienna Malt
1 lb. (0.45 kg) Caramel Malt (120°L)
0.5 lb. (0.23 kg) Briess Cherrywood Smoked Malt

Hops: 1.3 oz. (37 g) Summit pellets at 17% alpha acid

Yeast: White Labs WLP 1084 Irish Ale yeast. You should aim to pitch about 600 billion cells. This is best done as a starter using two packets, starting each separately then doubling each twice. Use a nutrient as recommended and oxygenate when pitching.

Procedure: Mash grain at 148–150°F (64.4–65.6°C), using 17 qt. (16 L) water (ratio 1.2 qt./lb., 2.5 L/kg). At 90 minutes perform a starch-iodine test and mash a further 30 minutes if positive for starch. If the test is negative and conversion is complete, run off and sparge with water at about 170°F (77°C) to collect 6 gallons (23 L) of wort at a specific gravity about ± 1.060 (14.7°P). Bring to a boil, add the Summit hops, and boil down to 4.5 gallons (17 L). Cool to about 70°F (21°C) and pitch the yeast. Ferment 10–14 days as close to 70°F (21°C) as possible, rack to secondary for 4 weeks, rack again, and leave for 6–8 months. Serve from stainless steel soda keg or bottle, force carbonating (keg) or priming if desired (bottles), preferably allowing the beer to age a further 6 months or more.

Projected parameters: 4.5 gallons (17 L) final volume
Original gravity: 1.085 (20.3°P)
Final gravity: 1.023 (5.8°P)
Apparent attenuation: 73.0%
Alcohol: 8.2% abv
Bitterness: 55 IBU (calculated on 15% utilization)
Color: deep red-gold

Notes

This introduces smoked character in the barley wine family—but see under Scotch ales.

Comments

Quite a light barley wine, but full-flavored enough to nicely balance its gentle smoky character.

SMOKY THE BEARLEY WINE

METHOD 1 (malt extract plus partial mashing)

Malt: 9 lb. (4.1 kg) Rye malt extract syrup
0.8 lb. (0.36 kg) Amber DME
1 lb. (0.45 kg) Pale 2-row Malt
0.5 lb. (0.23 kg) Briess Cherrywood smoked Malt.

Hops: 0.75 oz. (21 g) Summit pellets at 17% alpha acid

Yeast: White Labs WLP 1084 Irish Ale yeast. You should aim to pitch about 600 billion cells. This is best done as a starter using two packets, starting each separately then doubling each twice. Use a nutrient as recommended and oxygenate when pitching.

Procedure: Mash the grains (using a muslin bag) in 4 qt. (3.8 L) water at about 150°F (65.6°C) for 45 minutes. Remove the liquid to the boil pot, and rinse the grain in the bag twice, using 2 qt. (1.9 L) hot water. Collect the washings in the boil pot, stir in the DME and 4 lb. (1.8kg) of the rye malt extract, adding warm water as necessary to a total volume of 5 gallons (19 L). Add the hops and boil for 60 minutes; turn off heat, stir in the remainder of the rye extract (with care and protection!), cool to about 70°F (21°C), and pitch yeast. Ferment 7–10 days as close to 70°F (21°C) as possible, rack to secondary for 2 weeks, rack again, and leave for 3–4 months. Serve from stainless steel soda keg or bottle, force carbonating (keg) or priming if desired (bottles), preferably allowing the beer to age a further 6 months or more.

Projected parameters: 4.5 gallons (17 L) final volume
Original gravity: 1.086 (20.4°P)
Final gravity: 1.026 (6.6°P)
Apparent attenuation: 70.0%
Alcohol: 7.9% abv
Bitterness: 53 IBU (calculated on 25% utilization)
Color: red-brown

Notes

I assumed that this smoked malt needed to be mashed rather than just steeped, since it has significant diastatic power. Note that the rye malt extract is made from 25% rye malt, base malt, and some 40°L caramel malt.

Comments

This does not match the previous brew, although similar to it in OG. It has typical rye spiciness blending with smoke flavor as well as "normal" barley wine character. I kept the smoke flavor down but you can use more of the smoked malt if you want to accentuate this flavor—Briess says "up to 60% of the grist" but I consider that to be excessive.

BIG BOY BARLEY WINE

METHOD 2 (grain mash but plus extract)

Malt: 14 lb. (6.4 kg) Great Western American Pale Malt
   3 lb. (1.4 kg) Golden Light Malt extract syrup

Hops: 2.25 oz. (64 g) Summit pellets at 18% alpha acid

Yeast: SAFALE S-04 Ale yeast, 55 g, about 1,000 billion cells. Rehydrate according to instructions on package. Use a nutrient as recommended and oxygenate when pitching.

Procedure: Mash grain at 148–150°F (64.4–65.6°C), using 21 qt. (20 L) water (ratio 1.2 qt./lb., 2.5 L/kg). At 90 minutes perform a starch-iodine test and mash a further 30 minutes if positive for starch. If the test is negative and conversion is complete, run off and sparge with water at about 170°F (77°C) to collect 6 gallons (23 L) of wort at a specific gravity about ± 1.060 (14.7°P). Dissolve the malt extract syrup in this, stirring very thoroughly. Bring to a boil, add the Summit hops, and boil down to 3 gallons (11.4 L). Cool to about 70°F (21°C) and pitch the yeast. Ferment 10–14 days as close to 70°F (21°C) as possible, rack to secondary for 4 weeks, rack again, and leave for 6–8 months. Serve from stainless steel soda keg or bottle, force carbonating (keg) or priming if desired (bottles), preferably allowing the beer to age a further 6 months or more.

Projected parameters: 3 gallons (11.4 L) final volume
Original gravity: 1.156 (35.3°P)
Final gravity: 1.040 (10°P)
Apparent attenuation: 74.4.0%
Alcohol: 15.3% abv
Bitterness: 100 IBU (calculated on 10% utilization)
Color: deep dark red

Notes

I had to finish the "standard" barley wine section with two very big beers. You might need to add a champagne yeast at racking in order to get the desired attenuation.

Comments

A real sipping and savoring beer, one which will benefit from long maturation. It is well-suited to barrel-aging if that's to your taste; for my money, it does not need any extra flavor that a used spirit barrel might add.

ADULTS ONLY BARLEY WINE

METHOD 1 (all malt extract)

Malt: 12 lb. (5.4 kg) Briess CBW® Golden Light Malt extract syrup
1 lb. (0.45 kg) Golden Light DME

Hops: 2.25 oz. (64 g) Summit pellets at 18% alpha acid

Yeast: SAFALE S-04 Ale yeast, 55 g, about 1,000 billion cells. Rehydrate according to instructions on package. Use a nutrient as recommended and oxygenate when pitching.

Procedure: Stir extracts into 2 gallons (7.6 L) warm water, taking care to see that all of it is thoroughly dissolved, then make to 3.5 gallons (13.2 L). Add the hops and boil for 60 minutes; turn off heat, cool to about 70°F (21°C), and pitch yeast. Ferment 7–10 days as close to 70°F (21°C) as possible, rack to secondary for 2 weeks, rack again, and leave for 3–4 months. Serve from stainless steel soda keg or bottle, force carbonating (keg) or priming if desired (bottles), preferably allowing the beer to age a further 6 months or more.

Projected parameters: 3 gallons (11.4 L) final volume
Original gravity: 1.155 (35°P)
Final gravity: 1.042 (10.5°P)
Apparent attenuation: 72.9.3%
Alcohol: 14.8% abv
Bitterness: 100 IBU (calculated on 10% utilization)
Color: Deep red

Notes

You might need to add a champagne yeast at racking in order to get the desired attenuation.

Comments

Keep it till your first child is twenty-one, barrel age it if you wish, but when you drink it do give it the respect it deserves.

One of Connecticut's more venerable craft brewers in Amity.

VARIATIONS ON THE THEME

BURTON ALE?

METHOD 2 (grain mash and boil down)

Malt: 13 lb. (5.9 kg) Briess Ashburne® Mild Malt

Hops: 2 oz. (57 g) UK Goldings pellets at 4.5% alpha acid

Yeast: White Labs WLP 023 Burton Ale yeast. You should aim to pitch about 600 billion cells. This is best done as a starter using two packets, starting each separately then doubling each twice. Use a nutrient as recommended and oxygenate when pitching.

Procedure: Mash grain at 150–152°F (65.6-66.7°C), using 16 qt. (15.1 L) water (ratio 1.2 qt./lb., 2.5 L/kg). At 90 minutes perform a starch-iodine test and mash a further 30 minutes if positive for starch. If the test is negative and conversion is complete, run off and sparge with water at about 170°F (77°C) to collect 6 gallons (23 L) of wort at a specific gravity about ± 1.060 (14.7°P). Bring to a boil, add the Goldings hops, and boil down to 3.5 gallons (13.2 L); the boil should last at least 3–4 hours, topping up with water if necessary. Cool to about 70°F (21°C) and pitch the yeast. Ferment 10–14 days as close to 70°F (21°C) as possible, rack to secondary for 4 weeks, rack again, and leave for 6–8 months. Serve from stainless steel soda keg or bottle, force carbonating (keg) or priming if desired (bottles), preferably allowing the beer to age a further 6 months or more.

Projected parameters: 3.5 gallons (13.2 L) final volume
Original gravity: 1.104 (24.5°P)
Final gravity: 1.030 (7.6°P)
Apparent attenuation: 71.1%
Alcohol: 9.8% abv
Bitterness: 29 IBU (calculated on 15% utilization)
Color: deep red-brown

Notes

I used Mild Malt instead of pale malt, because modern versions of the latter are probably paler than was the case in the late nineteenth century. The long boil was designed to give a high level of Maillard reaction products, since it seems those early Burton ales were boiled for several hours.

Comments

This was just a guess as to what nineteenth-century Burton ales might have been like, but it is certainly a good fruity, chewy, toffee-flavored barley wine.

TRUE MAN'S BURTON ALE

METHOD 1 (all malt extract)

Malt: 12 lb. (5.4 kg) Golden Light malt extract syrup

Hops: 2 oz. (57 g) UK Goldings pellets at 4.5% alpha acid

Yeast: White Labs WLP 023 Burton Ale yeast. You should aim to pitch about 600 billion cells. This is best done as a starter using two packets, starting each separately then doubling each twice. Use a nutrient as recommended and oxygenate when pitching.

Procedure: Dissolve the extract in warm water and make to 4.5–5 gallons (17–19 L). Add the hops and boil for at least 3 hours; turn off heat, cool to about 70°F (21°C), and pitch yeast. Ferment 7–10 days as close to 70°F (21°C) as possible, rack to secondary for 2 weeks, rack again, and leave for 3–4 months. Serve from stainless steel soda keg or bottle, force carbonating (keg) or priming if desired (bottles), preferably allowing the beer to age a further 6 months or more.

Projected parameters: 4.5 gallons (17 L) final volume
Original gravity: 1.105 (24.8°P)
Final gravity: 1.033 (8.3°P)
Apparent attenuation: 68.6%
Alcohol: 9.6% abv
Bitterness: 29 IBU (calculated on 15% utilization)
Color: dark red-gold

Notes

Note the long boil as for the all-grain version to intensify the "savory" flavors of Maillard reaction products.

Comments

I used a straightforward pale malt extract, because those nineteenth-century Burton ales probably used only pale malt, with no added crystal malt. This was a little thinner in taste than the all-grain version, but still with good body and mouthfeel.

GONE FOR A BURTON ALE

METHOD 2 (grain mash and boil down)

Malt: 11 lb. (5 kg) Maris Otter Pale Malt
1.5 lb. (0.68 kg) Weyermann® CaraAmber Malt
0.5 lb. (0.23 kg) Fawcett Pale Chocolate Malt

Hops: 1 oz. (28 g) First Gold pellets at 7.5% alpha acid

Yeast: White Labs WLP 023 Burton Ale yeast. You should aim to pitch about 600 billion cells. This is best done as a starter using two packets, starting each separately then doubling each twice. Use a nutrient as recommended and oxygenate when pitching.

Procedure: Mash grain at 150–152°F (65.6–66.7°C), using 16 qt. (15.1 L) water (ratio 1.2 qt./lb., 2.5 L/kg). At 90 minutes perform a starch-iodine test and mash a further 30 minutes if positive for starch. If the test is negative and conversion is complete, run off and sparge with water at about 170°F (77°C) to collect 6 gallons (23 L) of wort at a specific gravity about ± 1.060 (14.7°P). Bring to a boil, add the First Gold hops, and boil down to 3.5 gallons (13.2 L). Cool to about 70°F (21°C) and pitch the yeast. Ferment 10–14 days as close to 70°F (21°C) as possible, rack to secondary for 4 weeks, rack again, and leave for 6–8 months. Serve from stainless steel soda keg or bottle, force carbonating (keg) or priming if desired (bottles), preferably allowing the beer to age a further 6 months or more.

Projected parameters: 3.5 gallons (13.2 L) final volume
Original gravity: 1.101 (23.9°P)
Final gravity: 1.027 (6.8°P)
Apparent attenuation: 73.3%
Alcohol: 9.8% abv
Bitterness: 24 IBU (calculated on 25% utilization)
Color: dark red

Notes

No excessively long boil, with caramel and chocolate malts to give toasted and roasted character to the beer.

Comments

A modern-style version of this beer, with raisin-like, toffee, and fruity ester flavors. The specialty malts give the beer some German and West Yorkshire character!

GONE FOR ANOTHER BURTON

METHOD 1 (malt extract plus steeping)

Malt: 9 lb. (4.1 kg) Amber malt extract syrup
1.5 lb.(0.68 kg) Weyermann® CaraAmber Malt
0.5 lb. (0.23 kg) Fawcett Pale Chocolate Malt

Hops: 1 oz. (28 g) First Gold pellets at 7.5% alpha acid

Yeast: White Labs WLP 023 Burton Ale yeast. You should aim to pitch about 600 billion cells. This is best done as a starter using two packets, starting each separately then doubling each twice. Use a nutrient as recommended and oxygenate when pitching.

Procedure: Steep the grain (using a muslin bag) in 2 qt. (2 L) water at about 160°F (71°C) for 30–45 minutes. Remove the liquid to the boiling pot, and rinse the grain in the bag twice, using 2 qt. (1.9 L) hot water. Collect the washings in the boiling pot, stir in the Amber extract, adding warm water to a total volume of 4 gallons (15.1 L). Add the hops and boil for 60 minutes; turn off heat, cool to about 70°F (21°C), and pitch yeast. Ferment 7–10 days as close to 70°F (21°C) as possible, rack to secondary for 2 weeks, rack again, and leave for 3–4 months. Serve from stainless steel soda keg or bottle, force carbonating (keg) or priming if desired (bottles), preferably allowing the beer to age a further 6 months or more.

Projected parameters: 3.5 gallons (13.2 L) final volume
Original gravity: 1.103 (24.4°P)
Final gravity: 1.028 (7.1°P)
Apparent attenuation: 72.8%
Alcohol: 10.0% abv
Bitterness: 24 IBU (calculated on 15% utilization)
Color: Deep red-brown

Notes

More or less a match of the previous brew; the use of Amber malt extract, rather than Golden Light extract as in Adults Only Barley Wine (page 221), may well give a flavor more like Burton ale might have been in the 1890s.

Comments

All the expected barley wine characteristics are here, with some added ester character from the yeast; very satisfying.

ARCTIC ALE?

METHOD 2 (grain mash and boil down)

Malt: 15 lb. (6.8 kg) Briess Ashburne® Mild Malt
2.5 lb. (1.1 kg) Crisp Brown Malt

Hops: 1 oz. (28 g) Admiral pellets at 15% alpha acid

Yeast: White Labs WLP 023 Burton Ale yeast. You should aim to pitch about 800 billion cells. This is best done as a starter using two packets, starting each separately then doubling each twice. Use a nutrient as recommended and oxygenate when pitching.

Procedure: Mash grain at 150–152°F (65.6–66.7°C), using 21 qt. (20 L) water (ratio 1.2 qt./lb., 2.5 L/kg). At 90 minutes perform a starch-iodine test and mash a further 30 minutes if positive for starch. If the test is negative and conversion is complete, run off and sparge with water at about 170°F (77°C) to collect 6 gallons (23 L) of wort at a specific gravity about ± 1.080 (19.3°P). Bring to a boil, add the Admiral hops, and boil down to 3.5 gallons (13.2 L). Cool to about 70°F (21°C) and pitch the yeast. Ferment 10–14 days as close to 70°F (21°C) as possible, rack to secondary for 4 weeks, rack again, and leave for 6–8 months. Serve from stainless steel soda keg or bottle, force carbonating (keg) or priming if desired (bottles), preferably allowing the beer to age a further 6 months or more.

Projected parameters: 3.5 gallons (13.2 L) final volume
Original gravity: 1.131 (30.2°P)
Final gravity: 1.031 (7.8°P)
Apparent attenuation: 76.3%
Alcohol: 13.1% abv
Bitterness: 39 IBU (calculated on 12% utilization)
Color: Dark brown with red tinges

Notes

If they used anything other than pale malt for Arctic Ale, then it might well have been brown malt.

Comments

A stronger version of the Burton ales above, more mouth-filling, still fruity with caramel notes, but also with a hint of licorice from the brown malt.

UNLIKELY ARCTIC ALE

METHOD 1 (all malt extract)

Malt: 12 lb. (5.4 kg) Amber malt extract syrup
1 lb. (0.45 kg) Amber DME

Hops: 1 oz. (28 g) UK Admiral pellets at 15% alpha acid

Yeast: White Labs WLP 023 Burton Ale yeast. You should aim to pitch about 800 billion cells. This is best done as a starter using two packets, starting each separately then doubling each twice. Use a nutrient as recommended and oxygenate when pitching.

Procedure: Dissolve the extract in warm water and make it to 4 gallons (15.1 L). Add the hops and boil 60 minutes; turn off heat, cool to about 70°F (21°C), and pitch yeast. Ferment 7–10 days as close to 70°F (21°C) as possible, rack to secondary for 2 weeks, rack again, and leave for 3–4 months. Serve from stainless steel soda keg or bottle, force carbonating (keg) or priming if desired (bottles), preferably allowing the beer to age a further 6 months or more.

Projected parameters: 3.5 gallons (13.2 L) final volume.
Original gravity: 1.133 (30.9°P)
Final gravity: 1.035 (8.8°P)
Apparent attenuation: 73.7%
Alcohol: 12.8% abv
Bitterness: 39 IBU (calculated on 12% utilization)
Color: dark red-brown

Notes

Called "unlikely" because these extracts are partly based on caramel malts, which would not have been used in the original Arctic Ale.

Comments

This is not, of course, anywhere near authentic but it would still be a warming and sustaining drink if you were stuck on an ice floe in the Arctic Ocean.

STINGO

METHOD 2 (grain mash and boil down)

Malt: 12 lb. (5.4 kg) Maris Otter Malt
2 lb. (0.91 kg) Caramel Malt (120°L)

Hops: 1.5 oz. (43 g) Admiral pellets at 15% alpha acid

Yeast: Wyeast 1469 West Yorkshire Ale yeast. You should aim to pitch about 600 billion cells. This is best done as a starter using two packets, starting each separately then doubling each twice. Use a nutrient as recommended and oxygenate for the main brew.

Procedure: Mash grain at 148–150°F (64.4–65.6°C), using 17 qt. (16 L) water (ratio 1.2 qt./lb., 2.5 L/kg). At 90 minutes perform a starch-iodine test and mash a further 30 minutes if positive for starch. If the test is negative and conversion is complete, run off and sparge with water at about 170°F (77°C) to collect 6 gallons (23 L) of wort at a specific gravity about ± 1.060 (14.7°P). Bring to a boil, add the Admiral hops, and boil down to 4 gallons (15.1 L). Cool to about 70°F (21°C) and pitch the yeast. Ferment 10–14 days as close to 70°F (21°C) as possible, rack to secondary for 4 weeks, rack again, and leave for 6–8 months. Serve from stainless steel soda keg or bottle, force carbonating (keg) or priming if desired (bottles), preferably allowing the beer to age a further 6 months or more.

Projected parameters: 4 gallons (15.1 L) final volume
Original gravity: 1.098 (23.6°P)
Final gravity: 1.025 (6.3°P)
Apparent attenuation: 74.5%
Alcohol: 9.7% abv
Bitterness: 51 IBU (calculated on 12% utilization)
Color: Deep red-brown to black

Notes

With this yeast you may get less attenuation as it is quite flocculent; if so, try adding a second dose of yeast (as a starter), or even a champagne yeast if you fancy.

Comments

Lots of malt and caramel flavors in this beer, but with noticeable hop bitterness as a balance to these.

JINGO STINGO

METHOD 1 (malt extract plus steeping)

Malt: 9 lb. (4.1 kg) Amber malt extract syrup
0.75 lb. (0.34 kg) Amber DME
2 lb. (0.91 kg) Caramel Malt (120°L)

Hops: 1 oz. (28 g) UK Admiral pellets at 15% alpha acid

Yeast: White Labs WLP 023 Burton Ale yeast. You should aim to pitch about 800 billion cells. This is best done as a starter using two packets, starting each separately then doubling each twice. Use a nutrient as recommended and oxygenate when pitching.

Procedure: Steep the grain (using a muslin bag) in 2 qt. (2 L) water at about 160°F (71°C) for 30–45 minutes. Remove the liquid to the boil pot, and rinse the grain in the bag twice, using 2 qt. (1.9 L) hot water. Collect the washings in the boil pot, stir in the Amber and DME extracts, adding warm water to a total volume of 4.5 gallons (17 L). Add the hops and boil for 60 minutes; turn off heat, cool to about 70°F (21°C), and pitch yeast. Ferment 7–10 days as close to 70°F (21°C) as possible, rack to secondary for 2 weeks, rack again, and leave for 3–4 months. Serve from stainless steel soda keg or bottle, force carbonating (keg) or priming if desired (bottles), preferably allowing the beer to age a further 6 months or more.

Projected parameters: 4 gallons (15.1 L) final volume
Original gravity: 1.098 (23.6°P)
Final gravity: 1.031 (7.8°P)
Apparent attenuation: 68.4%
Alcohol: 8.8% abv
Bitterness: 51 IBU (calculated on 12% utilization)
Color: Very dark red-brown

Notes

Like the all-grain version, you may need to add a second dose of yeast (champagne yeast if you like) at racking.

Comments

This is an excellent malty, well-balanced drink but it is only my idea of what Stingo ales might really have been like.

SCOTCH ALES

ROBERT'S RULES SCOTCH ALE

METHOD 2 (grain mash and boil down)

Malt: 16 lb. (7.34 kg) Golden Promise Pale Ale Malt

Hops: 2.75 oz. (78 g) UK Goldings pellets at 4.5% alpha acid

Yeast: Wyeast 1728 Scottish Ale yeast. You should aim to pitch about 700 billion cells. This is best done as a starter using two packets, starting each separately then doubling each twice. Use a nutrient as recommended and oxygenate for the main brew.

Procedure: Mash grain at 152–154°F (66.7–67.8°C), using 19 qt. (18 L) water (ratio 1.2 qt./lb., 2.5 L/kg). At 90 minutes perform a starch-iodine test and mash a further 30 minutes if positive for starch. If the test is negative and conversion is complete, run off and sparge with water at about 170°F (77°C) to collect 6 gallons (23 L) of wort at a specific gravity about ± 1.075 (18.2°P). Bring to a boil, add the Goldings hops, and boil down to 4 gallons (15.1 L). Cool to about 70°F (21°C) and pitch the yeast. Ferment 10–14 days as close to 65°F (18.3°C) as possible, rack to secondary for 4 weeks, rack again, and leave for 6–8 months. Serve from stainless steel soda keg or bottle, force carbonating (keg) or priming if desired (bottles), preferably allowing the beer to age a further 6 months or more.

Projected parameters: 4 gallons (15.1 L) final volume
Original gravity: 1.112 (25.1°P)
Final gravity: 1.042 (10.5°P)
Apparent attenuation: 62.5%
Alcohol: 9.7% abv
Bitterness: 35 IBU (calculated on 15% utilization)
Color: Deep crimson

Notes

This uses a slightly high mash temperature with a yeast giving low attenuation.

Comments

A true Scottish ale, much as it was in the nineteenth century, very full bodied, but low in hop bitterness and somewhat sweet. At this FG, be careful that fermentation really is complete before bottling.

REBELLION SCOTCH ALE

METHOD I (all malt extract)

Malt: 12 lb. (5.4 kg) Amber malt extract syrup
0.5 lb. (0.23 kg) Amber DME

Hops: 2.75 oz. (78 g) UK Goldings pellets at 4.5% alpha acid

Yeast: Wyeast 1728 Scottish Ale yeast. You should aim to pitch about 700 billion cells. This is best done as a starter using two packets, starting each separately then doubling each twice. Use a nutrient as recommended and oxygenate for the main brew.

Procedure: Dissolve the extracts in warm water and make up to 4.5 gallons (17 L). Add the hops and boil for 60 minutes; turn off heat, cool to about 70°F (21°C), and pitch yeast. Ferment 7–10 days as close to 65°F (18.3°C) as possible, rack to secondary for 2 weeks, rack again, and leave for 3–4 months. Serve from stainless steel soda keg or bottle, force carbonating (keg) or priming if desired (bottles), preferably allowing the beer to age a further 6 months or more.

Projected parameters: 4 gallons (15.1 L) final volume
Original gravity: 1.111 (26°P).
Final gravity: 1.044 (11°P)
Apparent attenuation: 60.4%
Alcohol: 8.8% abv
Bitterness: 35 IBU (calculated on 15% utilization)
Color: Red-brown

Notes

Again, be sure fermentation is complete before bottling—kegging with occasional release of pressure is a much safer procedure.

Comments

Despite the nontraditional ingredients, this comes out as a typical Scotch ale, malty and sweet.

HIGHLAND PROMISE SCOTCH ALE

METHOD 2 (grain mash and boil down)

Malt: 12 lb. (5.4 kg) Golden Promise Pale Ale Malt
1 lb. (0.45 kg) Simpson's Dark Crystal Malt (80°L)

Hops: 1.25 oz. (35 g) Admiral pellets at 15% alpha acid

Yeast: White Labs WLP 028 Edinburgh Ale yeast. You should aim to pitch about 500 billion cells. This is best done as a starter using two packets, starting each separately then doubling each. Use a nutrient as recommended and oxygenate for the main brew.

Procedure: Mash grain at 152–154°F (66.7–67.8°C), using 16 qt. (15.1 L) water (ratio 1.2 qt./lb., 2.5 L/kg). At 90 minutes perform a starch-iodine test and mash a further 30 minutes if positive for starch. If the test is negative and conversion is complete, run off and sparge with water at about 170°F (77°C) to collect 6 gallons (23 L) of wort at a specific gravity about ± 1.060 (14.7°P). Bring to a boil, add the Admiral hops, and boil down to 4 gallons (15.1 L). Cool to about 70°F (21°C) and pitch the yeast. Ferment 10–14 days as close to 65°F (18.3°C) as possible, rack to secondary for 4 weeks, rack again, and leave for 6–8 months. Serve from stainless steel soda keg or bottle, force carbonating (keg) or priming if desired (bottles), preferably allowing the beer to age a further 6 months or more.

Projected parameters: 4 gallons (15.1 L) final volume
Original gravity: 1.090 (21.5°P)
Final gravity: 1.035 (8.8°P)
Apparent attenuation: 61.1%
Alcohol: 7.2% abv
Bitterness: 53 IBU (calculated on 15% utilization)
Color: Deep red-brown

Notes

The high mash temperature coupled with a yeast gives low attenuation, so be careful that fermentation really is complete before bottling.

Comments

Moderately full-bodied with caramel/toffee notes, sweetish but with a hop bitterness on the high side for a Scotch Ale.

OLD PRETENDER SCOTCH ALE

METHOD 1 (all malt extract plus steeping)

Malt: 9 lb. (4.1 kg) Amber malt extract syrup
1 lb. (0.45 kg) Simpson's Dark Crystal Malt (80°L)

Hops: 1.25 oz. (35 g) Admiral pellets at 15% alpha acid

Yeast: White Labs WLP 028 Edinburgh Ale yeast. You should aim to pitch about 500 billion cells. This is best done as a starter using two packets, starting each separately then doubling each. Use a nutrient as recommended and oxygenate for the main brew.

Procedure: Steep the grain (using a muslin bag) in 2 qt. (2 L) water at about 160°F (71°C) for 30–45 minutes. Remove the liquid to the boiling pot, and rinse the grain in the bag twice, using 2 qt. (1.9 L) hot water. Collect the washings in the boiling pot, stir in the Amber extract, adding warm water to a total volume of 4.5 gallons (17 L). Add the hops and boil 60 minutes; turn off heat, cool to about 70°F (21°C), and pitch yeast. Ferment 7–10 days as close to 65°F (18.3°C) as possible, rack to secondary for 2 weeks, rack again, and leave for 3–4 months. Serve from stainless steel soda keg or bottle, force carbonating (keg) or priming if desired (bottles), preferably allowing the beer to age a further 6 months or more.

Projected parameters: 4 gallons (15.1 L) final volume
Original gravity: 1.090 (21.5°P)
Final gravity: 1.037 (9.3°P)
Apparent attenuation: 58.9%
Alcohol: 6.9% abv
Bitterness: 53 IBU (calculated on 15% utilization)
Color: Deep Red-brown

Notes

Again, be sure fermentation is complete before bottling—kegging with occasional release of pressure is a much safer procedure.

Comments

Very low attenuation on this one, so quite sweet but with some hop bitterness to balance the sweetness.

AULD REEKIE SCOTCH ALE

METHOD 2 (grain mash and boil down)

Malt: 17 lb. (7.7 kg) Crisp Floor-malted Maris Otter Malt
1 lb. (0.45 kg) Briess Caramel Malt (60°L)
0.75 lb. (0.34 kg) Simpson's Peated Malt

Hops: 1.5 oz. (43 g) Nugget pellets at 13% alpha acid

Yeast: White Labs WLP 028 Edinburgh Ale yeast. You should aim to pitch about 800 billion cells. This is best done as a starter using two packets, starting each separately then doubling each twice. Use a nutrient as recommended and oxygenate for the main brew.

Procedure: Mash grain at 152–154°F (66.7–67.8°C), using 23 qt. (22 L) water (ratio 1.2 qt./lb., 2.5 L/kg). At 90 minutes perform a starch-iodine test and mash a further 30 minutes if positive for starch. If the test is negative and conversion is complete, run off and sparge with water at about 170°F (77°C) to collect 6 gallons (23 L) of wort at a specific gravity about ± 1.085 (20.3°P). Bring to a boil, add the Nugget hops, and boil down to 3.5 gallons (13.2 L). Cool to about 70°F (21°C) and pitch the yeast. Ferment 10–14 days as close to 65°F (18.3°C) as possible, rack to secondary for 4 weeks, rack again, and leave for 6–8 months. Serve from stainless steel soda keg or bottle, force carbonating (keg) or priming if desired (bottles), preferably allowing the beer to age a further 6 months or more.

Projected parameters: 3.5 gallons (13.2 L) final volume
Original gravity: 1.138 (31.7°P)
Final gravity: 1.045 (11.2°P)
Apparent attenuation: 67.4%
Alcohol: 12.1% abv
Bitterness: 42 IBU (calculated on 10% utilization)
Color: Red-brown

Notes

The high mash temperature coupled with a yeast gives low attenuation, so be careful that fermentation really is complete before bottling. The peated malt can vary quite a lot in its smoke flavor, so be careful not to overdo it.

Comments

A big Scotch ale, lots of malt body, medium hop bitterness, overlain with some smoked character.

THANE OF CAWDOR SCOTCH ALE

METHOD 1 (malt extract plus partial mashing)

Malt: 12 lb. (5.4 kg) Maris Otter Malt extract syrup
0.5 lb.(0.23 kg) Amber DME
1 lb. (0.45 kg) Pale 2-row Malt
1 lb. (0.45 kg) Briess Caramel Malt (60°L)
0.75 lb. (0.23 kg) Simpson's Peated Malt

Hops: 1.5 oz. (43 g) Nugget pellets at 13% alpha acid

Yeast: White Labs WLP 028 Edinburgh Ale yeast. You should aim to pitch about 800 billion cells. This is best done as a starter using two packets, starting each separately then doubling each twice. Use a nutrient as recommended and oxygenate for the main brew.

Procedure: Mash the grains (using a muslin bag) in 4 qt. (3.8 L) water at about 150°F (65.6°C) for 45 minutes. Remove the liquid to the boiling pot, and rinse the grain in the bag twice, using 2 qt. (1.9 L) hot water. Collect the washings in the boiling pot, stir in the extracts, and make up to 4 gallons (15.1 L). Add the hops and boil for 60 minutes; turn off heat, cool to about 70°F (21°C), and pitch yeast. Ferment 7–10 days as close to 65°F (18.3°C) as possible, rack to secondary for 2 weeks, rack again, and leave for 3–4 months. Serve from stainless steel soda keg or bottle, force carbonating (keg) or priming if desired (bottles), preferably allowing the beer to age a further 6 months or more.

Projected parameters: 3.5 gallons (13.2 L) final volume
Original gravity: 1.140 (32.1°P)
Final gravity: 1.047 (11.7°P)
Apparent attenuation: 66.4.0%
Alcohol: 12.1% abv
Bitterness: 42 IBU (calculated on 10% utilization)
Color: Dark red-brown

Notes

The peated malt contains starch and has to be mashed; see previous brew for comments on its variability.

Comments

Similar in character to the previous brew, just a tad sweeter, but with the smoke overlaying the flavor palate.

INDEPENDENCE SCOTCH ALE

METHOD 2 (grain mash and boil down)

Malt: 17 lb. (7.7 kg) Briess Ashburne® Mild Malt
0.5 lb. (0.23 kg) Weyermann® CaraAmber Malt
0.5 lb. (0.23 kg) Dingeman Special B Malt

Hops: 1.5 oz. (43 g) Warrior pellets at 16% alpha acid

Yeast: Wyeast 1728 Scottish Ale yeast. You should aim to pitch about 700 billion cells. This is best done as a starter using two packets, starting each separately then doubling each twice. Use a nutrient as recommended and oxygenate for the main brew.

Procedure: Mash grain at 152–154°F (66.7–67.8°C), using 23 qt. (22 L) water (ratio 1.2 qt./lb., 2.5 L/kg). At 90 minutes perform a starch-iodine test and mash a further 30 minutes if positive for starch. If the test is negative and conversion is complete, run off and sparge with water at about 170°F (77°C) to collect 6 gallons (23 L) of wort at a specific gravity about ± 1.085 (20.3°P). Bring to a boil, add the Warrior hops, and boil down to 4 gallons (15.1 L). Cool to about 70°F (21°C) and pitch the yeast. Ferment 10–14 days as close to 65°F (18.3°C) as possible, rack to secondary for 4 weeks, rack again, and leave for 6–8 months. Serve from stainless steel soda keg or bottle, force carbonating (keg) or priming if desired (bottles), preferably allowing the beer to age a further 6 months or more.

Projected parameters: 4 gallons (15.1 L) final volume
Original gravity: 1.120 (28°P)
Final gravity: 1.036 (9°P)
Apparent attenuation: 70%
Alcohol: 10.9% abv
Bitterness: 55 IBU (calculated on 12% utilization)
Color: Deep red

Notes

The high mash temperature coupled with a yeast gives low attenuation, so be careful that fermentation really is complete before bottling.

Comments

Yes, it is still a sweet, strong Scotch ale but with added nuttiness and biscuit flavors from the specialty malts, neither of which would have been used by nineteenth-century Scots brewers.

ST. ANDREW'S BONES SCOTCH ALE

METHOD 1 (all malt extract plus steeping)

Malt: 12 lb. (5.4 kg) Amber malt extract syrup
0.75 lb. (0.34 kg) Amber DME
0.5 lb. (0.23 kg) Weyermann® CaraAmber Malt
0.5 lb. (0.23 kg) Dingeman Special B Malt

Hops: 1.5 oz. (43 g) Warrior pellets at 16% alpha acid

Yeast: Wyeast 1728 Scottish Ale yeast. You should aim to pitch about 700 billion cells. This is best done as a starter using two packets, starting each separately then doubling each twice. Use a nutrient as recommended and oxygenate for the main brew.

Procedure: Steep the grain (using a muslin bag) in 2 qt. (2 L) water at about 160°F (71°C) for 30–45 minutes. Remove the liquid to the boiling pot, and rinse the grain in the bag twice, using 2 qt. (1.9 L) hot water. Collect the washings in the boiling pot, stir in the extracts, adding warm water to a total volume of 4.5 gallons (17 L). Add the hops and boil for 60 minutes; turn off heat, cool to about 70°F (21°C), and pitch yeast. Ferment 7–10 days as close to 65°F (18.3°C) as possible, rack to secondary for 2 weeks, rack again, and leave for 3–4 months. Serve from stainless steel soda keg or bottle, force carbonating (keg) or priming if desired (bottles), preferably allowing the beer to age a further 6 months or more.

Projected parameters: 4 gallons (15.1 L) final volume
Original gravity: 1.119 (27.8°P)
Final gravity: 1.038 (9.3°P)
Apparent attenuation: 68.1%
Alcohol: 10.5% abv
Bitterness: 55 IBU (calculated on 12% utilization)
Color: Deep red-brown

Notes

Again, be sure fermentation is complete before bottling—kegging with occasional release of pressure is a much safer procedure.

Comments

Much like its all-grain counterpart, sweet, alcoholic, biscuity, nutty, delicious!

APRÉS CAIRNGORMS SCOTCH ALE

METHOD 2 (grain mash and boil down)

Malt: 18 lb. (8.2 kg) Fawcett Pearl Pale Malt

Hops: 1.75 oz. (50 g) Newport pellets at 16% alpha acid

Yeast: Lallemand Nottingham Ale yeast, 50 g, about 800 billion cells. Rehydrate according to instructions on package. Use a nutrient as recommended and oxygenate when pitching.

Procedure: Mash grain at 150–152°F (65.6–66.7°C), using 22 qt. (21 L) water (ratio 1.2 qt./lb., 2.5 L/kg). At 90 minutes perform a starch-iodine test and mash a further 30 minutes if positive for starch. If the test is negative and conversion is complete, run off and sparge with water at about 170°F (77°C) to collect 6 gallons (23 L) of wort at a specific gravity about ± 1.085 (20.3°P). Bring to a boil, add the Newport hops, and boil down to 3.5 gallons (13.2 L). Cool to about 70°F (21°C) and pitch the yeast. Ferment 10–14 days as close to 65°F (18.3°C) as possible, rack to secondary for 4 weeks, rack again, and leave for 6–8 months. Serve from stainless steel soda keg or bottle, force carbonating (keg) or priming if desired (bottles), preferably allowing the beer to age a further 6 months or more.

Projected parameters: 3.5 gallons (13.2 L) final volume
Original gravity: 1.144 (33°P)
Final gravity: 1.035 (9°P)
Apparent attenuation: 75.7%
Alcohol: 14.3% abv
Bitterness: 60 IBU (calculated on 12% utilization)
Color: Red-gold

Notes

The Nottingham yeast is preferred since it gives good attenuation, which I wanted here because of the high OG for this beer.

Comments

It has the sweetness of a Scotch ale, balanced by high alcohol and hop bitterness. But is it really much different from a "standard" barley wine?

WHEAT WINES

NEW WORLD WHEAT WINE

METHOD 2 (grain mash, collect all)

Malt: 9 lb. (4.1 kg) Wheat malt
3 lb. (1.4 kg) pale 2-row malt
1.5 lb. (0.68 kg) Munich malt (10°L)
1.5 lb. (0.68 kg) Caramel malt (80°L)
1.5 lb. (0.68 kg) rice hulls, in addition to malts

Hops: 1.75 oz. (50 g) Millennium pellets at 14% alpha acid

Yeast: Wyeast 1084 Irish Ale yeast. You should aim to pitch 500 billion cells. As described above, this would require five packets of fresh yeast. The best approach would be to prepare a starter from two packets of yeast, each in a separate vessel and doubling up twice. That means you would have to prepare the starter several days in advance of brewing. Use a nutrient as recommended and oxygenate the wort at pitching.

Procedure: Mash grain at 152–153°F (66.7–67.2°C), using 18 qt. (17 L) water (ratio 1.2 qt./lb., 2.5 L/kg); add a portion (about one-quarter) of the rice hulls to the water first, and evenly as possible mixing the remainder with the rest of the grain. At 60 minutes perform a starch-iodine test and mash a further 30 minutes if positive for starch. If the test is negative and conversion is complete, run off and sparge with water at about 170°F (77°C) to collect 6 gallons (23 L) of wort. Specific gravity of this wort should be about 1.070 (17.1°P). Bring to a boil, add the bittering hops, and boil down to 4.5 gallons (17 L); this took about 2 hours in my case. Cool to about 70°F (21°C) and pitch the yeast starter. Ferment 10–14 days as close to 70°F (21°C) as possible, rack to secondary for 4 weeks, rack again, and leave for 6–8 months. Serve from stainless steel soda keg or bottle, force carbonating (keg) or priming if desired (bottles) as soon as the beer has clarified and reached the desired carbonation level.

Projected parameters: 4.5 gallons (17 L) final volume
Original gravity: 1.092 (22°P)
Final gravity: 1.025 (6.3°P)
Apparent attenuation: 72.8%
Alcohol: 8.8% abv
Bitterness: 62 IBU (calculated on 15% utilization)
Color: pale orange

Comments

I used a relatively high mash temperature plus Munich malt and a high color caramel malt to try to ensure this beer had a decent level of mouthfeel. That is because some of the commercial versions I have tried, especially those at higher alcohol levels, have tasted somewhat thin and allowed the heat of the alcohol to stand out too strongly.

OLD WORLD WHEAT WINE

METHOD 1 (all malt extract)

Malt: 12 lb. (5.4 kg) Briess CBW® Bavarian wheat malt extract

Hops: 1 oz. (28 g) Millennium pellets at 14% alpha acid

Yeast: White Labs WLP 1084 Irish Ale yeast. You should aim to pitch about 600 billion cells. This is best done as a starter using two packets, starting each separately then doubling each twice. Use a nutrient as recommended and oxygenate when pitching.

Procedure: Dissolve the extract in warm water and make up to 5 gallons (19 L). Add the hops and boil for 60 minutes; turn off heat, cool to about 70°F (21°C), and pitch yeast. Ferment 7–10 days as close to 70°F (21°C) as possible, rack to secondary for 2 weeks, rack again, and leave for 3–4 months. Serve from stainless steel soda keg or bottle, force carbonating (keg) or priming if desired (bottles), preferably allowing the beer to age a further 6 months or more.

Projected parameters: 4.5 gallons (17 L) final volume
Original gravity: 1.093 (22.2°P)
Final gravity: 1.030 (7.6°P)
Apparent attenuation: 67.7%
Alcohol: 8.3% abv
Bitterness: 46 IBU (calculated on 20% utilization)
Color: Yellow to gold

Notes

Use of a "Bavarian" extract may seem out of place in an American style of beer, but the extract is made in the United States!

Comments

A relatively light version of this beer, but still with some good malt character.

WARM-WEATHER WHEAT WINE

METHOD 2 (grain mash, collect all)

Malt: 9.5 lb. (4.3 kg) Great Western White Wheat malt
8.5 lb. (3.9 kg) Briess Pilsen Malt
1.5 lb. (0.68 kg) rice hulls, in addition to malts

Hops: 1 oz. (28 g) Warrior pellets at 16% alpha acid

Yeast: Lallemand Nottingham Ale yeast, 40 g, about 700 billion cells. Rehydrate according to instructions on package. Use a nutrient as recommended and oxygenate when pitching.

Procedure: Mash grains at 152–153°F (66.7–67.2°C), using 18 qt. (17 L) water (ratio 1.2 qt./lb., 2.5 L/kg); add a portion (about one-quarter) of the rice hulls to the water first, and evenly as possible mixing the remainder with the rest of the grain. At 60 minutes perform a starch-iodine test and mash a further 30 minutes if positive for starch. If the test is negative and conversion is complete, run off and sparge with water at about 170°F (77°C) to collect 6 gallons (23 L) of wort. The specific gravity of this wort should be about ±1.080 (19.3°P). Bring to a boil, add the bittering hops, and boil down to 4.5 gallons (17 L); this took about 2 hours in my case. Cool to about 70°F (21°C) and pitch the yeast starter. Ferment 10–14 days as close to 70°F (21°C) as possible, rack to secondary for 4 weeks, rack again, and leave for 6–8 months. Serve from stainless steel soda keg or bottle, force carbonating (keg) or priming if desired (bottles) as soon as the beer has clarified and reached the desired carbonation level.

Projected parameters: 4.5 gallons (17 L) final volume
Original gravity: 1.112 (26.3°P)
Final gravity: 1.025 (6.3°P)
Apparent attenuation: 77.7%
Alcohol: 11.4% abv
Bitterness: 40 IBU (calculated on 15% utilization)
Color: pale yellow

Notes

I wanted this beer to be as pale in color as possible, hence the use of pilsen malt.

Comments

This is somewhat lacking in mouthfeel for such a strong beer, and the alcohol does tend to come through on the palate a bit more than I would like.

WISHING WELL WHEAT WINE

METHOD 1 (all malt extract)

Malt: 9 lb. (4.1 kg) Wheat Malt extract syrup
6 lb. (2.7 kg) Pilsen Malt extract syrup

Hops: 1 oz. (28 g) Warrior pellets at 16% alpha acid

Yeast: White Labs WLP007 Dry English Ale yeast. You should aim to pitch about 700 billion cells. This is best done as a starter using two packets, starting each separately then doubling each twice. Use a nutrient as recommended and oxygenate when pitching.

Procedure: Dissolve the extract in warm water and make up to 5 gallons (19 L). Add the hops and boil 60 minutes; turn off heat, cool to about 70°F (21°C), and pitch yeast. Ferment 7–10 days as close to 70°F (21°C) as possible, rack to secondary for 2 weeks, rack again, and leave for 3–4 months. Serve from stainless steel soda keg or bottle, force carbonating (keg) or priming if desired (bottles), preferably allowing the beer to age a further 6 months or more.

Projected parameters: 4.5 gallons (17 L) final volume.
Original gravity: 1.117 (27.2°P)
Final gravity: 1.032 (8.1°P)
Apparent attenuation: 72.7%
Alcohol: 11.1% abv
Bitterness: 40 IBU (calculated on 15% utilization)
Color: Yellow

Notes

I used the pilsen extract to lighten the color as in the all-grain version.

Comments

Again, a really pale version of this beer which could do with a little more body and mouthfeel.

WHOPPER WHEAT WINE

METHOD 2 (grain mash plus extract)

Malt: 7 lb. (3.2 kg) Briess Red Wheat malt
5 lb. (2.3 kg) Great Western American Pale 2-row Malt
3 lb. (1.4 kg.) Wheat Malt extract syrup
1.5 lb. (0.68 kg) rice hulls, in addition to malts

Hops: 1.5 oz. (43 g) Summit pellets at 17% alpha acid

Yeast: GigaYeast GY001 British Ale yeast #1.You should aim to pitch about 700 billion cells. This is best done as a starter using two packets, starting each separately then doubling each twice. Use a nutrient as recommended and oxygenate when pitching.

Procedure: Mash grains at 148–150°F (64.4–65.6°C), using 14 qt. (12 L) water (ratio 1.2 qt./lb., 2.5 L/kg); add a portion (about one-quarter) of the rice hulls to the water first, and evenly as possible mixing the remainder with the rest of the grain. At 60 minutes perform a starch-iodine test and mash a further 30 minutes if positive for starch. If the test is negative and conversion is complete, run off and sparge with water at about 170°F (77°C) to collect 5.5 gallons (21 L) of wort. The specific gravity of this wort should be about ±1.060 (14.7°P). Add the extract syrup and stir thoroughly until dissolved. Bring to a boil, add the bittering hops, and boil down to 3.3 gallons (12.5 L); this took about 2 hours in my case. Cool to about 70°F (21°C) and pitch the yeast starter. Ferment 10–14 days as close to 70°F (21°C) as possible, rack to secondary for 4 weeks, rack again, and leave for 6–8 months. Serve from stainless steel soda keg or bottle, force carbonating (keg) or priming if desired (bottles) as soon as the beer has clarified and reached the desired carbonation level.

Projected parameters: 3.3 gallons (12.5 L) final volume
Original gravity: 1.134 (30.9°P)
Final gravity: 1.035 (8.8°P)
Apparent attenuation: 73.9%
Alcohol: 13.0% abv

Bitterness: 80 IBU (calculated on 15% utilization)
Color: Deep yellow with hints if red

Notes

A mix of extract and grains was used to get a high OG.

Comments

This beer was much more full-bodied than the previous ones, and with a high level of bitterness so as to maintain a balance.

The only wheat wine I could find locally.

WIZARD'S WAND WHEAT WINE

METHOD 1 (all malt extract)

Malt: 12 lb. (5.4 kg) Bavarian Wheat Malt extract syrup

Hops: 1.5 oz. (43 g) Summit pellets at 17% alpha acid

Yeast: Wyeast 1056 American Ale yeast. You should aim to pitch about 600 billion cells. This is best done as a starter using two packets, starting each separately then doubling each twice. Use a nutrient as recommended and oxygenate when pitching.

Procedure: Dissolve the extract in warm water and make up to 3.5 gallons (13.2 L). Add the hops and boil for 60 minutes; turn off heat, cool to about 70°F (21°C), and pitch yeast. Ferment 7–10 days as close to 65°F (18.3°C) as possible, rack to secondary for 2 weeks, rack again, and leave for 3–4 months. Serve from stainless steel soda keg or bottle, force carbonating (keg) or priming if desired (bottles), preferably allowing the beer to age a further 6 months or more.

Projected parameters: 3 gallons (11.4 L) final volume
Original gravity: 1.140 (32.1°P)
Final gravity: 1.038 (9.5°P)
Apparent attenuation: 72.9%
Alcohol: 13.4% abv
Bitterness: 77 IBU (calculated on 12% utilization)
Color: Golden yellow

Notes

An extract designed for a Hefeweizen works well for a wheat wine, too.

Comments

A simple-to-brew beer which is a good match for the previous grain/extract beer, with perhaps even a little more body.

WISE WORDS WHEAT WINE

METHOD 2 (grain mash, collect all)

Malt: 12 lb. (5.4 kg) Great Western White Wheat malt
7 lb. (3.2 kg) Rahr 2-row Pale Malt
1.5 lb. (0.68 kg) Briess Bonlander® Munich Malt (10°L)
0.5 lb. (0.23 kg) Dingemans Special B Malt
1.5 lb. (0.68 kg) rice hulls, in addition to malts

Hops: 1.5 oz. (43 g) Columbus pellets at 15% alpha acid

Yeast: SAFALE US-05 American Ale yeast, 40 g, about 700 billion cells. Rehydrate according to instructions on package. Use a nutrient as recommended and oxygenate when pitching.

Procedure: Mash grains at 152–153°F (66.7–67.2°C), using 18 qt. (17 L) water (ratio 1.2 qt./lb., 2.5 L/kg); add a portion (about one-quarter) of the rice hulls to the water first, and evenly as possible mixing the remainder with the rest of the grain. At 60 minutes perform a starch-iodine test and mash a further 30 minutes if positive for starch. If the test is negative and conversion is complete, run off and sparge with water at about 170°F (77°C) to collect 6 gallons (23 L) of wort. The specific gravity of this wort should be about ±1.095 (19.3°P). Bring to a boil, add the bittering hops, and boil down to 4.5 gallons (17 L); this took about 2 hours in my case. Cool to about 70°F (21°C) and pitch the yeast starter. Ferment 10–14 days as close to 70°F (21°C) as possible, rack to secondary for 4 weeks, rack again, and leave for 6–8 months. Serve from stainless steel soda keg or bottle, force carbonating (keg) or priming if desired (bottles) as soon as the beer has clarified and reached the desired carbonation level.

Projected parameters: 4.5 gallons (17 L) final volume
Original gravity: 1.126 (29.2°P)
Final gravity: 1.031 (7.8°P)
Apparent attenuation: 75.4%
Alcohol: 12.4% abv
Bitterness: 57 IBU (calculated on 15% utilization)
Color: Reddish-yellow

Notes

The use of Munich and Special B provides both extra body and color in this beer.

Comments

Lots of mouthfeel, malty and bready flavors make this one of the best wheat wines I have brewed.

WET-WEATHER WHEAT WINE

METHOD 2 (grain mash, collect all)

Malt: 11 lb. (5 kg) Great Western White Wheat malt
8.5 lb. (3.9 kg) Briess Pale Ale Malt
0.5 lb. (0.23 kg) Briess Rye Malt
1.5 lb. (0.68 kg) rice hulls, in addition to malts

Hops: 1.75 oz. (50 g) Nugget pellets at 13% alpha acid

Yeast: Imperial Organic Yeast B51 Workhorse yeast. You should aim to pitch about 700 billion cells. This is best done as a starter using two packets, starting each separately then doubling each twice. Use a nutrient as recommended and oxygenate when pitching.

Procedure: Mash grains at 152–153°F (66.7–67.2°C), using 24 qt. (23 L) water (ratio 1.2 qt./lb., 2.5 L/kg); add a portion (about one-quarter) of the rice hulls to the water first, and evenly as possible mixing the remainder with the rest of the grain. At 60 minutes perform a starch-iodine test and mash a further 30 minutes if positive for starch. If the test is negative and conversion is complete, run off and sparge with water at about 170°F (77°C) to collect 6.5 gallons (24.6 L) of wort. The specific gravity of this wort should be about ±1.085 (20.3°P). Bring to a boil, add the bittering hops, and boil down to 5 gallons (19 L); this took about 1.5 hours in my case. Cool to about 70°F (21°C) and pitch the yeast starter. Ferment 10–14 days as close to 70°F (21°C) as possible, rack to secondary for 4 weeks, rack again, and leave for 6–8 months. Serve from stainless steel soda keg or bottle, force carbonating (keg) or priming if desired (bottles) as soon as the beer has clarified and reached the desired carbonation level.

Projected parameters: 5 gallons (19 L) final volume
Original gravity: 1.112 (26.2°P)
Final gravity: 1.028 (7.1°P)
Apparent attenuation: 75%
Alcohol: 10.9% abv
Bitterness: 52 IBU (calculated on 15% utilization)
Color: Yellow with a hint of orange

Notes

A yeast I hadn't tried before, and an out-of-style use of rye malt.

Comments

A different take on the style with the rye malt adding its typical spicy character to an otherwise straightforward wheat wine.

WILLOW WARBLER WHEAT WINE

METHOD 2 (grain mash, collect all)

Malt: 13 lb. (5.9 kg) Great Western White Wheat malt
8 lb. (3.6 kg) Ashburne® Mild Malt
1 lb. (0.45 kg) Briess Caramel Malt (120°L)
1.5 lb. (0.68 kg) rice hulls, in addition to malts

Hops: 3 oz. (85 g) Apollo pellets at 18% alpha acid

Yeast: White Labs WLP 007 Dry English Ale yeast. You should aim to pitch about 1000 billion cells. This is best done as a starter using three packets to make two starters, then doubling each twice. Use a nutrient as recommended and oxygenate when pitching.

Procedure: Mash grains at 148–150°F (64.4–65.6°C), using 24 qt. (23 L) water (ratio 1.2 qt./lb., 2.5 L/kg); add a portion (about one-quarter) of the rice hulls to the water first, and evenly as possible mixing the remainder with the rest of the grain. At 60 minutes perform a starch-iodine test and mash a further 30 minutes if positive for starch. If the test is negative and conversion is complete, run off and sparge with water at about 170°F (77°C) to collect 6 gallons (23 L) of wort. The specific gravity of this wort should be about ±1.095 (19.3°P). Bring to a boil, add the bittering hops, and boil down to 4 gallons (15.1 L); this took about 2 hours in my case. Cool to about 70°F (21°C) and pitch the yeast starter. Ferment 10–14 days as close to 70°F (21°C) as possible, rack to secondary for 4 weeks, rack again, and leave for 6–8 months. Serve from stainless steel soda keg or bottle, force carbonating (keg) or priming if desired (bottles) as soon as the beer has clarified and reached the desired carbonation level.

Projected parameters: 4 gallons (15.1 L) final volume
Original gravity: 1.154 (35°P)
Final gravity: 1.037 (9.3°P)
Apparent attenuation: 76%
Alcohol: 15.4% abv
Bitterness: 100 IBU (calculated on 10% utilization)
Color: Yellow with red hints

Notes

A straightforward recipe, with Mild Malt to add a little more body and color, as does the high roast caramel malt.

Comments

A very big, alcoholic wheat wine with a high hop bitterness to balance the full malty body of this beer. This beer will keep for years and would be suited to barrel-aging.

WHAT THE W WHEAT WINE

METHOD 2 (all malt extract)

Malt: 15 lb. (6.8 kg) Wheat Malt extract syrup
3 lb. (1.4 kg) Munich Malt extract syrup

Hops: 1.5 oz. (43 g) Apollo pellets at 18% alpha acid

Yeast: White Labs WLP 007 Dry English Ale yeast. You should aim to pitch about 1000 billion cells. This is best done as a starter using three packets to make two starters, then doubling each twice. Use a nutrient as recommended and oxygenate when pitching.

Procedure: Dissolve the Munich extract and 6 lb. (2.7kg) Wheat Malt extract in warm water and make to 4.5 gallons (17 L). Add the hops and boil 60 minutes; turn off heat, and carefully dissolve the remaining 9 lb. (4.1 kg), cool to about 70°F (21°C), and pitch yeast. Ferment 7–10 days as close to 70°F (21°C) as possible, rack to secondary for 2 weeks, rack again, and leave for 3–4 months. Serve from stainless steel soda keg or bottle, force carbonating (keg) or priming if desired (bottles), preferably allowing the beer to age a further 6 months or more.

Projected parameters: 4 gallons (15.1 L) final volume
Original gravity: 1.158 (36°P)
Final gravity: 1.041 (10.2°P)
Apparent attenuation: 74%
Alcohol: 15.4% abv
Bitterness: 100 IBU (calculated on 20% utilization)
Color: Yellow-brown with red tinges

Notes

I used the Munich Malt extract to provide a little more body and color than would be obtained from plain pale extract.

Comments

This is an extract version of the previous all-grain beer, very simple to make yet really full-flavored, chewy, and with a high hop bitterness to balance the high level of alcohol. This beer will keep for years.

Another detail from the mural on the outside of Brewport Brewing Co. Go see the complete painting for yourself and sample the beers.

BIBLIOGRAPHY

Accum, Fredrick. *A Treatise on the Art of Brewing*. 2nd ed. Longman, Hurst, Rees, Orme and Brown, London, 1821.

Allen, Fal, and Dick Cantwell. *Barley wine: History, Brewing Techniques, Recipes*. Boulder, CO: Brewers Publications, 1998.

Amsinck, George Stewart. *Practical Brewings: A Series of Fifty Brewings in Extenso*. London, 1868.

Arnold, Richard. *The Customs of London, Otherwise Called, Arnold's Chronicle*. London: Printed for F. C. and J. Rivington, etc., 1503.

Avis, Anthony. "A Brewery's Price List of a Century Ago." *The Journal of the Brewery History Society*, Spring 2002, no. 107, n.d.

Barnard, Alfred. *The Noted Breweries of Great Britain and Ireland*. London: Sir Joseph Causton & Sons, 1889.

Baron, Stanley Wade. *Brewed in America*. North Stratford, NH: Ayer Company Publishers Inc., 1962.

Baverstock, James. *Hydrometrical Observations and Experiments in the Brewery*. London: G. G. J. and J. Robinson, 1785.

Beer Judge Certification Program. "BJCP Style Guidelines," n.d. https://www.bjcp.org/bjcp-style-guidelines/.

"Beer Talk: Thomas Hardy's Ale, Vintage 2003." *All About Beer*, July 2004.

BeerSmith Home Brewing Software. "BeerSmith Recipe Cloud," n.d. https://beersmithrecipes.com/.

Bennett, Judith M. *Ale, Beer and Brewsters in England*. New York: Oxford University Press, 1996.

Berg, Maxine L. *Luxury and Pleasure in Eighteenth Century Britain*. Oxford: Oxford Univ. Press, 2010.

Black, William. *A Practical Treatise on Brewing*: 3rd ed. London: Longman, Brown, Green and Longman, 1844.

Blake, George. *Observations and Remarks on the Construction and Important Uses of Blake's Former and New Saccharometer*: Designed Principally for the Brewery, 1811.

Blake, George. *Strictures on a New Mode of Brewing*. London: Printed for the author and sold by J. Johnson, 1791.

Blichmann, John, and John J. Palmer. "Sequential Mashing." *Brew Your Own* 23, no. 5 September 2017.

Brande, W. *The Town and Country Brewery Book; Or, Every Man His Own Brewer, Etc*. 1830. Reprint edition. Chagrin Falls, OH: Raudins Publishing, 2018.

"The Breweries of England." *Brewery History*, no. 168 (2017): 8.

Brewers Association. "2023 Brewers Association Beer Style Guidelines," n.d. https://www.brewersassociation.org/edu/brewers-association-beer-style-guidelines/.

Bruning, Ted. "Prince of Ales Back on Its Throne." *What's Brewing*, December 1996.

Buckler, Benjamin, and Samuel Rolleston. *Oinos Krithinos: A Dissertation Concerning the Origin and Antiquity of Barley Wine*. Oxford: James Fletcher, 1750.

Bushnan, John Stevenson. *Burton and Its Bitter Beer*. London: William S. Orr, 1853.

Chadwick, William. *A Practical Treatise on Brewing*. London: Whittaker and Co, 1835.

Colby, Chris. "'Feeding' the Biggest Beers." *Beer & Gardening Journal*, 2015.

Combrune, Michael. *An Enquiry into the Prices of Wheat, Malt, and Occasionally of Other Provisions: Of Land and Cattle, &c*. London: Longman, 1768.

———. *An historical account of the English brewery*. Unpublished manuscript: Beinecke Library, Yale University, Osborn, [1768?].

Compton-Davey, John A.R. "Audit Ales: A Short History." *Brewery History*, no. 128 (2008): 2–48.

Coppinger, Joseph. *The American Practical Brewer and Tanner*. 1815. Reprint, Cleveland, OH: BeerBooks.com, 2007.

Cornell, Martyn. *Amber, Gold and Black*. Teddington, Middlesex: Zythography Press, 2008.

——. "Arctic Ale." *Zytophile*, January 10, 2010. https://zythophile.co.uk/2010/01/10/arctic-ale-a-158-year-old-adventure-revived/.

——. "Contending Liquors." *Brewery History*, no. 144 (2011): 33–40.

——. "'A Glass of Something Very Treble Extra.'": *Brewery History*, no. 153 (2013): 2–10.

——. "The Mystery of the Vanishing 2016 Vintage Ale." *Zytophile*, February 20, 2017. https://zythophile.co.uk/2017/02/20/the-mystery-of-the-vanishing-2016-vintage-ale/.

——. "Only the Strong Survive." *What's Brewing*, April 2007.

Cornell, Martyn, and Anthony Hayes. "Burton Ale." *Zymurgy*, January 2011, 22.

Crumplen, Rena M., ed. *Laboratory Methods for Craft Brewers*. American Society of Brewing Chemists, 1997.

Daniels, Ray. *Designing Great Beers: The Ultimate Guide to Brewing Classic Beer Styles*. Brewers Publications, 1996.

Donnachie, Ian L. *A History of the Brewing Industry in Scotland*. Edinburgh: John Donald Publishers, Ltd., 1797.

Ellis, William. *The Country Housewife's Family Companion*. 1750. Reprint, Blackawton, Devon: Prospect Books, 2000.

——. *The London and Country Brewer*. London: J. and J. Fox, 1736.

An Essay Upon Excising Several Branches That Have Hitherto Escaped the Duty of the Brewing Trade. London, [1699?].

Evans, Jeff. "Cool Customer." *What's Brewing*, July 2002.

"Focus on Brakspear & Sons Ltd." *The Brewer*, August 1982.

Foster, Terry. "50 Years of Maris Otter." *Brew Your Own*, November 2015.

——. *Brewing Porters and Stouts*. New York: Skyhorse Publishing, 2014.

——. *The Hydrometer Code*. Self-published, 2011.

———. "Queen's College Chancellor Ale." *Brewery History*, 132 (2009): 58–66.

Glasse, Hannah. *The Compleat Confectioner*. Dublin, 1769.

———. *First Catch Your Hare*. 1747. Reprint, Backawton, Devon: Prospect Books, 1995.

"Gleanings." Brewery History Society Newsletter, no. 77 (July 2017): 12.

Glover, Brian. "Antifreeze for the World's Frozen Waste." *What's Brewing*, January 2004.

Gourvish, T. R., and R. G. Wilson. *The British Brewing Industry, 1830–1980*. Cambridge University Press, 1994.

A Guide to Gentlemen and Farmers, for Brewing the Finest Malt-Liquors, Much Better and Cheaper than Hitherto Known. London: J. Niet, 1703.

Harrison, John, and Durden Park Beer Circle. *Old British Beers and How to Make Them*, 2003.

Harrison, William, and Georges Edelen. *The Description of England*. Reprint. 1587. Reprint, New York: Dover Publications Inc, 1994.

Herbert, James. *The Art of Brewing India Pale Ale and Export Ale, Stock & Mild Ales, Porter & Stout*. Burton-on-Trent: Self-published, 1866.

Hind, H. Lloyd. "Brewing at Queen's College, Oxford." *Brewer's Journal*, no. 15 (1927).

———. *Brewing Science and Practice*. New York: John Wiley & Sons, 1938.

Hitchcock, Thomas. *A Practical Treatise on Brewing*. London: R. Boyd, 1842.

Hornsey, Ian S. *A History of Beer and Brewing*. Cambridge: Royal Society of Chemistry, 2003.

Gillman, Gary. "The Arc of American Musty Ale." *Brewery History*, no. 169 (2016): 36–59.

Jackson, Michael. *Michael Jackson's Beer Companion*. Philadelphia: Running Press, 1990.

———. *The New World Guide to Beer*. Philadelphia: Running Press, 1988.

Kish, Jules. *Beer Cans of Connecticut Breweries, 1935-2013*. Self-published, 2013.

Knoblock, Glenn A., and James T. Gunter. *Brewing in New Hampshire*. Charleston, SC: Arcadia Publishing, 2004.

Lightbody, James. *Every Man His Own Gauger*. London: Baldwin, 1695.

Lynch, Patrick, and John Vaizey. *Guinness's Brewery in the Irish Economy, 1759-1876*. Cambridge University Press, 1960.

Markham, Gervase. *The Husbandman's Jewel*. London: G. Conyers, 1619.

Martin, Benjamin. *A Description of the Nature, Construction, and Use of the Torricellian, Or Simple Barometer*. London: Self-published, 1766.

Mathias, Peter. *The Brewing Industry in England, 1700-1830*. Cambridge University Press, 1959.

Meyers, Will. "Barleywine Designed for the Occasion." *Craft Beer and Brewing*, December 2017.

Miller, Norman. *Boston Beer*. Charleston, SC: Arcadia Publishing, 2012.

Molyneux, William. *Burton-on-Trent: Its Waters and Its Breweries*. Trübner Co, 1869.

Moynihan, Peter. *Kentish Brewers and the Brewers of Kent*. Brewery History Society, 2011.

Noonan, Greg. *Scotch Ale*. Boulder, CO: Brewers Publications, 1993.

Owen, C. C. *The Development of Industry in Burton upon Trent*. Chichester: Phillimore & Co., 1978.

Palmer, John J. *How To Brew*. Fourth edition. Boulder, CO: Brewers Publications, 2017.

Parry, David Lloyd. *South Yorkshire Stingo: A Directory of South Yorkshire Brewers, 1758-1995*. Brewery History Society, 1997.

Pattinson, Ronald. *The Home Brewer's Guide to Vintage Beer: Rediscovered Recipes for Classic Brews Dating from 1800 to 1965*. Beverly, MA: Quarry Books, 2014.

———. *Numbers!* Amsterdam: Kilderkin, 2009.

Pike, Frank. "Fifty Years on: Hall & Woodhouse Ltd, 1945–1995. Part I." *Brewery History*, no. 142 (2011).

Ploughman, William. *Oeconomy in Brewing.* Second edition. Romsey: Self-published, 1797.

Protz, Roger. "Dawn Chorus Welcomes Ale Bubble-Brain." *What's Brewing*, December 1997.

———. *The Real Ale Drinker's Almanac.* Fifth edition. Glasgow: Neil Wilson Publishing Ltd, 1997.

Reddington, William. *A Practical Treatise on Brewing, Etc.* London: John Clarke, 1760.

Redman, Nicholas. "Wise Man from North's Fine Ale." *What's Brewing*, December 1996.

Rich, H.S. *One Hundred Years of Brewing.* Reprint edition. 1903. Reprint, Arno Press, 1974.

Richardson, John. *Statistical Estimates of the Materials of Brewing.* London, 1784.

Roberts, William Henry. *The British Wine Maker and Domestic Brewer.* Edinburgh: Oliver & Boyd, 1835.

———. *The Scottish Ale-Brewer and Practical Maltster.* Reprint. 1847. Reprint, Chagrin Falls, OH: Raudins Publishing, 2003.

Sambrook, Pamela. *Country House Brewing in England, 1500–1900.* London: Hambledon Press, 1996.

Scot, Reginald. *A Perfite Platforme of a Hoppe Garden.* London, 1572.

The Secrets of the Mash Tun; or, The Real Causes of Failure in Producing Good Ale or Beer Exposed: By a Brewer of 25 Years' Standing. London: Kessinger Publishing Legacy, 1847.

Smith, Gregg. *Beer in America: The Early Years--1587-1840: Beer's Role in the Settling of America and the Birth of a Nation.* Boulder, CO: Brewers Publications, 1998.

Southby, E. R. *A Systematic Handbook of Practical Brewing.* Third edition. London: Brewing Trades Review, 1889.

Sumner, James. *Brewing Science, Technology and Print, 1700–1880.* London: Pickering & Chatto, 2011.

The Theory and Practice of Malting and Brewing. London: William Creech, 1793.

Tryon, Thomas. *A New Art of Brewing Beer, Ale, and Other Sorts of Liquors.* London: Thomas Salisbury, 1691.

Turczyn, Amahl. "Seasonal Brews, A Tale of Arctic Ale." *Zymurgy,* November/December 2006.

Wahl, Robert, and Max Henius. *American Handy Book of the Brewing, Malting and Auxiliary Trades.* Third Edition. Chicago, 1908.

Ward, Edward. *A Vade Mecum for Malt-Worms.* London: T. Bickerton, [1715?].

Ward, Ian L. "Clear Beer through Finings Technology." Bsgcraft, 2017. https://bsgcraft.com/Resources/Craftbrewing/PDFs/Brewing _Processes_and_Techniques/ClearBeerTechnology.pdf

Watkins, George. *The Complete English Brewer; Or, the Whole Art and Mystery of Brewing, Etc.* London, 1768.

Wheeler, Graham, and Roger Protz. *Brew Your Own British Real Ale at Home.* St. Albans: CAMRA, 1993.

Whitaker, Edward. *Directions for Brewing Malt Liquors. By a Country Gentleman, with a Satyr upon Brandy by Another Hand.* London: Nutt, 1700.

White, Chris, and Jamil Zainasheff. Yeast: *The Practical Guide to Beer Fermentation.* Boulder, CO: Brewers Publications, 2010.

White, Jerry. *London in the Eighteenth Century.* London: Vintage Books, 2013.

Van Wieren, Dale Philip. *American Breweries II.* West Point, PA: Eastern Coast Breweriana Association, 1995.

Worth, William Y. *Cerevisiarii Comes; or, the New Art of Brewing.* London: J. Taylor, 1692.

The Young Brewer's Monitor. London: Baldwin, Craddock, and Joy, 1824.

A SELECTION OF OTHER SOURCES SEARCHED

Acitelli, Tom. *The Audacity of Hops: The History of America's Craft Beer Revolution*. Chicago: Chicago Review Press, 2013.

Arnold, John Paul. *Origin and History of Beer and Brewing*. Reprint. 1911. Reprint, Cleveland, OH: BeerBooks.com, 2005.

Byrn, Marcus Lafayette. *The Complete Practical Brewer*. Reprint. 1852. Reprint, Chagrin Falls, OH: Raudins Publishing, 2002.

Corran, H. S. *A History of Brewing*. Newton Abbot, Devon: David & Charles, 1975.

Foster, Terence. *Doctor Foster's Book of Beer*. London: A & C Black, 1979.

Garetz, Mark. *Using Hops: The Complete Guide to Hops for the Craft Brewer*. Danville, CA: HopTech, 1994.

Hieronymus, Stan. *For The Love of Hops: The Practical Guide to Aroma, Bitterness and the Culture of Hops*. Boulder, CO: Brewers Publications, 2012.

Monckton, Herbert Anthony. *A History of English Ale and Beer*. London: Bodley Head, 1966.

Noonan, Gregory J. *New Brewing Lager Beer*. Boulder, CO: Brewers Publications, 1996.

Oliver, Garrett, ed. *The Oxford Companion to Beer*. New York: Oxford University Press, 2012.

Tomlan, Michael A. *Tinged with Gold*. University of Georgia Press, 1992.

Unger, Richard W. *Beer in the Middle Ages and the Renaissance*. University of Pennsylvania Press, 2004.